HIS PERFECT VICTIM

His Perfect Crime Trilogy
Book I

By
BARBARA H. MARTIN

This is a work of fiction. Names, characters, businesses, places, events and incidents are either the products of the author's imagination or used in a fictitious manner. Any resemblance to actual persons, living or dead, or actual events is purely coincidental.

Dedicated to my husband Edward

Acknowledgements
Michael E. Martin gave his expert advice on weapons and technical issues.
Katherine E. Busbee helped with computer terminology and gave advice on overall content.
My special thanks to Delores Chancellor who spent countless hours editing the manuscript.

Copyright © 2014 by Barbara H. Martin

All rights reserved under International and Pan-American Copyright Conventions. By payment of required fees, you have been granted the non-exclusive, non-transferable right to access and read the text of this e-book on-screen. No part of this book may be reproduced, transmitted, downloaded, decompiled, reverse engineered, or stored in or introduced into any information storage and retrieval system, in any form or by any means, whether electronic or mechanical – except in the case of brief quotations in articles or reviews - without the express written permission of Barbara H. Martin. To contact the author, please send an email to Barbara Martin at barbara@BarbaraHMartin.com.

Cover artist credit: SelfPubBookCovers.com/diversepixel

Other titles by Barbara H. Martin:

When the East Wind Blows

Silk Sheets and Other Things That Don't Work

The Little Book of Miracles

Walking in Power

Contact Barbara directly at:

barbara@BarbaraHMartin.com

www.BarbaraHMartin.com

Prologue

He stood in the shadow and waited until heavy clouds plunged the forty foot sleek yacht into darkness. A tiny sliver of light could be seen from below deck through the half open door of the small cabin. It was still two hours before daylight, plenty of time to get everything done.

He had waited a long time for this. His heart raced and he trembled with anticipation. Finally, he would reach the goal he had dreamed of ever since he found out who he really was. Remembering the rejection first and after that the hatred as if it was yesterday. The idea began to form slowly at first until it consumed his entire being. Today he had no doubt he would succeed. After months of meticulous planning and countless hours of considering every aspect of his perfect plan, it was justice, plain and simple.

The yacht rocked gently on the calm waters of the ocean. A warm breeze drifted off the coast line in the far distance. It had been easy to sneak on the boat. The man he sought to kill had come on board late last night and gone straight to bed after he carried his small bag into the cabin below. The intruder knew the man was alone and would get up early to fish just off the coast until midmorning. He had observed him many times over the last few months, but this was the first time he was actually on the boat with him. The intruder had been on "The Tranquility" many times before, but always alone when it was safely moored in the harbor. He felt at home here and knew every inch of this beautiful vessel. There was nothing left to chance in his plan, he had made sure of that. It was hard to believe this was finally the day he would do what needed to be done. Sometimes he wondered how he could hate someone he didn't know with such intensity.

When the motor cranked into action early in the morning, he realized he had actually fallen asleep. He felt a little stiff from lying on the hard deck, but stayed hidden as the yacht slowly made its way out into the open ocean. It seemed a long time until the motor was suddenly still and the boat drifted gently on the calm sea. As he started moving toward the covered part of the cabin, his heart hammered in his chest and he felt his knees give way. He sat back against the wall of the deck, going over one more time how it would happen. In his mind every step was planned, every precaution taken and the timing was perfect. And so would his future be. *It will be like stepping into a new life, a life of happiness and security. Everything he never had before,* he thought. A sudden calm filled him as he waited patiently. He held the gun close to his body.

Then he heard the footsteps. This was it! With a feeling of strange exhilaration he rose and grabbed the gun and held it firmly in his right hand as he released the safety. He waited until the man was on the open part of the deck, close to the railing. He strained to make out his victim's face and took in a sharp breath as it came into full view. This was harder than he thought, almost surreal. Hesitating for what seemed a long time, he slowly lifted the gun and stepped closer.

The sound of the shot was lost in the expanse of the vast ocean. The man had a look of total surprise on his face as he faced his assailant and then slumped down on the deck in a heap. A pool of blood began to seep out in slow motion from under his upper body. The shooter stood motionless, his gun still in his hand. His breathing was labored as he whispered,

"It is done. I'm somebody now."

Chapter 1

The Anscott Estate lay well hidden at the far end of a tree lined driveway in the upscale suburb of Glenridge. It was a stately three-story building with huge columns reaching up to the second floor in the front. A four car garage stood connected to one side. The building gave the feeling of solidity and comfortable wealth. To get to the large oak front door one had to step inside the portico between two massive columns. Large planters, filled with meticulously maintained lush, green ornamental plants, filled the spaces in between. They gave the mostly gray exterior of the house a splash of color. The white window frames across the entire building added a touch of class and even grandeur.

Marten Anscott hesitated before he reached for the ornate doorbell. They would wonder why he had come home early. It had been a hectic drive from the airport with five o'clock traffic at its worst. The chime seemed to be going on forever as he stood there waiting for someone to let him in.

"It is you, Sir!" The butler stood with a surprised smile as he stepped aside to let Marten in. "We did not expect you till Sunday. Please, come in." Marten loved the crisp British accent.

"Thank you, Richard. I decided to come back early."

"May I get your luggage?" The butler stepped outside and without waiting for an answer walked toward the shiny new sports car.

"That won't be necessary Richard. I left it at the beach house. Mom and Cassie can bring some of it, the rest can stay."

Marten stood in the middle of the great entrance hall as if unable to tear himself away from the view before him. The floor was covered with Venetian tile. The beautiful antique furniture was placed strategically by an expert decorator and expensive works of art covered the walls. They gave the foyer an air of quiet elegance. His eyes were drawn to the marble staircase winding in a graceful curve to the floor above.

"I love this place," he thought. *"I belong here."*

"Your room is ready Sir," the butler said. "Emily did not disturb anything when she cleaned it."

"That is great Richard. I will need to change for dinner before I greet Mom and Cassie."

The butler stopped abruptly.

"But Sir, they are at the beach until Sunday as you know."

"Of course, I'm tired from the trip. Where is my mind? Let Mom and Cassie know I'm home will you? And don't forget to tell them to bring my things."

"Of course, Sir. Will you take dinner at the usual time or should Emily bring you something now?" The butler stood waiting.

"I will have something in my room for now and then have dinner at the regular time, Richard."

"Very well, Sir. I will let Emily know."

Marten slowly walked up the stairs, hesitating before he opened the first door on the left.

"Are you looking for something, Sir?" asked Lilly Messner. The young maid was a tiny woman with a pert smile and beautiful black hair tied in a bun. Her dark blue uniform accentuated a nice, trim figure.

"Well no, not really. I'm heading for my room." He hesitated a moment and then went on almost as an afterthought. "Why don't you go ahead of me and see if the towels are laid out for my bath."

"But Sir, they're always laid out for when you come home from one of your trips." She looked puzzled.

"Just humor me girl and do as you are told." He waved her on impatiently. "I'm too tired to argue about it."

"Of course, Sir."

"Lilly, I'm sorry. I have a terrible headache. I didn't mean to snap at you."

"That's quite alright, Sir." She was still puzzled by his outburst.

Marten entered his bedroom. It was large with an oversized bed and a sitting area arranged around a fireplace. A solid oak desk, littered with papers, stood in front of a big window. Heavy curtains were drawn wide to let in fresh air.

"The towels are all laid out for you, Sir. Will there be anything else?"

"No, that's all, you can leave. I will take that shower now." Marten headed for the bathroom and locked the door behind him. He felt annoyed.

Standing for a long time, he let the hot water wash away the stress he felt about coming home. He relaxed as he dried himself off and walked to the desk in the sitting area of the bedroom. He picked up some of the papers without thinking and arranged them in neat little stacks to one side. He stood for a long time looking out the window. Because of his blinding headache, his eyes were not focused anywhere in particular. He turned and folded back the luxurious bed covers and lay down with a deep sigh, falling asleep almost instantly.

The knock on the door startled him. He felt disoriented until he came fully awake and realized he was home.
"Come in!"
"Here is ye something to eat, Master Marten. I fixed you your favorites, a ham and cheese sandwich with relish and a glass of cold milk." The short, rotund, middle aged woman smiled at him with true affection. "Ye must be hungry after such a long trip. A young lad like you needs to eat."
She put the tray on the small table in front of the love seat.
"I don't want milk. Don't you have coffee?" Marten was annoyed again.
"But you love milk in the afternoon," She said with a puzzled frown on her face.
"Just get me coffee, will you?" Marten said in a sharp voice.
"Of course, Sir, right away. I'm sorry." She almost ran out the door, her face a mixture of hurt and bewilderment.
Milk, for crying out loud, he was 28 years old. Why would she treat him like a child? That would have to change for sure. Marten devoured the food and even drank the milk. Just when he was done, the woman emerged with a steaming cup of hot coffee.

Emily was still flustered and studied him closely after she put the beverage in front of him on the table. *He looks the same*, she thought. She had always loved his brown, curly hair with those deep warm hazel eyes to match. His nose was a little too big and his cheekbones too pronounced. A chin made up for it and gave his face a strong, handsome appearance. His lanky, long, slender frame made him look much younger than his 28 years. *But there is something in his eyes today that is different,* she thought. *I can't put my finger on it.* That is when her look went over to the desk to see the mess from before, tidied into neat stacks. She started to say something, but thought better of it and left the room.

She met up with Lilly, the young maid, on the way down.
"The young Sir is in a bad mood today. He has never snapped at me like that before, Miss Emily," Lilly said in a hushed tone. "Usually

he's happy after one of his trips down to the beach. But he did say he had a real bad headache."

"Don't worry, lass, he's just tired. All he needs is a good night's sleep and he'll be his usual self." Emily stopped at the bottom of the stairs. "Lilly, we need to make the rooms ready for Mrs. Anscott and Miss Cassie. They will be here before we know it."

"Yes, Miss Emily, I will get on it first thing in the morning if that is ok with you. I still have some laundry to do for the rest of the afternoon." She took a deep sigh. "There is no end to the chores around here."

It was late Friday evening when Patrick Anscott drove up and stopped his BMW by the front door. Richard was there to greet him and took the brief case.

"Good evening, Sir. It has been a long day for you. I have your brandy ready in the library and Emily will serve your dinner as soon as you say the word."

"Thank you, Richard. You make it a pleasure to come home," he answered with a tired smile. "Is that Marten's car in the driveway? I thought he was still at the beach."

"He came home today ahead of the ladies, Sir. You will find him in the drawing room." Richard headed for the office to pour the brandy and handed it to Patrick, who had taken a seat behind the large, ornate, mahogany desk.

"Thank you Richard, I need this tonight. It has been a terrible day," he said with a deep sigh.

"I'm sorry to hear that, Sir. Your wife and daughter will be home soon and that will surely make you feel better."

"They seem to have been gone a long time, or is it just me? Richard, why don't you ask Marten to come see me, I need to talk to him." He leaned back and sipped the brandy in small increments, enjoying the warmth filtering through his body. He loved this time right after coming home. It was a ritual he and his wife Helen enjoyed together while talking over the events of the day.

Patrick Marten Anscott looked and acted very much like his father did. With his piercing blue eyes, heavy dark eyebrows and a well-trimmed mustache, he looked more like a man from the turn of the century. He had always hated his stocky frame and wished he had been taller ever since he could remember. His receding hairline had started

8

early in life and in spite of his financial prowess there was nothing he could do to change that. To this day he had often wondered why the most beautiful girl in his senior class in college had paid any attention to him. But she did and before she could change her mind he had asked her to marry him.

He smiled. After thirty-five years, what a wonderful marriage it turned out to be. He still loved her as much now as the day he met her under that big oak tree on campus. She had worn a white dress with a flowing skirt and a red sweater draped over her shoulders.

He took another sip of brandy. Where have the years gone? It is time to retire and enjoy the last years they might have left together.

His thoughts were interrupted by Richard's discreet cough.

"I spoke with young Mr. Anscott, Sir. He says he does not have time to meet with you."

"Why not?"

"He did not say Sir," Richard said quietly.

"What the heck is he doing that is so important he cannot talk to me?" Patrick said with irritation in his voice.

"I don't know Sir." The butler shuffled uncomfortably, but remained in the room.

"Well, I guess I will talk to him tomorrow then. After Emily brings me dinner, both of you feel free to retire for the night, Richard."

"Thank you, Sir. Good night."

Patrick took the empty brandy glass and twirled it on its base. It was strange Marten did not want to talk to him tonight. The time had come to bring things out in the open. Things he had hoped he would never have to discuss. It was so long in the past and seemed unreal to him. After the phone conversation he had today with his lawyer, he could not wait any longer. Maybe he should wait until Helen came home to speak to Marten. She would know how to handle it better than he. While he had no trouble talking about business matters, this was something he truly had no idea how to handle.

He was still shaken up by the visitor he had today. The woman had come unannounced and would not leave until Glenda, his assistant, informed him of her presence. The name brought up unpleasant and long forgotten memories. It was more or less a one-sided conversation as usual, with her doing all the talking. He stood behind his desk in silence as she made her demands known. It was blackmail, clear and simple.

She had called it setting things straight. As soon as she left he had called his lawyer and old friend, Conner Matthews.

Patrick sat with his head in his hands and sighed deeply. After a while he stood up and walked over to a cabinet in the corner of the large room. He pulled out a small key on his key chain and stuck it in the door. At that same moment a knock interrupted him and Emily walked in with his dinner hidden under an ornate silver warmer.

"Here we are, Sir. It's lamb chops this evening with young carrots and mashed potatoes, just the way you like it."

"You spoil me, Emily. Thank you. Just put it down. I told Richard you can retire. I will take care of this."

"Thank you, Sir. I will see you in the morning." With that she closed the door gently behind her.

He ate his dinner mechanically, without tasting the food. When he finished he put the tray on the table and walked back to the cabinet and opened the door. Inside was a small safe. He turned the tumbler without having to think of the numbers or turns and pulled the safe door open. Carefully he took out some papers slightly yellowed by age.

Patrick never saw the man in black looking into the window of the library, watching him as he started reading.

Chapter 2

The phone rang early the next morning and jolted Helen Anscott out of her sleep.

"Yes, Richard, what is it?"

"Madam, I just want to let you know that Master Marten arrived here late yesterday."

"Really, I wondered where he was. We haven't seen him yet today and he did not join us at the restaurant for dinner last night. Did he say why he went back?"

"No Madam, he did not, but wanted me to let you know he was here."

"Thank you, Richard. We will be home by Sunday as planned. Make sure my husband remembers to come home in time to have dinner with us."

"Yes, Madam. Have a good flight home."

Helen Anscott put the receiver down with a puzzled look. This was not like Marten to leave without saying a word of goodbye. He loved the beach and normally would have complained about leaving.

She was still beautiful in spite of her fifty something years. Her face had a straight nose, large blue eyes and high cheek bones. She had kept most of the signs of aging at a minimum with the help of a nip and tuck here and there. Her auburn hair was still full with soft curls, giving her a kind, almost gentle look. She was a tall woman, her slender figure held erect at all times. Even when tired, she would never allow herself to slouch.

Why would Marten go home without telling her? It wasn't like him. Oh well, he is a grown man, let him do what he wants. It probably has to do with the company. He was really getting involved in Anscott Laboratories lately. *It's about time if he wants to take over some day,* she thought. Her heart felt a surge of love and warmth just thinking about Marten. *He turned out to be such a wonderful young man,* she thought and smiled.

"Mom, who was that on the phone?" Cassie shouted from the other room.

"It was Richard, sweetheart. He let me know Marten is already home."

"Really, without saying goodbye, that's weird."

Cassie bounced into the bedroom wearing a swimsuit. Water was dripping on the white carpet.

"Please, dry yourself off, you are getting everything wet." Helen said, slightly annoyed with her vivacious daughter.

"What's with him anyway, leaving like that? I wanted to ride in his new sports car on the way from the airport." She grabbed a towel from the adjoining bathroom and wrapped it around her. "I hate to leave. It was fun at the beach, Mom. We have to do this more often. I just wish Dad could have been with us."

"You know how hard it is for him to get away, honey. He tries, but it takes a lot to run the company. I was thinking it is high time Marten steps in more to help him. He is old enough." Helen got up from the bed and put on a pair of white slacks and a stunning red top with lots of "bling" on the front as her daughter called it.

"That looks great on you, Mom," Cassie said with admiration in her voice. She was proud of how good her mother looked. She would never be that pretty in spite of her mother telling her she looked exactly like her when she was her age. At 26, Cassandra Helen Anscott was a pretty girl with wavy auburn hair and a beautiful complexion. While there was a family resemblance, she had not inherited her mother's classic features. Her light blue eyes were from her father. She was like him in many ways. *I may not be pretty like Mom, but I have a head for business like Dad.* She had loved working at the company from the day she finished college a year ago. Deep down she wished she was the one to take over, but Marten was the oldest and a boy. Then again, that should not stop her in today's world.

On Sunday afternoon their plane arrived on time and Helen and Cassie were met by Richard as usual. He stood out in the waiting crowd at 6' 4', dressed impeccably in his dark suit and tie, his shoes shined to perfection. With his white hair he was a good looking man, serious and formal, in every way the British butler. While still in good shape for his 62 years, his middle was beginning to broaden somewhat to the point he was thinking of taking up walking every morning. Somehow, with all his duties, he never seemed to find the time. He and his wife Emily had been working for the Anscott family for nearly twenty years. No one could imagine life without either of them.

"Richard, how good to see you. How is everything at home?" Helen asked as they walked to the car.

"Things are well, Madam. Master Marten is waiting for you at home and Mr. Anscott promised to be home in time for dinner."

"Wonderful. It's great to go somewhere, but it is even greater to come back." Helen sank into the car seat with a sigh.

"Mom, I'm going in to work tomorrow," Cassie said as she settled into the back seat. "I miss it now that we're home."

Helen was thinking Cassie was getting more like her father about the company. It would be nice if Marten showed such enthusiasm. On the other hand, he had been nothing but a joy growing up and his father's pride. It made it easier for Patrick to work so hard when he knew both of his children would one day take over the company. She looked forward to that day so they could enjoy their later years together.

Marten stood outside the front door as they drove up. He seemed tense, but relaxed when Cassie ran up to him to give him a big hug.

"Why did you run off on us, big brother," she scolded him with a twinkle in her eyes.

"Just couldn't take your sassiness any longer I guess," he said with a forced smile.

"Hello, Mother, how good you made it back safe." He hugged Helen with a short hug. "Come on in, it's getting ready to rain."

Emily stood right inside the door, her face crinkled with a bright smile.

"How good to have ye home at last," she cried and hugged Cassie to her short, rotund figure. "It has been mighty lonely around here without you Lassie."

"Oh, Emily, I missed you too and your cooking," Cassie said with a big grin as she made her way up the stairs.

"Welcome back Mrs. Anscott. I hope you had a good flight," Emily said.

"It was ok. I'm just glad to be back. Is Patrick home yet?"

"No Madam, but he promised he would make it for dinner." Emily did not sound convinced. She knew how things usually went.

Marten stood apart and watched closely. He seemed slightly ill at ease and decided to go upstairs to his room. The whole scene had made him nervous and on edge.

Patrick Anscott arrived just in time for dinner Sunday evening as promised. He sighed as he got out of the car. He should have stayed to finish up some things at the office. Then again, it was Sunday, and he didn't feel like disappointing his family today. Besides, he had been working too hard lately and it was time to spend more time with them. He really hated coming home to an empty house while they were gone this time. Maybe when Marten took over, he would be able to join them more often at the beach in the future.

"Dad, we are back!" Cassie greeted him at the door with her usual enthusiasm and it felt good.

"Hi sweetheart, I'm so glad you're home." He gave her a big hug and then headed toward the dining room.

"Patrick, I'm so glad you made it in time for dinner. I missed you dear," Helen said as she got up to kiss him on the cheek. "How nice we are all together tonight," she added and then noticed Marten was not there.

"Richard, please tell Marten to come down for dinner."

"Yes, Madam."

Marten felt all eyes on him as he entered the dining room.

"Hi Dad, you made it," he said with a slight smile and sat down.

"Since when are you sitting in that chair, Marten?" Cassie asked with a big question mark on her face. "You know nobody ever sits there unless we have company."

"Sorry, I don't know why either," Marten mumbled and moved over to the other chair, opposite Cassie. "I'm not feeling all that well today," he went on, staring down on his empty plate. "I have a terrible headache."

"You are not ill, are you son?" Helen asked, suddenly concerned.

"No, Mom. It's nothing I'm sure. I will be as good as new in the morning." All during the meal he remained quiet and withdrawn.

"How was your time at the beach?" Patrick asked as he looked around the table. "I promise, the next time you go, I'm planning to go with you." Then he looked at Marten. "That means, young man, you will have to take on more of the responsibility at the company in the near future. You are old enough and I'm ready to cut back. Between you and Cassie, I'm certain you two can start running things without me. So that in just a few years your mother and I can travel the world together." He reached over to take Helen's hand and squeezed it lovingly.

"Patrick, that sounds wonderful." Helen leaned over and kissed him on the cheek. "I can't wait to live a life of travel and adventure."

"I don't know how much adventure we will have, but at least we will travel and see parts of the world we have always dreamed of."

"It sounds like a second honeymoon to me," Cassie laughed. "Go for it you two. Marten and I will be just fine slaving away while you have the time of your life." She looked at Marten, but he pretended to be busy with his food.

"Boy, you are in a bad mood today, aren't you brother?" Cassie said, leaning over toward him. "Cat got your tongue?"

"I'm sorry, please excuse me. I don't feel at all well. I'm going up to my room." With that he abruptly got up and left the room.

"Good grief, what's with him?" Cassie laughed.

"I'm concerned, this is not like Marten," Helen said. "I hope he's not real sick. He left the beach early without saying a word and came home. That is not like him and he hardly said a word during dinner and didn't finish his food either."

"He will be ok, Helen. It's time he gets out and becomes his own man. Maybe I will get him a condo or a house in town," Patrick said. "I was on my own long before his age and did ok. A man has to make it without his mother's apron strings. I'm afraid, as hard as that will be for you Helen that time has come for our son."

"I know, Patrick, make sure he understands he is always welcome to live right here," Helen said, trying to hide the panic in her voice. "He has never mentioned that he was unhappy living here," she added, stunned at the sudden turn of events.

There was silence around the table until Emily came in with her delicious home-made apple pie with ice cream.

Cassie walked into the kitchen after her parents had gone upstairs. She loved to talk to Emily when something troubled her.

"What do you think is wrong with Marten, Emily?"

"Well Lassie, I don't know. He's not his own self, that's for sure. I noticed it when he came back from the beach. I brought him his favorite ham and cheese sandwich with milk and he nearly did me an injury." She wiped her hands on her apron and started loading the dishwasher.

"What did he do, Emily?" Cassie asked.

"He said he was too old to drink milk and why had I not brought him coffee. He always likes milk in the afternoons with his sandwich. There was something in his eyes that was different, strange so to speak."

Her face had taken on a reddish hue as she went on. "Then I saw his desk. You know how it's always messy and he dares any of us to touch anything on there? So help me Holy Mary, the desk was perfectly straightened out with every bit of mess gone and everything in neat piles." She wiped her face with the dish towel. "Lassy, it just ain't like him. As long as I've been around, and that is since he was eight, our Marten has been the absolute messiest boy I've ever known." She turned to face Cassie with her hands on her hips. "I saw his room this morning. It was as neat as a pin. The bed was made and the desk was completely clean. In the sitting area every cushion was arranged on the love seat as if no one had ever sat there. I swear neither Lilly nor I had been in to do the cleaning." She sank into a kitchen chair as if totally exhausted from the stress.

Cassie took another chair.
"Emily, why would he have changed like that?"
"The saints only know." She crossed herself three times.
"Maybe he will be back to normal in the morning," Cassie said and took Emily's hand. "Don't upset yourself so. He'll be ok, you'll see."

Chapter 3

The precinct was in turmoil as usual for a Monday morning. Robert Latimer had just come in with a freshly brewed cup of coffee in one hand and a file folder in the other. In spite of the pandemonium, the world looked good. In just a few months he would be in Florida somewhere on the beach, playing shuffle board with the seniors and winning big at bingo at the church hall. Nobody would care how many crimes he had solved in his career or how he caught the famous railroad strangler several years ago. All they cared about was what to do all day when there was nothing to do. At least that is what Bob Latimer thought retirement was all about. How could he know? He had never spent a day at the beach, played shuffle board or bingo, and definitely had never seen a day with nothing to do.

He really didn't feel he was old enough to retire. At barely 64, he was still amazingly healthy and in good shape. He had kept up with a healthy diet when duty and time permitted and exercised regularly. With his full head of gray hair, a well-trimmed gray beard and mustache which matched his steely gray eyes, he presented a picture of self-confidence. There was something about him that exuded authority and made him look much taller than he was. Very few people dared argue with him, except his wife Mary. She had died ten years ago of breast cancer and he still missed her terribly.

His record on the force was legendary. When he was assigned a case, the powers to be pretty well left him to his own devises, following the old adage that if something works, don't fix it.

The phone interrupted his thoughts and he almost spilled his coffee.

"Latimer." He listened intently while drinking.

"Ok, I will get right on it." He leaned back with a sigh. Another murder in Glenridge, so what's new?

"Brighton, get yourself in here. We have a case."

Sgt. Kevin Brighton counted himself lucky to be assigned to Bob Latimer. It wouldn't hurt his career in the force one bit to learn from the master. He had joined the force ten years ago and worked himself up to Sergeant with tenacity and diligence. He looked much younger than his 29 years. That's why Latimer called him Kid. He didn't like it at first, but then he got used to it as time went on.

Ever since he could remember he was taller than everyone else. In school he towered over the other kids. When he graduated they voted him the friendliest tall person in the class. He did have a smile that could melt the heart of every young girl he met, complete with dimples. It was the dimples that gave cause to constant ribbing among his peers. With his lanky, thin body, straight blond hair and baby blue eyes, he presented the perfect picture of a friendly cop. They used to send him to lecture first graders about the trustworthiness of policemen, until he proved himself to be a valuable asset in an unsolved murder case. It was then he got the chance to join the Glenridge Major Crime Unit and proved to be better than anyone had thought.

To this day he had no idea why Latimer requested him to be his sidekick and he never tried to find out.

"What's the case, Sir?" he asked as he approached Latimer's desk.

"Some big shot business executive got murdered last night. That's all I know right now. Headquarters wants to make sure things are done by the book."

"It must be someone important. What's the name?" Sgt Brighton asked.

"Anscott. Patrick Marten Anscott."

"Holy Moses, that's the guy from Anscott Laboratories. This is big."

"That's right, Kid, we got us a really big fish this time." It was the first time Sgt. Brighton knew Latimer to be impressed with a case. "Let's go to Anscott Estate down on Kensington Road and see what this is all about," Latimer said as he got up and grabbed his coat from the worn out coat stand in the corner. This is bound to get interesting."

It was a half hour later they drove up to the main house at the Anscott Estate. The big, black, wrought iron gate stood wide open and they drove through unhindered. Latimer waved at a cop just inside as they made their way down the tree-lined driveway. Brighton whistled as he looked up at the impressive mansion. There were several cars from the coroner's office, EMS and other official vehicles. Dozens of people were rushing in and out of the open front door.

"Can't wait to see what it looks like inside," Brighton said, getting out of the car.

"Remember, these are important people. No need to upset them needlessly with dumb talk, Kid. Try to act like you see this kind of house every day." Latimer smiled his crooked little smile as he walked on ahead. He liked the Kid.

"Hi Inspector. It's a mess in there." It was one of the policemen who stood guard at the entrance.

"I'm sure it is, Officer Keller," Latimer said as he walked past him into the main foyer. "These things are always a mess," he mumbled to no one in particular. "Where is the coroner?" he asked one of the technicians.

"He's in the library with the body Sir, over there to your left."

Latimer looked at Brighton and said, "Let's go and see what we can find out."

The body lay in the middle of the floor. Blood had seeped out from under it and dried in a pool on the expensive oriental carpet. There was a look of total astonishment on the dead man's face as if he could not believe what was happening. Nothing was out of place, no sign of struggle or evidence of an intruder.

"This was murder by someone close to the victim," the coroner said. "Good to see you, Latimer. Cause of death is obvious as you can see," he added and pointed to the gunshot wound in the middle of the victim's chest. "It was as easy as taking candy from a baby. The perpetrator probably used a silencer because the family didn't hear a thing. No shell casings or gun. The housekeeper found the body this morning. She's in the kitchen completely hysterical."

"Thanks George, thorough as usual. Can you determine the time yet?"

"It was at 11:43 last night to be absolutely precise." He looked up at Latimer with a grin. "Am I good or what?" He pointed to the broken wrist watch on the victims arm. "It's nice when that happens."

Latimer introduced Brighton to the coroner.

"Nice to meet you, Sir." Sgt. Brighton always appreciated how polite Latimer was in introducing him to everyone new. Most other inspectors wouldn't have bothered.

Latimer looked around the room. The walls were filled from floor to ceiling with books on three sides. Many had beautiful leather bindings. Others seemed very old and probably valuable. He was most impressed with the exquisite, large mahogany desk in the middle of the room. He could have spent some time examining the intricate carvings further if it had not been for the body lying in front of it. An old cabinet in the corner to the left stood with the door open. It showed a small safe which was empty.

He stepped around the desk and took a close look at Patrick Marten Anscott. He looked like a man of substance and intelligence, with a solid look of respectability. He was not that old, maybe in his early sixties. His body seemed a little on the heavy side. His empty eyes had the bluest color he had ever seen on a man. His suit was definitely not bought in a regular store. The silk tie was a picture of understated elegance.

"What are you thinking, Sir?" Brighton asked, his voice filled with awe. "Who would kill a nice man like him?"

"Let's find out if he really was nice or if he just looks it by talking to the rest of the household." Latimer said.

"They are in the drawing room," Dr. Richter said.

"Thanks, George. Let me know if you find anything interesting." Latimer said on the way out.

As they made their way to the drawing room, Brighton had a chance to look at his surroundings.

"I could learn to live like this, Sir."

Latimer did not have time to answer. They had reached the open door to the large, yet comfortable room filled with two sets of seating arrangements. Three people sat in stoic silence, showing no reaction when they entered.

"I beg your pardon. I'm Inspector Latimer and this is Sgt. Brighton with the Major Crime Unit of the Glenridge police department. Please accept our deepest condolences for your loss."

Helen looked up with a tear stained face.

"I'm Helen Anscott, and this is my daughter Cassie and my son Marten. Please forgive us for not getting up. I'm sure you understand." Her voice trailed off into a whisper as she wrung her hands as if that would help with her grief.

"Ma'am, are you able to answer a few questions?" Latimer asked in his most gentle manner.

"I will try. The doctor has given me some medicine. I don't know how well I will do," she said, her hands still in the same wringing motion.

"Can you think of anyone who would want to kill your husband?"

"No. Patrick was a wonderful, kind and loving man." She was sobbing now. "This is so terrible."

"I think that is enough for now. I'm Marten Anscott and I demand that you leave my mother alone." His voice was menacing in spite of the grief.

"Will you answer a few questions then, Sir?" Latimer asked.

"Of course."

"When was the last time you saw your father alive, Mr. Anscott?"

"At dinner, around seven last evening. I was not feeling well and left the table early and went to bed."

"Did you hear any noise last evening?"

"No, I was out like a light the minute I hit the pillow. I slept till this morning when the housekeeper's screams woke me up."

"Can someone verify your statements, Sir?" Latimer braced himself before he asked the question.

"What kind of a ridiculous thing is that to ask? I'm not in the habit to have my family check on me when I'm asleep. And no, I don't have an alibi if that's what you mean." His eyes were cold as he spewed out the words with surprising venom.

"Marten, you don't have to be so mean to the Inspector, he is just doing his job." Cassie reached over to her brother and put her hand on his arm. "I apologize for my brother, Inspector. He is usually not like this. I guess we're all in shock."

"Can you tell me where you were between ten and twelve last night, Miss Anscott?"

"Like my brother, I went to bed early because mother and I had returned from the beach that day and I was tired. After dinner I talked to my friend Andrea for a while and then watched TV. I fell asleep and woke up at one in the morning and turned it off. With it running, I would not have heard anything going on in the house." Cassie slumped back into the chair and stared out the window, seeing nothing.

"I'm sure we will have more questions as time goes on. Please keep yourselves available." Latimer turned to Marten. "Where can I find the staff?"

"That would be in the kitchen. I will show you there if you'll follow me. I'm going up to my room. I have had enough of all these questions." His tone was icy.

It was quite a long way down hallways and corridors until they entered the kitchen. It was a large room with an island in the middle. In the one corner a group of people sat around a large, wooden table. Everyone fell silent when they walked in.

Before Latimer could thank him, Marten Anscott had turned and left without a word.

After introducing himself and Brighton, Latimer asked to speak to Emily.

"My wife is not able to talk to you, Inspector. The doctor gave her some medicine because she was close to a collapse. She found Mr. Anscott, you see. I don't know if she will ever get over it." He got up and shook Latimer's hand. "I'm Richard McAllister, the butler. My wife Emily is the housekeeper and we have been in service to the Anscott's for nearly twenty years." He wiped his eyes with one hand. "I'm sorry to act so unprofessional, but Mr. Anscott was very special to all of us. He was a good and kind man who treated us with respect at all times. It was an honor to serve him." He sat down with a deep sigh. "This is Lilly Messner, the maid. "Get up girl, and talk to the Inspector."

"Lilly, is there anything you can tell me that was different yesterday or in the evening?" Latimer was very gentle.

"No Sir, all was as it always is. We fixed dinner, Miss Emily and I, and then I cleaned up afterwards. It was my weekend to work and I went home at about nine o'clock the way I always do. Nothing was different." She started to cry. "There was no better employer than Mr. Anscott. He would always give us presents for birthdays and Christmas and such. He never lost his temper or was harsh in any way. I don't know why anyone would want to kill him." She was sobbing uncontrollably by now and Latimer motioned to Brighton to do something.

"Come now, Lilly, it will be alright," Brighton said after he laid down his notebook and pen. "You must be strong for the family." He patted her on the shoulder until she calmed down. He had no idea why the Inspector thought he had any idea how to deal with a crying female.

"I will want to question your wife tomorrow, Mr. McAllister," Latimer said to Richard. "Thank you for your cooperation. Sgt. Brighton and I will return first thing in the morning."

"Well, Sir, do you have any idea who did it?" Brighton asked as soon as they got into the car.

"It's way too early, Kid. I can tell you one thing already, this is a difficult case. Everything about that house and the family is so nice, it's unreal. There is something we're missing from this idyllic family portrait. I just don't know what it is." He put the seat belt on as he looked back to glance at the beautiful mansion one more time.

"I agree, I can't say I see anything amiss with the family or the staff. They do seem nice, like you say." Brighton stopped before he entered the main road and then headed for the precinct. "You don't think it was robbery or an intruder, do you Sir?"

"Like I said, it's too early to tell. From what I've seen, it doesn't seem to be." He turned to Brighton. "You never know with these cases until you dig deeper into the dynamics of a family. Everybody has secrets and it's our job to find them, Kid."

"We have to wait for the coroner's report anyway. I hope that will not take too long." Brighton sounded between hopeful and skeptical.

"It won't take long with this case. The brass is anxious to find the murderer. Anscott Laboratories gives a lot of money to good causes and the Police Benevolent Fund is one of them. He is one of their biggest contributors," Latimer said.

Several people stood outside the gate, held back by a cop from entering.

"I bet they are reporters, Sir," Brighton said as they turned on the main road.

"I bet it will be a circus by tomorrow. I can feel it in my old bones," Latimer said with a deep sigh.

Latimer got out of the car at the precinct's front entrance and walked to his office without stopping to talk to anyone along the way. He knew it was early in the case, but usually he had some idea where to go from here. He had an uneasy feeling that with this being his last case, he might just not be able to solve it. That would really mess up his retirement in a big way. He had only failed to solve 5 cases in his 30 years and could clearly remember every one of them. They happened early on and to mess up the last one would not be good. He sat behind his desk with his head in both hands, wishing he was already on the beach in Florida.

"What is your first impression, Latimer?" Chief Carson filled every inch of the door and came right to the point. "The brass is really antsy about this one, wants it solved real fast before the media has a field day with our behinds." He was a huge man in every way of the word. His voice alone sounded overpowering and together with a 6'2' frame and a circumference to match, he had given some on the force nightmares just being in the same room with him.

"Don't you think it's a little early to try to force me into early retirement, Chief?" Latimer didn't sound the least intimidated. "Seriously though, it's a strange case. I can't wrap my head around it from what I've seen so far."

"You realize the Anscotts are one of the most prominent families in this State," the Chief said. "There isn't a single big shot politician or any other well-known person who is not in some way connected to Patrick Anscott. It all boils down to big money. The guy was extremely generous to the Governor's campaign, the party and all the hundreds of charities who feed at the trough of Anscott Laboratories." Chief Carson slumped into the chair in front of Latimer's desk. "This is a mess. Honestly, the guy couldn't have been nicer, he or his family. My wife met Helen Anscott at a police benefit. She came home raving what a great lady she is. Who the heck would have reason to do away with such a good man?" He scratched his sparse hair with vigor and looked at Latimer with almost pleading eyes. "Don't let me down on this one, Latimer. Use all the resources you need and more to get to the bottom."

"I wish it was a matter of money, Chief." Latimer said in a tired voice. "This is a much deeper issue somehow. I don't know why I feel this way, I just do." He leaned over toward the Chief. "For now you can tell forensics to make this case a priority. For the rest, I will certainly take you up on your offer if the need should arise."

"I'm relying on you Latimer. You have never let me down in all these years. Don't go soft on me now." The Chief raised his huge frame from his chair with surprising ease and turned toward the door. "I want an update every day."

"I will give you one if I have anything new, Chief. I promise," Latimer said and leaned heavily on his desk as he watched him leave.

A minute later Brighton walked in, cheerful as ever.

"What are you smiling about, Kid?" he growled.

"The Chief is on your case already, hey? Can't say as I blame him, the story is all over the news. Maybe you will get famous, Sir." He draped his lanky frame over the chair in a way that was more like a contortionist. "I talked with Smith over in human resources. He thinks the butler did it." The smile on his face was so open and friendly it made Latimer smile in return.

"You are something, Kid, always seeing something funny in every situation. I wish I could feel like you look." He sighed heavily.

"You told me it was too early to come to any conclusion, Sir. I think even the Chief knows that. He just feels pressure from the top down and the media. I heard even the Governor called him an hour ago. Did he tell you that?"

"No he didn't and I can't say it makes me feel any better." Latimer frowned. "I don't need the whole world breathing down my neck five minutes after the crime has been committed, just because one rich guy was murdered." He turned his swivel chair to face Brighton head on. "I'm going to work just as hard on this case as I have done all my cases. No matter who or what the victim is. A rich man dies just as easy as a poor guy from the slums, darn it." He slammed his fist down on the desk. "I'm going home Kid and we will start fresh in the morning. I always think best after I get a good night's sleep."

He got up, grabbed his coat and walked out the door, leaving Brighton sitting by himself.

Chapter 4

The man stood staring out the window into the darkness. His mind was in turmoil. He had not slept much since that night on the yacht. Things had not turned out as good as he had thought they would. Nightmares haunted him relentlessly, even during the day. It was as if his mind was in a loop from which there was no escape.

In his dreams he is on the boat listening for the footsteps coming from below. His hands shake as he holds the gun and yet he can't release the safety. His victim stands before him and laughs at him. The kind of laugh kids in school used to taunt him with. He looks at the victim's face clearly and it is his own image he sees. That's when he tries to scream and fire the gun, but it will not fire, even when he releases the safety. Instead of a scream, only a gurgling sound escapes his throat. No matter how hard he tries, he cannot make the gun fire as the victim continues to walk toward him, laughing.

He held on to the bed post, trembling uncontrollably and with a loud moan fell back onto the bed. He wiped the sweat off his forehead and remembered again how it really had been that night. It was as if a second video tape was rolling in his head, but this one was showing the events as they really happened.

There was so much blood. He realized he better get rid of the body the way he had planned. He walked over to where he had hid the emergency anchor. He looked around. There was no other boat or ship in sight. No one would ever find the victim, he was sure of that.

He rested for a while and then dragged the victim closer to the railing. He tied the rope around the chest underneath both arms as secure as he could. It was long enough so he could heave the body overboard and then throw the anchor after it. Sweat soaked his shirt. He wanted to rest but knew he couldn't wait any longer. Someone was bound to come this way sooner or later.

The body was heavier than he thought and it was difficult to lift it up to the railing. With extreme effort he finally got it halfway up. Before he lifted the legs to toss it all the way, he took the anchor and hung it onto the railing, up close to the body. With supreme effort he lifted the legs and swung them upward until gravity did the rest. The body splashed over the railing into the water and with a swift motion he threw the anchor after it. Both sank easily and were gone from view in seconds. The waves covered the spot as if nothing had ever disturbed them.

He slumped to the floor of the deck, totally exhausted. A feeling of relief washed over him. After a while he finally got up and walked the whole length of the vessel. Everything had gone according to plan. It seemed impossible, but he had done it. Tears streamed down his face and then came the laughter. He couldn't stop either one and began to shake uncontrollably. His time had come. No more living in the shadows. The world was his and no one would ever make him feel little and insignificant again.

It took a long time to clean up any signs of blood. Finally he decided it was good enough and started the motor. He steered the yacht back to the harbor. He threw his blood stained clothes into the sea and put on the fresh ones he had brought for just this purpose. It was as if the change of clothing signified his change into a new man, leaving the old life behind in the forgetfulness of the vast ocean.

That is why he could not understand the endless nightmares now, the fear and the anger. When would they end and his new life begin?

Chapter 5

The next morning Inspector Latimer didn't feel any better than before he went to bed. No revelation during the night, no fresh insight in the morning. Nothing. It was as if his brain was on neutral. He rummaged around the fridge to find something for breakfast and found a lonely boiled egg sitting in the egg tray in the door. He put it on the table and watched with strange fascination as it wobbled to the edge and landed on the floor.

"That just about sums up my situation right now," he mumbled as he bent over to pick it up. "Well, maybe things aren't so bad. This makes it easier to peel." He laughed a silent laugh and reached over to fill his coffee cup with the delicious smelling brew. He wondered how maybe one or two people on the planet lived without this heavenly stuff. Of all the things he could ever give up, coffee would never be one of them he told himself. No matter what some doctor in Florida planned to tell him.

"Well, Florida will have to wait until I solve this case," he said out loud. "I refuse to go out with a whimper. He slammed his cup on the table and spilled half of its content. This would not be one of his easy days he realized with a certain resignation. Surely the forensics report would shed some light on the case. It had to. There was nothing else he could think of. The only people left to question were the housekeeper, and she was totally loyal to the victim. There was the wife. She didn't seem to fit the image of a cold blooded murderer and neither did the little maid Lilly. He sighed. It was still early in the game. Something would come up today.

He turned the news on the minute he got into the car. The first item was the murder of Patrick Anscott with the assurance by Chief Carson they were following several leads. *I wish they would let me in on what they are,* Latimer thought. He turned to his favorite music station with easy listening sounds and leaned back into his seat. Traffic was heavy this morning and he knew he would be late. Not that anyone cared when he arrived, just so he solved the case. It always came back to that.

"Good morning, Inspector. I hear you have several leads on the case."

If looks could have killed, Ginny, his secretary, would have fallen over dead instantly. "I'm just going by what I heard on the news this morning, Sir." She smiled at him with her brightest smile and continued typing on her computer, well aware when to lie low.

"Is Brighton in yet, Ginny?" It was more like a bark than a question.

"He has a dental appointment this morning. He should be back any time," she added hastily before Latimer could start another outburst.

Of all mornings the Kid had to go to the dentist. He had actually looked forward to hear if Brighton had come up with something. He walked to the employee lounge to get another cup of coffee, hoping to stall for time until he actually had to come up with a plan for today. If all else failed, a cup of coffee could never hurt.

"Hey Latimer, I hear you have some leads already." The voice was unmistakable. His old nemesis, Harold Brown, was standing by the coffee machine. It wasn't that they were real enemies, just rivals. They had sparred for years over who would solve the most cases before retirement. Brown was a year younger and never failed to mention that fact, no matter the occasion. They really quite liked each other when not in a competitive mode and had been on good social terms when Mary was alive. Brown's wife, Alice, was a wonderful woman and a great cook. Latimer wished she would still invite him for one of her home-cooked meals sometimes. It had been a long time since he had been to their house.

"You will have to work hard on this case, Latimer. There isn't much to go on in spite of what the Chief said on the radio this morning. This might be the case that will leave you in the dust before retirement."

Latimer mumbled something under his breath as he filled his coffee cup.

"I see I'm right on target." Brown tried hard to suppress a laugh. "You keep trying old man, you don't have much time left and I'm right on your tail."

Why are there days like this? Latimer thought as he walked back to his office. He slumped into his chair. Brighton walked in, disgustingly cheerful as ever.

"Still have all your teeth?" Latimer looked at the young man with a sour face. "It's about time you got here. We have to go to the Anscott Estate first thing to finish up questioning the housekeeper and the wife, although I don't expect much." He took another sip of coffee. "I'm ready as soon as I finish this," he pointed at his cup.

"I'm ready any time you are, Sir. I've been thinking about this case last night and this morning."

"Did you come up with anything?"

"Nope." Brighton looked at Latimer. "It looks like you have, according to Chief Carson. I heard him on the radio on the way to the dentist."

Latimer answered with a grunt that spoke volumes.

"I guess the Chief was just blowing smoke as usual when the brass is on his neck."

"I guess you are right, Kid. That is how he gets to be Chief while we remain little Indians." Latimer got up from the chair, reached for his coat and headed for the door without saying another word. Brighton followed right behind him after grabbing his note pad.

When they arrived at Anscott Estate they found a large group of people peering through the closed gate.

"Reporters Sir, lots of them," Brighton said. "How are we going to get in there?"

"There is a bell and a speaker box over on the side, let's try that, Kid. Someone will let us in." Latimer motioned for Brighton to get out of the car.

He had a hard time getting through the crowd until he finally pushed the button on the box. He heard a faint crackling sound and then recognized the butler's voice.

"What can I do for you?"

"It's Inspector Latimer and Sgt. Brighton, Richard. We need to get in for some more questioning."

"Wait a moment and I will open the gate, Sgt. Brighton."

Dozens of reporters surrounded the car, shouting questions. Brighton had a terrible time moving the car without hurting anyone.

"No comments guys," he shouted through the open window as he slowly drove through the gate, which closed silently behind them.

There were no cars in front of the house. The place looked almost deserted. Latimer saw a curtain move in one of the windows upstairs, but couldn't make out who it was.

Richard opened the door before they could ring the bell.

"Come on in gentlemen. Good morning."

"I'm sorry we have to disturb your wife so early in the day, Richard. I hope she is up to it," Latimer said in a compassionate tone.

"She will be glad to answer any of your questions as best she can today, Sir. I told her you would be here first thing. Please follow me to the kitchen. Emily is waiting for you." He seemed composed and calm. Nothing showed in his attire or demeanor showed that he was upset about the events from yesterday. He was a true man of his profession.

Emily sat at the table in the corner with a cup of coffee in her hand. She stood up to greet them.

"Good morning, Mrs. McAllister. I'm Inspector Latimer and this is Sgt. Brighton with the Glenridge Central Crime Unit."

"Good morning, gentlemen. I'm sorry I was not able to talk to ye yesterday. Finding the body of dear Mr. Anscott was such a shock. I still can't believe it." She wiped a single tear from her eye and sat back down.

"What can you tell us, Mrs. McAllister?" Latimer asked gently.

"Oh, please call me Emily, Inspector," she said with a sad smile. "It's less formal."

"Thank you, Emily. Now tell us exactly what happened."

"Well Sir, it was early in the morning yesterday. I get up at the same time, and that would be six o'clock, to get breakfast ready for the family. On my way to the kitchen I saw the light on in the library and stopped to turn it off. I thought it was unusual for Mr. Anscott to leave it on." She wiped her forehead with her apron. "In spite of all the money he had, he was very frugal with everything. Funny that. Well, anyway. The door to the library was open just maybe an inch and that was unusual as well. He always kept it closed, whether he was in the room or not." She stopped to take a sip of coffee and then went on. "I called out his name, just in case he was in the room. When I heard no answer, I walked in slowly." Her eyes misted over and she started to breathe in short breaths. "There he was. I will never forget that horrible sight in all my born days. He lay on the floor in front of the big desk on his back." She was crying now. "He had this look of total surprise on his face as if he couldn't believe the person who shot him would do such a dreadful thing. Then I saw the blood all over the floor and started screaming until everyone in the house came running. After that I don't remember much."

She leaned back with a big sigh and took another sip of coffee. "Why would anyone want to kill this wonderful man? What is this world coming to?"

"Thank you Emily, you did very well." Latimer leaned over toward her. "Did you notice anything unusual the day before or in the evening?"

"No Sir, I can't think of anything."

"Do you know of anyone who does not like Mr. Anscott? Maybe his neighbors, people in his business or anyone else?"

"Sir, I swear to you he was one of the most well liked men I have ever known. All the money he has given to charity, church and the many people he helped, without anyone ever knowing about it." She raised herself up to full height. "But I knew about it. When one lives with a person for a long time one has a greater insight into what they're like." She seemed to have spent all her energy and leaned heavily over the table. "Now we will all have to pick up the pieces and help poor Mrs. Anscott go on without him. She is such a dear." Emily looked exhausted. It was as if sharing about this horrible ordeal had taken her last strength.

Latimer reached over and put his hand on her arm.

"You did great Emily, thank you. Do you think we can speak with Mrs. Anscott now?"

"Of course, Sir, she would be in the morning room. I know it's early, but she is one to be down first and read quietly before breakfast. I saw her there earlier. Richard, would you be so kind and take these gentlemen?"

The morning room was filled with bright sunlight let in by a big window facing a beautiful fall flower garden in the back of the house. It presented a picture of peace and tranquility and fully lived up to its name. Helen Elizabeth Anscott sat on a white leather couch facing the window. She had a small book in her hand and did not seem to notice the visitors as she stared out into the profusion of colors outside.

Latimer and Brighton hesitated to interrupt this peaceful scene and remained still just inside the door.

"It's alright, gentlemen, I'm prepared to talk to you today," she said as she got up to greet her visitors. Her face was very white and drawn. She wore a gray dress held at the waist with a black and silver belt. Latimer was not easily intimidated. Yet this woman, standing there with such poise and dignified elegance, blew him away. Here was a lady in the truest sense of the word. He could have stood there and stared at her for a long time, but instead reached out his hand to shake hers.

"Ma'am, we have to continue our conversation from yesterday. Again, let me say how sorry we are about your loss. I want you to know we will do everything we can to apprehend the person who did this terrible thing."

"Thank you Inspector, that is very kind of you. I cannot imagine who would have wanted to kill my husband." She pointed to the two armchairs. "Please have a seat. It is good to see you, Sgt. Brighton. Can Lilly bring you both some coffee?"

"No thank you Ma'am, I've had my fill for this morning," Latimer said after settling into the chair. He could have used another cup, but it didn't seem the thing to do at the moment.

"I have to ask you, did your husband have any enemies, at work, among friends, business people, disgruntled staff or anyone else?" Latimer asked.

"There is no one I can think of, Inspector. I was not involved in his business dealings at all. We decided to keep our private life separate from the company. He would share at times if something important came up, but not on a regular basis, and certainly not about daily office details." She looked at him with a look of utter despair. "I don't know anyone who did not like him, because he truly was a good man."

"Is there anything in your private life that bears mentioning, anything unusual that happened yesterday during the day or in the evening," Latimer asked.

"Nothing. My daughter and I had returned from the beach and were picked up at the airport by Richard. My son Marten had left our condo three days earlier because he wasn't feeling well. Come to think of it, I never asked him if he was better. He never even told us he was leaving. We assumed he was fishing when Richard called to inform me he was already home."

"Where is your condo, Mrs. Anscott?"

"In West Palm Beach."

"Do you go there often?"

"I don't, but my son likes to go fishing down there. He takes his friends several times a year, especially in the winter months. Like I told you, we all just spent some two weeks at our condo at the beach."

"Did your husband join you during this time?"

"No, he could not get away as usual. It is rare that he found the time to go with us." Her eyes filled with tears. "And now he never will again."

"Does your son work at Anscott Laboratories?"

"Yes, he does actually, but it is not a steady position yet. He finished his Master's in business just a year ago and wanted to take some time off to enjoy life before he puts his nose to the grindstone. Patrick had just told me last night, he thought it was time for Marten to start getting involved more in the business. He wanted us to travel together and see the world as he put it." She dabbed at her eyes. "That's not going to happen now either, is it?"

"How did your son feel about all this, Mrs. Anscott?" Latimer was simply fishing by now.

"Patrick had not talked to him yet, so I don't know. Given the situation, he won't have a choice now, will he? However, my daughter is very much involved with the company. She has more of a business head than Marten actually, and loves to work as hard as her father did. At 26 she is quite enthusiastic about learning how to take on a responsible position at Anscott Laboratories. Sometimes I think she may even be more interested to take over than Marten."

"That brings me to another question, Mrs. Anscott. Who stands to inherit the bulk of your husband's business?"

"It will be divided into three parts with me holding the controlling shares. The two children will inherit equal shares. I will get the Estate naturally and all other properties we own, including the condo in West Palm Beach. It will be up to me to decide which one of the children gets to run Anscott Laboratories when the time comes." She shook her head in sudden disbelief. "The time is here, isn't it?"

"Do your children know about the details of the Will?"

"Oh yes. We have always been very open about that. Like I said, Marten is not set on being a CEO, but Cassie is. I will have to talk to them both and let them decide which one wants to take Patrick's place. I'm afraid neither one is old enough, or experienced enough, for such a responsible position right now. I will have to ask Patrick's best friend and business associate Mark Lenhart to train them both for a few years." She sat back with a deep sigh. "There is so much to think about."

"Mrs. Anscott, you have been very helpful, thank you so much." Latimer stood up. "Please don't get up. I still would like to talk to both of your children if I may."

"Richard will see to it they are available, Inspector," Helen said. "Hopefully Marten is well enough to see you in the small library."

Latimer and Brighton followed Richard into a small study just off the morning room. The only window faced the side of the house and allowed a splendid view of a manicured lawn interspersed with several large oak trees. Four comfortable leather chairs were grouped around a round table filled with magazines and various books. One wall was lined with book shelves from bottom to ceiling. Knick knacks and family pictures broke up the countless rows in a cheerful way.

"Please, make yourselves comfortable," Richard said, pointing to the chairs. "I will inform Miss Cassie and Master Anscott you are here."

Latimer walked to the shelves to study the pictures. There were many of the children when they were small. One was of Marten on his boat in West Palm Beach and another in football uniform with the Stanford logo on it. He looked happy and exceedingly handsome. The one of Cassie was from her teenage years in a tennis outfit. She looked very much like her mother, judging from a picture of Helen Anscott right next to hers. Latimer looked for a family resemblance in Marten, but couldn't find any. The young man in the picture looked at him with a bright smile, showing flawless teeth and a healthy tan. Other than he was tall and lanky like his mother, nothing else in his features suggested a family likeness.

"Good morning, Inspector Latimer. I can't say I'm particularly happy to see you again." Marten Anscott looked much calmer and in control this morning as he stretched out his hand to Latimer. "I will be glad to answer any questions you might have. Although I can't imagine what I can say to help you find my father's killer." He sat down in a chair and totally ignored Brighton.

"Well Sir, you never know. Even the slightest detail can sometimes make the difference between success and failure in these cases." Latimer was relieved to find the young man more amiable this morning. "I believe you remember Sgt. Brighton."

"Of course." Marten merely glanced in Brighton's direction. "Let's get this over with. I have a lot of things to do with the preparations for the funeral." He leaned forward toward Latimer. "When will my father's body be released by the coroner's office, Inspector? Surely they are finished with their work by now. I simply must know in order to schedule the service. As you can imagine, this will be a large event with statewide media coverage." His face took on a frown. "Can't you do something about the reporters outside the gate? They are relentless and it upsets my mother and sister."

It upsets you even more, Latimer thought and ignored the request.

"I have not spoken with the coroner's office this morning, Sir. I imagine it will take a few more days until all the results are in." Latimer leaned back in his chair. "I want you to know that our office is pulling out all the stops trying to bring the murderer to justice. Unfortunately, these things take time. I will inform you the minute I hear anything definite."

Marten relaxed somewhat.

"I expect no less, Inspector."

"Now, let's get to the questions." Latimer's voice took on a more professional tone. "Your mother tells us you are aware of the details of the Will. Do you think you will want to run the company when things settle down?"

"I have not given it any thought, Inspector. Don't you think it's a little early to be concerned about that?" The sharp edge in his voice surprised Latimer.

"Well then, let's go over the evening of the murder again. Tell me exactly what happened."

"Wouldn't it be easier if you taped these interviews? You seem to be forgetting that I already told you what little there is I know." Latimer ignored the arrogance behind the remark.

"Humor me. And yes, as you can see, Sgt. Brighton takes notes while we talk, if you must know." Latimer's voice was even and nothing showed that he thought this man broke the mold of "nice" in the family, but then, everyone handles stress in different ways.

"Like I said before, I had dinner with the family that night and left the table early because I didn't feel well. I went to my room and stayed there till morning."

"What was wrong with you, Sir?"

"I never figured it out, because I feel better today. It must have been a bug I picked up somewhere."

"You didn't hear anything during the time of the incident?"

"I already told you, I didn't. I took some medicine and went to sleep."

"What kind of medicine? You didn't mention that last time."

"Some kind of antacid, I don't remember. Why would that be important?"

"So it was not sleeping medicine?" Latimer asked.

"No, it wasn't."

Latimer could see the beginning of anger in the young man's face.

"It must have been early in the evening when you went to bed. Are you sure you went to sleep right away?"

"Yes I did, how many times do I have to say it? Your line of questions is outrageous. Next you will accuse me of murdering my father." His face had taken on a red hue and he was trembling slightly as he held on to the edge of the chair.

Latimer did not answer and looked at him with a stony face. Brighton kept his head down, scribbling furiously.

"Well, never mind then, am I done here?" Marten started to get up.

"I'm afraid not, Sir, I have a few more questions." Latimer's voice was steady. "I still need to know why you came back from the beach early."

"I simply got bored and didn't feel all that great. There was no need for me to stay. Besides, I had things to do here. Two weeks at the beach is too long. I had done all the fishing I was going to do and so I left."

"Why did you leave without telling your mother and sister?"

"I didn't feel like having a discussion about it. I do what I want and when I want. Just because I live in this house doesn't mean I owe everyone an explanation for my actions." He was much more in control now and leaned back in his chair. He looked at Latimer with a hint of arrogance.

"Well, Mr. Anscott, that will be all for now. Please hold yourself available in case I need to tie things up if necessary."

Everyone rose.

"Would you please tell the maid I need to talk to her," Latimer said.

"I will let Richard know," Marten said and left the room.

In a few minutes Lilly knocked on the door.

"Inspector, Richard says you want to talk to me." She was shy and nervous and had trouble placing her hands.

"Come in, Lilly. You remember Sgt. Brighton, don't you?"

"Oh, yes Sir. It all seems a bit of a haze since yesterday. I don't know what I might be able to tell you."

"Have a seat, Lilly. We'll figure it out together," Latimer said with that infectious smile he knew to put on when the situation demanded.

Lilly carefully sat on the edge of the chair.

"Now tell me again what you saw yesterday, Lilly."

"Well Sir, I came running to the library after hearing Emily screaming something awful. I couldn't see at first what the trouble was, but then I saw Mr. Anscott on the floor. It was gruesome the way he stared up in surprise with those empty, blue eyes of his. He was such a nice man." She had relaxed as she talked and scooted back in her chair. It seemed a little big for her small frame.

"Is there anything unusual that happened that day or evening?" Latimer was fishing again.

"Nothing I can think of." She frowned a little as if deep in thought and then went on. "Maybe there is something. But no, that wouldn't have anything to do with the murder, I wouldn't think."

"Go ahead and tell us anyway," Latimer said with sudden interest.

"You know I've been employed in this house for three years now and never had any reason for complaints. The whole family treats all of us with great kindness and consideration, even young Mr. Anscott." She moved uneasy in the chair. "Maybe I shouldn't say anything, it being such a hard time right now."

"That is ok Lilly. What you tell us won't go any further. I'm sure you mean well." Latimer was really interested now. Finally something that wasn't perfect.

"The day young Mr. Anscott came home early I saw him enter an empty bedroom at the landing of the first floor. No one ever goes in there because it's never used for anything. He seemed lost somehow. When I asked him if everything was alright, he asked me to go ahead of him to his bathroom to make sure all the towels were laid out for his bath."

"What would be so unusual about that, Lilly," Latimer asked.

"For heaven's sake, the towels are laid out every morning when I clean. It's part of my job and I take my responsibilities very serious, Inspector. Why would he think I didn't do it on that day? When I told him I was sure they were ready for him to use he snapped at me in a most unkind way and told me to do as he asked."

"Had he ever acted that way before, Lilly?"

"No Sir, never." She rose up to full height with indignation. "I could understand if I had done something wrong, but I hadn't." Suddenly she moved to the edge of the chair again and her face became even more animated. "That brings to mind something I had forgotten. Young Mr. Anscott was rude to Emily too that day.

"How so?"

"Well, when he came back from the beach that day he told Richard he wanted a snack brought up to his room. Emily knew what he liked and fixed him a ham and cheese sandwich with a tall glass of milk. When she took it in to him he told her in no uncertain terms he didn't want the milk and to bring him some coffee. Emily was quite put out about it when she came back into the kitchen and told me what happened." She hesitated before she went on. "You know, that was before all this happened so it couldn't have been because his father died. Emily also said that she thought his eyes looked really mean that day. Young Mr. Anscott has never been mean in the years I've been here." She leaned over to Latimer. "You promise you won't say anything to anyone."

"I promise Lilly, unless it is necessary to solve the case. You would not mind it then, would you?" There was that disarming smile again.

"Of course in that case Inspector, it would be ok I guess."

"Thank you, Lilly. I think we have everything for now. You can go back to your duties." He rose and walked ahead of her to open the door.

Back at the precinct Latimer asked Brighton to check with forensics. Maybe something had come up they could use. He sat behind his desk, looking at his notes and going over every statement from yesterday and today. He was always pleased with the thorough notes Brighton managed to jot down. It was helpful too that he could read them easily. There certainly wasn't anything that unusual or helpful as far as he could see in what he found out. Even the Will did not contain any surprises. Everyone seemed so darn cordial and normal, except for the son. He felt frustrated. No family was that nice. There had to be skeletons somewhere. He just hadn't found them yet. Of course he still had to interview some of the people at Anscott Laboratories this afternoon. Maybe something would come up.

He could also talk to the family's personal attorney. He knew he couldn't say too much but at least he could give a hint of anything out of the ordinary that could be a motive for murder.

"Ginny, can you come in here please?"

She appeared at the door almost instantly.

"What can I do for you, Inspector?" She was all business this morning after that display of foul mood earlier by her usually amiable boss.

"I need an appointment with the personal attorney of the Anscott family. I have no idea who that is, but I'm sure you can find out."

"Right away, Sir. Do you want that for today or does it matter?"

"Try to get it as soon as possible. Tell him I just need ten minutes of his time."

"Ok, will do."

"When Brighton comes back I want to see him right away."

"Ok boss."

"Why are you in a snit, Ginny?"

"Because you were in a snit first thing this morning."

"Sorry, I didn't mean to take it out on you. I'm just frustrated with this case." He looked at her with the charming grin he used when he had done something wrong.

"It's alright, Bob. I know you have a lot on your plate. Try to let me know when you are mad about something other than me."

"I also need you to call the main office at Anscott Laboratories and let them know I need to talk to certain management personnel. Tell them this might take several days and be available after lunch."

"Will do, boss." She gave him her brightest smile and walked back to her desk.

"You are the best, Ginny!" he shouted after her.

"I know."

Brighton walked in, holding the coroners preliminary report in his hand.

"Here it is, boss. I had to wait a few minutes to get it."

"Let's see what we have here," Latimer said as he settled back and started reading. "There is no doubt the victim was shot at close range." He rubbed his forehead as he always did when things did not add up. "According to the coroner, Anscott was shot with a Walther PK 380. It's a common hand gun, which can be purchased anywhere. Since there was no break-in, no alarm went off and no foot prints around the perimeter of the house, it had to be someone on the inside, Brighton. It also means the perp had to have used a silencer since no one heard the shot."

"I can't see anyone in the family or the staff doing this," Brighton said. "The only one who could possibly have it in him is the son, but what would his motive be? The old man was going to ask him to take over the business sooner rather than later. That meant everything was his for the taking, without the need for murder."

"You are so right, Kid. This guy has been groomed from childhood to take over, yet was not that eager to do it, according to his mother. Remember, she told us he wanted to have some fun before starting down that road."

"There is no motive, Sir."

"You are right on, no motive whatsoever. We are going to talk to the people in charge at the company this afternoon. I will insist they go over the books to see if any money is missing. That could be a motive if young Mr. Marten had dipped his fingers in the till before Daddy was ready to give it to him. Having fun can be expensive, Kid."

"I wouldn't know, Sir, all I do is work for a few bucks. Some day when I grow up big and strong like you, I will get to play at the beach in Florida." Brighton grinned.

"That actually sounds real good right about now," Latimer grumbled. "Feel like going to the burger joint across the street for a grease infested meal, Kid? I'm buying."

"Yes Sir, that sounds good, I'm hungry."

"You're always hungry. I guess it takes a lot to fill up that long bean pole of a body at your age. Instead of French fries, get me a salad with Ranch dressing. Make sure you get the burger with everything on it."

"Ok Sir, I will be right back," Brighton said, holding out one hand for the money.

Chapter 6

Anscott Laboratories was housed in one of the tallest buildings in Glenridge. It was an impressive glass tower in the middle of downtown. The company occupied the top ten floors which served as headquarters. Anscott Labs could be found in every major city of the East and even in some smaller communities. It was an old business, handed down for three generations. The first Patrick Marten Anscott started out small in Glenridge around 1900. It was his son who branched out first to New York and Washington, DC and then to many of the major cities along the East Coast. It was when he ventured into medical research facilities, the company made a name for itself. By the time the present Mr. Anscott took over, it was one of the most prestigious companies of its kind in the East. However, unlike his father and grandfather, he did not wish to branch out into the Midwest or California. There were several people on his management team who had urged him to reconsider over the years. He stuck to his guns with the reason his family was more important to him than owning a nationwide business.

Latimer knew these latest facts from his wife Mary, who had gotten to know Helen Anscott during a charity fundraising event. Mary had really been into these kinds of things. While she could not contribute large sums of money, she made up for it by giving freely of her time. He remembered her telling him about meeting Helen and spending several days with her, where she had shared some of these personal facts. He also remembered telling his wife to be careful, because Helen Anscott was clearly out of their league. Mary had brushed him off, saying she was one of the nicest women she had ever met. He wished he could tell his deceased wife how right she had been.

They were on their way to see Mark Lenhart, Senior VP for Anscott Laboratories. Ginny had done a good job lining up several managers for this afternoon.

"Let's see if we can't make some headway here," Latimer said more to himself than to Brighton who walked close behind him. He pushed the button on the elevator to the top floor. Chrome and glass everywhere spoke of money. Even one side of the elevator was all mirrors. Brighton took the opportunity to check his hair. When the door finally opened they were looking down a long hallway lined with heavy carpet and expensive wood paneling on the walls. To the left sat a large, opulent desk with two chairs in front and a young secretary talking on the phone. She waved them over when she spotted them.

"Gentleman, you must be from the police. I'm Greta. I'll ring you through to Mr. Lenhart." She pushed a button on her large console and waited. "The police are here, Sir. Yes Sir, right away." She looked at Latimer with a friendly smile and rose from her desk. "I will take you to Mr. Lenhart's office. Please follow me."

Their shoes sunk into the plush carpet as they walked by several closed doors until she opened one of the last ones.

"Please go on in. Mr. Lenhart is ready to see you."

"Thank you, Greta," Brighton said with his best smile as he let Latimer go in first.

"You must be Inspector Latimer." The tall, handsome man got up from his chair and stretched out his hand across the desk. He looked the typical executive dressed in an expensive gray suit.

"That is correct Sir, and this is my assistant Sgt. Brighton. It is good of you to see us under, what I'm sure, are extremely trying circumstances." Latimer was all business.

"We are all still in shock Inspector about this tragedy. Patrick and I went to college together and have been joined at the hip in this business since we graduated. He was not just an employer, but more so a good friend for all these many years. I talked with Helen this morning and told her I would do anything to help in whatever way she needed me." He sat back down and folded his hands neatly on the desk.

"I have a few questions I need to ask you Sir," Latimer said after a slight pause. "First of all, we are certain he was shot in his home at close range in the study. There are no defensive wounds or signs of a struggle. That means he knew his assailant well and had no idea of his intentions. As a matter of fact, even in death there was a look of total surprise on his face." Latimer cleared his throat. "My question to you is this Sir, can you think of anyone here at the company who had a grudge against him or would have benefited from Mr. Anscott's death?"

"I have thought long and hard about this, Inspector. Patrick was one of those rare men liked by most people in spite of his high position and the unlimited power he wielded in this company. I can't honestly think of anyone who disliked him, least of all hated him enough to want to kill him." His hands had not moved. "Besides, surely someone would have heard the doorbell or the car drive up if he let a visitor in the house that late at night. I cannot imagine anyone in the family or the staff doing such a horrible thing." He leaned back in his chair and looked at Latimer for conformation.

"It looks like you have really been thinking about this a lot, Mr. Lenhart," Latimer said, surprise in his voice.

"I make a lot of money in my job to solve problems and put out fires every day, Inspector." He had a tiny smile on his face. "It comes with the territory."

"You certainly make my job easy, Sir." Latimer showed one of his polite smiles he used when the other guy was right, but he hated to admit it. "There is one area I will need your further help with though."

"Anything I can do Inspector, just name it."

"I think it will be necessary to check the financial side of the company and see if there are any discrepancies anywhere. We are looking at funds missing or anything else that would indicate a motive for murder by a company employee."

"Do you have any specific person in mind?" Mark Lenhart shifted slightly in his seat. "If you do it would certainly help with our search."

"At this point I don't. It could be anyone, even a member of the family, given the circumstances of the murder."

"Oh, goodness gracious, I can't imagine any member of that nice family being involved, Inspector. I have known them all for a long time." He really looked uncomfortable now.

"I'm going to come right out and ask you about Marten Anscott. Was he in any kind of a financial bind that you know of?" Latimer asked.

"I don't think so. He has a large trust fund at his disposal and has no need to go to such measures as murdering his father. We expect him to join our top management team at any time. Marten sure is ready for it. Cassie is already well on her way to take on certain responsibilities and is doing well. She also has access to her own trust fund since she turned 25 last year. So you see, there is no need for either of them to murder their father for money." He seemed relieved to have solved the problem of family involvement. "I think you are barking up the wrong tree Inspector."

"It seems that I have to agree with you. Nevertheless, look into it and see if any unusual transactions have occurred within the last year." Latimer rose from his chair. "You've been most helpful, Mr. Lenhart. I hope I can call on you again if I have any more questions."

"You certainly may, Inspector. You must excuse me. I'm late for a meeting. Have a good day."

"That went well, Sir."

"Almost too well, if you ask me Kid. I see another perfect setting with lots of perfect people and no one capable of murder. Why do I feel almost angry with so much perfection? What are we missing?"

"I agree with you, Sir. But you will admit, so far we have not come across anyone who looks like your typical murderer." Brighton's smile actually made Latimer feel better.

They stopped at Greta's desk. She had been on the phone with what seemed to be a private call and hung up the moment she saw them walk up.

"I have Mrs. Goldsmith for you next. She is another senior VP in charge of quality control. Let me ring her for you."

Henrietta Goldsmith was old school, in her sixties, beautiful white hair arranged perfectly and wearing a dark blue business suit. She was waiting for them as they came down the hallway.

"Come on in gentlemen. I don't have but 15 minutes to spare, but I'm sure I can tell you what little I know about this dreadful business."

"Thank you for seeing us, Ma'am," Latimer said in his most polite tone. "I'm Inspector Latimer and this is Sgt. Brighton." He looked directly at her. "Did you know the deceased on a personal level rather than strictly business?"

"I knew him well, but did not associate with him or his wife socially. Our relationship, while friendly, was kept to business matters. Of all the men in high positions I have ever known, he was one of the kindest and most pleasant. He was a gentleman of the old school. They simply don't make them like that anymore." Her face had softened as she spoke. Latimer could tell she had respected Patrick Anscott. He continued for a while with routine questions, but realized she had nothing to add to the case.

"Thank you, Mrs. Goldsmith for your time. You were most helpful."

"This is getting worse by the minute," Brighton muttered under his breath as they walked toward Greta's desk. "There has got to be at least one mean old grouch in the bunch."

"You are back again so soon?" Greta was already dialing the next number. "You will be seeing Thomas Pelosi, head of HR next. Please, follow me Inspector."

We finally hit the jackpot, Latimer thought when he saw the bald, tiny man behind what seemed to be an oversized desk. He glared at them as they entered.

"I have no time for this kind of nonsense. What could I possibly know about the murder of Mr. Anscott? I didn't know the man other than to talk to him at meetings."

"Mr. Pelosi, I'm Inspector Latimer and this is Sgt. Brighton. Sorry to bother you, but it is necessary to ask you a few questions in this case."

"Well, if you must, but get on with it. I haven't got all day."

"Do you have a list of the people who were fired or laid off by Mr. Anscott or anyone in the offices of Anscott Laboratories within the last year?"

"Do you have any idea how many employees this company has? It will take valuable time for me to research this matter." His small, blue eyes pierced right through Latimer with total annoyance.

"I'm sure you are very competent in your job Mr. Pelosi, and will be able to give us an answer, if not today, then maybe tomorrow. Surely you know of someone who fits the description of an angry ex-employee." Latimer sounded the picture of patience.

"I can't say that I can think of anyone off hand, but I will look into it." His little body seemed to stretch a few inches higher as he added emphatically, "This is a reputable company and we treat our employees well."

Latimer could barely suppress a smile, thinking of this little man treating anybody well, least of all an employee.

"Well Sir, we will be in touch with you tomorrow. I will send someone over for the list if you will give it to Greta up front. We appreciate your time."

"That was funny, Sir." Brighton could barely refrain from laughing. "How does a guy like that end up in management?"

"He must be doing something right or he wouldn't be there. Look at you, Kid. How did you manage to end up with me?" They both started laughing until they once again ended up at Greta's desk.

She looked at them with a strange look on her face.

"I believe you are the first people that have ever left Mr. Pelosi's office laughing."

"It's a long story, Greta," Brighton said.

"I believe you. Are you ready for the next one?"

"How about Mr. Anscott's secretary or assistant, is she available?" Latimer said before she started punching in another number.

"Oh, of course, that would be Glenda Hinsley. She just walked in a few minutes ago. I will ring her. She was already dialing before she finished the last sentence.

A short time later a middle aged, well-dressed woman walked toward them.

"You must be Inspector Latimer and Sgt. Brighton. I'm Glenda Hinsley, Mr. Anscott's personal assistant. Please follow me to my office right down the hall."

Latimer was impressed. The woman was friendly yet professional with an air of efficiency in her movements. Her silver gray hair was styled in a short, expensive cut and her dark business suit covered any flaws or signs of age in her figure. Her office was neat yet cluttered enough to produce results. Her dark blue eyes sparkled with intelligence.

"I was wondering when the police would come and talk to me. I'm glad I had a few hours to gather my wits about me after I heard what happened to Mr. Anscott. I cannot tell you how shocked I was when I heard the news. I have worked for him for 12 years and have never heard a cross word out of his mouth." She sat down behind her desk. "Mind you, it's not that he never got mad, but he never let it out on those around him."

"Can you think of anyone in the company who would want to do something like this, Mrs. Hinsley?" Latimer had a good feeling about this interview.

"I have thought about this. I can honestly say I can't think of anyone who would want to kill a good man like that. It had to be someone who is deranged in some way. There simply is no other explanation, Inspector."

"Do you know anybody who fits that category among his family, friends, business associates or even his enemies?"

She thought carefully for a moment.

"His family is wonderful. I've known all of them for a long time. His friends are good people and have been close to him for years. His business associates respected him, even if they disagreed on some matters." She tilted her head slightly. "Let me see, his enemies. He didn't really have any that I know of except for one. I don't know anything about that one so I'm not even sure about her."

"Can you elaborate, Mrs. Hinsley?"

"Oh, please call me Glenda." She settled back in her chair and pushed an imaginary strand of hair behind one ear. "It happened the other day, Friday it was I think. A woman came into my office unannounced and demanded to see Mr. Anscott. She looked poorly dressed, although it was probably the best outfit she owned. Of course I inquired of her name and what her business was. I asked her if she had an appointment to see Mr. Anscott."

We are finally getting somewhere, Latimer thought.

"Go on Glenda," he said.

"The woman said her name was Lora Weston and she was an old acquaintance of Mr. Anscott. 'From years back,' were her words, and her business with him was private. I asked her if I could make an appointment to meet with him some other time since he was in a meeting, but she wouldn't hear of it. "He wouldn't dare not see me," she said in a smug tone. "I'll wait for as long as it takes.""

Glenda got up and walked to the window overlooking the city. "The woman gave me the creeps, Inspector. I had never seen her before or heard her name mentioned by Mr. Anscott or anyone in the family."

"Did you know the members of his family well?" Latimer asked.

"Yes, I spent many vacations with them at the condo in West Palm Beach and was invited to birthdays and other special occasions. They treated me almost like a member of the family."

"Tell me more about this woman, Glenda."

"Well, the strangest thing happened. About an hour later Mr. Anscott walked in the office. His face turned pale when he saw the woman and then he told me in a real harsh tone, "Cancel all my appointments for the afternoon." Then he waved the woman on to follow him into his office."

"Did you hear anything they talked about?" Latimer felt like a blood hound on a fresh trail.

"No, I didn't. I'm ashamed to say I listened at the door, but it is well constructed and sound proof. I couldn't hear a thing, no shouting or arguing."

"How long did the woman stay?"

About a half hour I would say. When she came out she had a real smug look on her face. "I'll be back, honey," she said to me in a real nasty way.

"Did you talk to Mr. Anscott about the visit?"

"I tried, but he cut me off and said he was going home. He then asked me to tell Mark Lenhart to take over the board meeting. He left about five minutes later."

"How did he look?"

"Funny you should ask. His face was like a mask, real drawn and pale. He didn't even say goodbye." She began to tear up. "That's so sad, because I never saw him again."

"Lora Weston you say was her name? You're sure it doesn't ring a bell?"

"I'm certain I've never heard it before. You see, I have a thing about names. Unlike most people, I never forget once I hear a name. It really helps me in my job."

"How old do you think the woman was?"

"Oh, I would think in her early sixties, maybe a little older, but not much. It was hard to tell because she looked like she has led a pretty tough life."

"Glenda, this is the first really helpful information we have gotten so far. We'll definitely try to find this woman. Thank you so much. You've been extremely helpful."

"I'm glad I finally talked about this to someone. I didn't know what to do, whether I was overreacting if I contacted the police or not. That's why I was so relieved when you asked to talk to me."

"I will schedule a session with our sketch artist tomorrow at the precinct so we can put out an APB on her." Latimer stood up. "For now, that is all we can do here. Thanks again Glenda, and goodbye."

"Remember Kid, crime investigation is usually short on glory and long on patience, perseverance and tenacity. Only in the movies does the hero ride on a white horse from one adventure to another." Latimer was in a good mood. "We have found the chink in the armor of perfection in Patrick Anscott's life."

Chapter 7

"Ginny!" Latimer yelled though the open door of his office.

"I'm not deaf, Bob. What is it I can do for you?"

She looked almost pretty this morning with her thick blond hair pulled back into a pony tail. Well, maybe not pretty, but pert and cheerful and young. He was glad they hadn't assigned him one of the older secretaries, who in his opinion equated efficiency with grouchiness. To be honest, they probably were more efficient, but he had trained the young girl to do things according to his ways.

"You are looking nice this morning."

"You must want something really bad telling me that." She smiled and he could tell she was pleased with his compliment.

"Did you ever get hold of the Anscott's lawyer?"

"I did. His name is Connor Mathews. He was not thrilled that you want to talk to him, citing client confidentiality and all that. I managed to get you an appointment later on this morning, shortly before noon. I guess he figures, if he doesn't like your questions, he can escape for lunch."

"Thanks, Ginny. If I could I would give you a raise every day."

"Yeah right." Her pony tail bounced as she turned around to go back to her desk.

Brighton looked his cheerful self when he walked in the door right after Ginny had left. He looked rested and rearing to go.

"What's up today, Sir? Are we going back to the company to interview a few more stuffed shirts?"

"I don't think so. I have to talk to the Chief in a few minutes and give him an update on this woman Lora Weston. What you can do is go into the data base and find out if she has a record of some kind. Narrow it down to women around sixty."

"Shouldn't we wait until we have the sketch?"

"You have a name that should do for the first try, Kid." He started to get up. "Before anything else, get our sketch artist and Glenda Hinsley together today."

"Ok boss."

Latimer walked by the lounge to grab another cup of coffee before heading for the Chief's office. Brown was there ahead of him, filling his cup.

"Well, well, what have we here? No news is good news, hey?" He looked at Latimer with big innocent eyes. "I have been praying for you. Has it done any good?"

"Thank you Brown, as a matter of fact it has. I'm on my way to the Chief's office to give him the good news. I will make sure to mention it was due to your inroads with the man upstairs."

For once Brown was speechless and stepped out of the way to let Latimer fill his cup. He didn't have a chance to say more because the Chief walked in the door.

"Good morning gentlemen." He turned to Latimer. "I hope you are on your way to see me with some good news. My phone keeps ringing and I don't have anything new to say. That is not good when one of the calls is from the Governor's office." He filled his cup and Latimer followed him down the hall.

"Tell me you have something, Latimer," he said before he sat down behind his desk.

"I do Sir."

"Really?" He leaned over the desk with interest.

"Well Sir, Brighton and I interrogated several people at Anscott Laboratories yesterday afternoon. At first nothing stood out until we talked with Mr. Anscott's assistant, a woman by the name of Glenda Hinsley. She told us about a visit her boss had last Friday by a very strange woman who called herself Lora Weston." Latimer then told the Chief the details of the rest of the interview.

"Brighton is scheduling her now as we speak to meet with our sketch artist. He is going over the data base to find a match," he added.

"Excellent, Latimer, excellent. That will give me something to feed to the wolves out there." He leaned back in his chair with satisfaction. The chair let out a painful moan.

"Chief, I don't know that we should share any of this with the public. It might scare the woman off and she could disappear. Who knows, she may have already left since Anscott's murder has been hashed over without letup in the news over the last few days."

"Don't worry Latimer. I did not get to be Chief because I'm an idiot." He smiled as he said it, which put Latimer at ease. No sense in alienating this guy before retirement.

"We should know more about the woman by this afternoon, Sir. I will go to the Estate and talk to Mrs. Anscott. Maybe she has an idea what this is all about." Latimer waited if the Chief had anything to add and got up. "I will definitely keep you informed, Sir."

"Good job, Latimer. I knew I could count on you," the Chief said and took another sip of his coffee. "I'll wait to hear from you."

Latimer hesitated at the door.

"One more thing Sir, would it be possible to let me know what you will share about this case with the media before you do it?" He held his breath.

"Why, don't you trust me Latimer?" His boss looked at him for a moment and then said, "I'll have my secretary send you a memo before the press conference this afternoon, how's that?"

"Thank you Sir, that is very kind of you." Latimer left before the Chief could change his mind. He had no idea what he would do if he disagreed with what his superior planned to say. At least he would be prepared or could try to change his mind.

Back in his office he found Brighton waiting for him.

"I found 17 Lora Westons in the city so far, Sir. Three seem to fit our suspect. One sticks out above the rest." He moved from behind the desk to let Latimer sit in his chair. "I have it on your computer right here." He waited until Latimer sat down and moved behind him and with a click brought up the picture of a woman on the screen.

"That's great, Kid, but we have to go back to the Estate to talk to Helen Anscott before anything else. I have a feeling she knows something about this."

Brighton's face fell.

"But this might be the one, Sir."

"She could be, but we will wait till this afternoon until Glenda Hinsley comes and can give us a positive ID."

"You are right, Sir. I hadn't thought of that."

"We will be back in two hours or so, Ginny. You know how to reach me," he said on the way out.

Ginny simply nodded.

There was still a group of reporters in front of the gate. Just like the last time, they stormed the car when they realized it was the police. Brighton drove in after Richard opened the gate.

Latimer studied the four cars in front of the house carefully. One was the florist unloading several large flower arrangements. The other was a black sedan with dark, tinted windows. Another was the little red Lexus belonging to Marten, plus a blue two door Honda Civic.

The front door to the house was open and the two detectives walked in after they rang the bell. Richard appeared almost immediately and greeted them with a warm smile.

"Good morning gentlemen, how good to see you again."

"I'm sorry we have to bother you one more time, Richard," Latimer said as he walked in. "We need to speak to Mrs. Anscott if that is possible."

"Of course Sir, I will let her know you are here. I'm afraid she is in with her minister at the moment. I'm sure she will see you after they are done. It will be a little while I'm afraid. Why don't you follow me to the small library and wait there. I will send Lilly with some refreshments. He turned and they followed him through the foyer and down the hallway to the back of the house.

"Madam, the police would have another word with you," they heard Richard say after a half hour. "Shall I ask them to come in?"

"Inspector, how good to see you. Sgt. Brighton, come and sit down over here." She pointed to the same chairs they had occupied the day before. "It looks like we are getting to know each other quite well, doesn't it?" A Bible was lying on the coffee table in front of her.

Latimer cleared his throat. He hoped he would not disturb her with his questions more than she already was.

"What can I do for you, Inspector?" she finally asked when he did not say anything.

"Ma'am, I will come right to the point. There has been a development. Sgt. Brighton and I went to the company yesterday and interviewed several people. Glenda Hinsley related an incident in your husband's office on Friday afternoon that might pertain to this case." He shifted uncomfortably in his seat.

"Really, what happened, Inspector?"

"Well Ma'am, it sounds very strange and even mysterious and we thought maybe you could shed some light on this." Then he told her what Glenda Hinsley had shared with them without leaving anything out, except the name of the woman.

"That does sound strange, Inspector. Did Glenda find out the name of this person?"

"Yes, she did, Ma'am. It is Lora Weston."

Right before his eyes Helen Anscott crumbled. Her face turned ashen and her hands trembled as she slumped over and buried her head in her arms. Sobs shook her body. Latimer and Brighton looked at each other, surprised and stunned into silence. They certainly had not expected such an emotional reaction.

"Mrs. Anscott, may I get Richard to bring you some water or anything else you need?" Brighton took the initiative. He was better at these things than his boss. Latimer just sat there, looking uncomfortable.

After what seemed a long time, Helen Anscott raised herself up and reached for a napkin on the table and wiped her face.

"You must forgive me, but I was not prepared for this." Her hands were still trembling just a little. "I'm usually not this emotional," she added.

"Do you feel like telling us who this woman is and what she wanted from your husband?" Latimer was coming alive again.

"I really don't want to talk about this, Inspector. This is a matter from many years ago and has nothing to do with my husband's death. I'm certain of that." She had collected her emotions by now and straightened herself.

"Mrs. Anscott, this is a murder investigation and we must insist you share with us all things relevant to your husband's life." Latimer had gone into his gentle, diplomatic mode. "I'm sure you understand our position."

"I understand, but I will not talk about this to anyone. Not now or in the future, not even to you, Inspector." She looked at him with fierce determination. "That is the way it is." She stood up suddenly and said as if remembering her manners, "Now if you will excuse me, I'm very busy with preparations for the funeral service." Just before she reached the door she turned around and said, "Richard will show you out." With that she left.

They sat in stunned silence as they watched the door close behind her.

"Well, that went well," Brighton muttered under his breath.

"You have a gift for understating the obvious, Kid."

"Now what, Sir?"

"How the heck should I know, I'm still in shock." Latimer was staring at the closed door. "Of all the things, I would have never expected this." He finally got up. "We might as well go. I'm certain none of the children or the staff will be able to shed a light on this secret." He turned to Brighton. "This is not just a chink in the armor, this is a big hole and we are going to find out what it is."

Richard stood in the door.

"I am to show you out gentlemen, if you will follow me." He was not smiling.

Back in the car Latimer realized it was just about time to go to the lawyer's office. The black car was gone. It must have been the minister's. He searched for the address and typed it into the GPS on his cell phone. It turned out to be not too far from where they were. They arrived fifteen minutes early in front of the law offices of Mathews, Hewitt, McCormick and Knowles. It was a pretty large, well-kept two-story building just outside the center of town. A large maple tree graced the front in the middle of a small patch of manicured lawn. The door to the office was made of solid oak with a brass slit for the mail. It opened without effort.

"Can I help you gentlemen?" The secretary looked young with a fresh, friendly face, long blond hair, blue eyes and a stick figure to complete the image of a model on the cover of Vogue. She interrupted filing her bright red nails when they stood in front of her desk.

"We are with the police and have an appointment with Mr. Mathews." Brighton said with his best smile.

"I will let Mr. Mathews know you are here. Please have a seat." She pointed to a seating area to the left. "Mr. Mathews, the police are here to see you", she said into an intercom device.

Before they could get comfortable in their chairs, a short, well-dressed man in his sixties entered the room. His suit reeked of money and a Rolex watch gleamed on his wrist. His thinning black hair was combed to one side to hide the bare spot on top of his head. *I bet it takes a lot of hair spray to keep that in place,* Latimer thought, grateful for his full head of hair.

"I'm Connor Mathews and you must be Inspector Latimer." He had a firm handshake.

"This is Sgt. Brighton. Thank you for seeing us, Mr. Mathews."

"Please follow me to my office, gentlemen. Have a seat." He pointed to a seating area with four heavy leather chairs arranged around a matching table with an expensive looking bowl of artificial fruit in the middle. The huge desk stood to the right filled with countless stacks of papers. Mr. Mathews apparently was not a man of order judging by the clutter everywhere. Book shelves lined the walls and seemed to pertain to the law mostly. There were several pictures of small children, probably his grandchildren. One was of a woman his age in a beautiful silver frame on his desk.

"What is it you wish to ask me about, Inspector? I can't imagine what I could add to your investigation of my good friend Patrick. I'm still shocked. We were college roommates at Stanford you know."

"I realize you cannot speak about matters pertaining to your client's business and legal matters, Mr. Mathews. Could you tell me if you know of a woman with the name of Lora Weston?"

Connor Mathews tried very hard not to show any emotion, but Latimer saw the twitch in his eye. It was the sharp intake of breath that really gave him away.

After a pause a fraction too long, he caught himself and said, trying to sound casual, "Like you said yourself, I'm bound by the law of client privilege and this would definitely fall into that category." He exhaled deeply.

"Then you know such a woman, Sir?" Latimer asked.

"I did not say that Inspector and unless there is anything else you want to ask me, our conversation is over. I have a busy schedule as you can imagine." He started to stand up.

"I do have another question, Mr. Mathews. Can you think of anyone who had a grudge against the victim? The woman called Lora Weston seems to have known your client for many years. According to Glenda Hinsley, she showed a lot of hostility when she visited him in his office last Friday."

"I cannot comment on this matter Inspector, for reasons I already stated."

"Can you tell me if the family has any knowledge about this mystery woman?"

"Again I cannot give you an answer." He started to sound agitated.

"We spoke to Mrs. Anscott this morning. To put it mildly, she fell apart when I mentioned Lora Weston's name." Latimer wasn't going to give up so easily. "This is a murder investigation and this woman is now our main person of interest."

"I fully understand your position, but I have spoken with Mrs. Anscott after you left her house. She instructed me unequivocally not to speak about this matter under any circumstances. As her family lawyer, I have no choice but to abide by her wishes." He got up and walked around the desk. "Our meeting is over Inspector. I'm truly sorry I could not be of more help. I'm as interested as you to find the killer of my good friend, but my hands are tied." He shook Latimer's hand. "I believe you know the way out."

"If I was given to cussing this would be the time to do it." Latimer said as he got in the car. "The hole in the chink keeps getting bigger." He put on his seat belt. "We can almost be sure this has to do with the past of the Anscott family. Infidelity is the most common reason for blackmail in the world. I guarantee you Patrick and this woman Lora Weston had a little fling going and Helen found out about it. They patched things up between them and paid the woman off to keep it from the kids and everyone else.

"Since both husband and wife know about it, how could anybody blackmail Anscott after all this time?" Brighton asked as he started the car.

"Could it be she ran out of money and came back for more? People like the Anscotts will do almost anything to hide those kinds of secrets in order to put up a perfect front for the world to see," Latimer said with renewed zeal in his voice. "That means we will have to ask Marten and Cassie Anscott about the woman. After that we have to find this Lora Weston."

Brighton turned onto Main Street and headed back to the precinct.

"Maybe Glenda can identify her this afternoon, Sir. She is pretty sharp and will definitely pick her out of the data base if she's there." Brighton looked encouraged.

"Make sure you look at as many different data bases as you can think of, even if it takes several days. She is our only hope right now. I'm sure the Chief is beginning to take some heat already. You know how these high profile cases are, they want them solved in a day or at least two." Latimer sighed deeply. "Florida is starting to look good again, Kid."

Glenda arrived promptly at two o'clock and Brighton took her to a special room with a computer hooked up to the precinct's data base.

"Thanks for coming, Glenda. It's important that you take your time as you study each face on the screen. I have instructed the program to sort out women from the age of 55 to 65." He turned to her with his disarming smile. "Are you ready?"

"Sure, this sounds interesting. Maybe I will find some people from my family on there. You never know." She laughed. "They all seem pretty normal with normal lives as far as I know."

She leaned back in the chair with a sigh. "I'm ready."

Picture after picture of women of all shapes and sizes flashed in a constant stream before their eyes. Glenda had stopped shaking her head after a while and just sat still as she studied each face. It seemed like hours had gone by when Brighton asked if she wanted a cup of coffee.

"I need one, I'm getting sleepy." She yawned.

He jumped up. "Let's go to the lounge and stretch our legs and find the coffee pot. Maybe somebody brought some good stuff today."

"I don't eat sweets. I want to keep my girlish figure you know."

"You are sure doing a good job of it." Brighton tried hard to say the right thing on this touchy subject with women. He never knew what the right thing was and had gotten in trouble several times with a girlfriend. His expertise with the opposite sex was not the greatest. Lately, he had wondered if it was time to find someone to spend the rest of his life with.

As if she had read his thoughts Glenda said, "Have you thought about finding the right girl for you, Sergeant? Or maybe you have already found her." She laughed a soft little laugh.

"No, but I've been thinking about it lately. It's not easy. Most girls want a career or a rich man. And a sergeant in the police force doesn't exactly guarantee a mansion down the road."

"Money isn't everything. You are such a wonderful young man. Surely there is a girl who would take you."

"Well, maybe there is hope for me, Mrs. Hinsley."

They had arrived at the lounge and Brighton poured two cups of coffee. It looked real strong by this time in the afternoon.

"Better put lots of cream and sugar in, otherwise it will blow you away," he said as he handed the cup to Glenda. On the other hand, it will keep you awake to look at some more pictures."

When five o'clock came, Glenda had not seen anyone who looked like the woman she encountered in Patrick Anscott's office.

"Can you come back in the morning?" Brighton asked when he turned off the computer. "The Inspector says it's very important we go through as many as we can. As a matter of fact, solving the case pretty well depends on it right now."

"I better show up then, shouldn't I?" She took her purse and waved Brighton goodbye. "I will try to be here at ten if that's ok."

Chapter 8

The next day Latimer got to the office around 7:30 a.m. He wanted to sift through the notes Brighton had made so far. He found them neatly typed on his desk and thanked God for Ginny.

After three cups of coffee and two donuts he had not made any headway. Let's face it, it all boiled down to finding out who this Lora Weston was. He decided to go back to the Estate as soon as Brighton showed up. They would ask Marten and Cassie, as well as Richard and Emily, if they had ever heard of her or seen her. There was a chance the old couple had been in on the secret since they had been with the family for 20 years.

"Let's get on the road, Kid," he said as soon as Brighton walked in.

"Can I get a cup of coffee first?"

"Make it snappy."

"Glenda is coming at ten to look at more profiles." Brighton said as they drove down the road.

"I don't think this will take long. I just want to ask everyone in the house if they have ever heard of Lora Weston."

Richard answered the door. His demeanor did not seem quite as friendly as before, but it was hard to tell.

"Richard, I will need to talk with you, your wife, Cassie and Marten this morning," Latimer said. "It will only take a moment of your time." Latimer looked for any sign of reluctance in the butler's face, but found none.

"Of course, Inspector, I will see to it everyone is available."

Cassie was the first to arrive. She wore jeans, a t-shirt and open sandals.

"Good morning Inspector, Sgt. Brighton. You are lucky you caught me. I usually go for a brisk walk before going to work." She sat down in a chair opposite from Latimer. "What can I do for you?"

"Miss Cassie, do you know a woman by the name of Lora Weston?"

She thought for a moment, "No, I don't believe I have ever heard that name."

"Thank you Ma'am, that's all we came to ask."

"For heaven's sake, you could have called me on the phone if that is all you have Inspector." She got up and headed for the door. "Have a good day and I hope you find out who she is. Goodbye."

Richard came in as if he had been waiting by the door.

"I'm available for you right now Sir, if that is alright with you." He hesitated before he sat down.

"Do you know a woman by the name of Lora Weston?"

Pausing for a fraction of a second he said, "No Sir, I don't believe I do. I would remember if I had ever met such a person."

"Thank you Richard, that's all. Can you ask your wife to come in next, please?"

Latimer looked at Brighton. "Not too promising so far, Kid."

It was the same with Emily. She could not recall ever having heard the name.

"Please, have young Mr. Anscott come next Emily, and we will be done."

Marten seemed in a foul mood. His hair was uncombed and his face rather pale. A black shadow showed he had not shaved in at least two days.

"What do you want now, Inspector?" he said and sat down on the chair Latimer pointed to. "I was yanked out of bed for this again?" He sounded agitated.

"We have just one question for you, Sir. Have you ever seen or heard of a woman named Lora Weston?"

Marten's face suddenly reddened and then went white. A twitch on the right side of his cheek appeared as he stared at Latimer. His hand went up as he tried to stop it. It looked like his mouth had gone dry and he could not speak. A sudden silence hung in the room like a heavy curtain.

"Sir, did you hear my question?" Latimer finally asked, although he knew better.

"Yeah, I heard you." Marten shifted in his chair as if to get up. "Why do you want to know if I know some stupid old woman?"

"I did not say she was old, Sir," Latimer answered in a low voice.

"Well, I don't care and I wish you would stop bothering me with these mindless questions." He had recovered somewhat and got up suddenly. "I have had enough of this. You can always arrest me if that's what you want."

"Thank you, Mr. Anscott, that will be all for today. We will show ourselves out." Latimer and Brighton had gotten up and headed for the door. Marten left the room without another word. For the first time Richard was nowhere to be seen as they walked out the front door.

"Pay dirt!" Brighton shouted once they drove down the drive way. "That boy knows her."

"Yes he does, Kid. The hole is getting bigger all the time, I should think." Let's get back to the precinct. You get to spend some more time with the lovely Glenda Hinsley."

"She is about the right age for you, Sir. I don't think she's married." He laughed when he saw Latimer's shocked expression.

Trying as hard as they might, Glenda failed to spot Lora Weston in the data base.

Afterwards, Glenda spent two hours with the sketch artist. The result was a woman of about sixty with motley gray hair, tired light blue eyes in a narrow, gaunt face. She looked old with a hint of mean in her eyes. Her chin was slightly pointed, which made the large nose seem smaller than it was. It was not a face one would want to remember.

When it was done, a technician fed the picture into the computer data base and everyone stood mesmerized as the machine scanned with lightning speed over hundreds of faces in seconds. After 15 minutes Latimer lost interest and went back to his office, disappointed. He had counted on Glenda finding the woman.

Brighton and Glenda stayed to watch for another ten minutes. Just as they were ready to give up, the computer stopped. A face appeared on the screen looking very similar to the one on the sketch. It was the face of Lora Weston. There was only one thing wrong according to the data base. Her name was Camilla Preston and she was dead.

"You've got to be kidding!" Brighton shouted.

"Let's not give up. Read what it says about her," Glenda said and leaned over to make out the information written in small letters. She reached into her purse and got out a pair of stylish reading glasses. "It's tough to get old."

"Camilla Preston was involved in a baby smuggling ring in 1986. She disappeared for a while until her body washed up in the river in 1987. Before that she lived in the slum area of Glenridge and was involved with prostitution. It showed she had several arrests and fines.

"Not the cream of society I must say," said Brighton. "It still leaves us with the big question, who is this Lora Weston you saw in your office, Glenda?"

"I don't know, but she looks exactly like this woman on the computer named Camilla Preston. I would know her anywhere."

Brighton got out his cell phone.

"Sir, you may want to come and take a look at this. We found something." He listened and then repeated more urgently, "No, Sir, you need to see this for yourself."

Latimer stood as if transfixed when he saw the picture and background of the woman called Camilla Preston. *Nothing about this case is easy,* he thought.

"What do you make of it, Sir?" It was Brighton. "Glenda says it's the woman from her office alright."

"You are sure, Glenda?" he asked.

"I'm absolutely sure Inspector. It's not a face one forgets easily."

"That is true. So there must be a rational explanation." Latimer said. Glenda could hear his frustration.

"Could the data base be wrong?" she asked.

"I have never heard that happening," Brighton said with conviction. "They are pretty good at what they do."

"Ok, this is what we are going to do, or rather what you are going to do, Kid. The Chief said we can ask for all the resources we need on this case. Go and ask him for several people to dig out this old case of the baby smuggling ring and any prostitution conviction of Camilla Preston, or Lora Weston while you're at it." There must be a connection. Find it." His voice sounded grim. "I'm tired of these dead ends everywhere we turn."

"Is there any way to make Mrs. Anscott talk, Sir?" Glenda asked.

"No, there isn't since she's not under arrest or likely will be. She's not even a suspect."

"How about Marten?" Brighton asked. "Surely he has looked suspicious from the start and especially today."

"And what would you charge him with hotshot, suspicious looks?" Latimer had a tiny smile on his face. "I have my doubts about that young man. There is definitely something not right about him. For the life of me I don't know what. He absolutely has no motive and a half way decent alibi."

"So where do we go from here, Inspector?" Glenda said.

"We?" He looked at her.

"I feel I started all this with Lora Weston. I would love to be a part of solving this mystery." She looked at Latimer as if it was a done deal.

"I don't believe they allow civilians on the force, Glenda. Even pretty ones like you." His face lit up with a big smile.

"If they ever do, you'll be the first one, I promise."

She blushed and fumbled with her glasses. "I bet you say that to all the old ladies who want to help you solve a crime."

"How did you know?"

"Is that a date, Sir?" Brighton chimed in.

Now it was Latimer's turn to be embarrassed. "Get back to work Kid, or I will have your hide for disrespecting a superior."

"Yes Sir, I'm gone." He sprinted out of the room.

"Well, is it a date, Inspector?" Glenda asked.

He looked at her for a second. "Do you want it to be? I haven't dated anyone since my wife died ten years ago. I'm a bit rusty with these things."

"That makes two of us. I have not had the time to date since my husband left me eight years ago. Maybe two rusty old folks make one shiny new date."

"How about coming to dinner with me this evening then? It's almost time to quit work anyway. I know a nice little restaurant about ten minutes from here. They have the best raw oysters in town. Are you game?"

"I love raw oysters," she said with a bright smile that made her look ten years younger.

"Come back with me to my office and I will tie up a few loose ends. Then we can go."

She watched him closely for the first time while he was making several phone calls. He was a good looking man, well preserved with a neatly trimmed gray beard and mustache. She liked that in a man. His voice was strong but not loud. There was no way she would ever date a man with a loud voice. But then ten minutes ago she was sure she was never going to go on a date with any man.

"Are you ready to go? You looked a million miles away, having second thoughts?" She knew he was teasing.

"Not yet, Inspector."

"Don't you think you can drop the Inspector and start calling me Bob now that we are off the clock?"

"That would be nice, Bob. Do you want me to take my car and follow you to the restaurant?"

"I'm not so rusty that I ask a lady out on a date and let her drive herself to the place I'm taking her. I know these are modern times, but I'm quite old fashioned when it comes to treating a woman right." He took her arm and steered her out the door toward the main entrance of the precinct building. "If you are real nice to me I will even bring you back here after dinner."

"I just thought of something," she said when they were sitting in the restaurant. "You won't get in trouble going out with me because of this case, will you?"

He looked at her for a moment. "Let's see. No, I guess you are not a suspect. If you were, I would have to arrest you now and take you to jail and then go out and eat by myself. You wouldn't want me to do that, would you?"

"Are you always this impossible?"

"Yes."

They both laughed. Latimer felt good about this. He had a fleeting thought about what Mary would think, but then decided she would want him to have a good time with a lovely woman after all these years. This whole dating thing came as a shock. *It's only one date, for heaven's sake!*

"Do you mind talking about the case, Bob? I find all this fascinating."

"I wish there was that much to talk about. Let's face it, except for a few things, I have no leads."

"What few things?"

"Marten Anscott is one. He has been behaving odd since the beginning. I thought at first it was because of grief, but that isn't the case."

"Marten? He is one of the nicest young men I can think of. In what way has he behaved odd?"

"Right from the start he has been uncooperative and downright rude at every turn. There is a deep anger in that young man that is dying to come out."

"You are kidding. Are we talking about the same Marten who is gentle, considerate and would never be rude to anyone? He's like his father in that way."

"Glenda, you've known him a long time. We are definitely not talking about the same person. Even his sister told him the other day to stop being so rude." Latimer frowned. "No one changes in such a drastic way overnight without cause."

"Are you sure it isn't because of the death of his father?" Glenda said. "Some people don't handle sudden grief very well."

"He does not show grief at all from what I can tell. I'm a pretty good judge of character after the experience I've had over the last 30 years. This is more than unresolved grief, Glenda. This is unresolved anger at something or someone."

"I'm afraid it absolutely does not sound like Marten." She shook her head. "Tomorrow I will pay a visit to the Estate. It's high time. I just didn't want to intrude too soon. While there I will make it a point to talk to Marten at length."

"I would appreciate if you will let me know what you find out. His behavior has bothered me from the start. It's the lack of grief in his demeanor that is so evident in comparison to the others in that house. I know I'm not wrong about that. I just thought that was the way the guy was." He lifted his glass to her. "Let's have a toast to us working together after all." His eyes twinkled.

Their glasses clanked and both took a sip.

"Do you like the wine?"

"It is great, but I will only have one glass since I have to drive home later. So will you, Mr. Inspector." She laughed and looked at him teasingly.

"I'm glad I asked you out, Glenda. I'm actually having fun. I thought I was too old for this."

"Why do you think that? You couldn't possibly be much older than I am and I'm still pretty young for my age."

"I'm getting ready to retire the middle of next year. I have plans to move to Florida and age gracefully in the midst of other old fogies, shuffle board and bingo.

"Are you kidding? There is no way you're ready to hang up your job, are you?"

"No, not really, but that is policy now. At 65 they shove you out the door with an imitation gold watch and a ticket to heaven called

Florida." His face turned serious. "I actually dread it. The thought of sitting around on my behind waiting to get old sounds terrible."

"I agree with you. There must be something else you can do when you have to leave this job." She thought for a moment. "How about being a private detective? With your experience that would be great."

"You know, I had never really considered that. It would keep the gray matter stirred up nicely wouldn't it? Not bad for a girl." He raised his glass to her. "You are quite a woman, Glenda."

When it was time to leave, he paid and drove her to the precinct parking lot.

"Call me tomorrow after you have been to the Estate. I'm anxious to hear what you think of Marten. If at all possible, ask him about Lora Weston. He was quite upset when I did this afternoon." He leaned over and kissed her on the cheek. "Thanks for a great evening."

"Thank you, Bob, I'll be in touch."

He watched her drive off and smiled.

Chapter 9

The next morning Brighton was busy going over the data base of the woman called Camilla Preston. He had gotten help from several departments. With a five member crew under his guidance, he planned to search the old paper files in the basement of the precinct. The Chief had kept his word, making the officers available.

Latimer was pleased to have the extra help. There had to be something there he could use. He had planned to go back to the company and get the list of ex-employees from Mr. Pelosi. A secretary had left a message on his phone saying it was ready for him Greta's desk. He would have a chat with Greta to see if she heard any rumors or gossip that might help the case.

Glenda had called him to say she was on the way to the Anscott Estate. Richard assured her the family would be glad to see her when she called ahead. She could not get Marten out of her mind. What could have happened to change him so, she wondered.

The reporters were still camped at the front gate. She looked at the mansion as she drove up and felt a profound sadness. Everything had changed. The house seemed empty somehow. Even at work there was a different feeling. Mark Lenhart had pretty well taken over. She knew he would do a good job. It would never again be like it was. She had no idea what would become of her. For the time being she was needed to ease the transition, but who knows how long that would last. Would she lose her job? At her age it would not be easy to find another, unless one of the managers wanted her. She hadn't heard anything, not even rumors.

"How good to see you, Miss Glenda," Richard said, standing in the door, waiting for her.

"How are things, Richard?"

"Pretty sad, I'm afraid. Nothing is the same. Do come in. Madam is waiting to talk to you in the morning room."

"I will manage, Richard," she said and walked past him toward the back.

"Glenda dear, I was wondering when you would come." Helen Anscott held out her arms and Glenda hugged her in a close embrace.

"I didn't want to be in the way, so I waited to come until things have settled somewhat. "I'm so sorry about Patrick, Helen. Please accept my heartfelt condolences. He was a wonderful man and I shall never know another boss like him."

"I'm still devastated Glenda, as you can imagine. This place feels empty and so does my life. He meant everything to me." She started to cry. "I feel so alone in the midst of a house full of people. They are preparing for the service and there will be a select group here at the house afterward. You are invited, of course, dear."

"Thank you, Helen. How are Cassie and Marten doing?"

"Amazingly, Cassie has been going in to work since yesterday. She says it keeps her from going mad. The one who worries me is Marten. He hardly leaves his room, behaves sullen and has actually been rude to the staff." She wiped her nose with a beautiful, embroidered handkerchief. "I hardly recognize him."

"Has he been in to work at all?"

"No, he stays mostly in his room and when he comes down for meals, barely speaks to anyone. I'm so worried he is not dealing well with his father's death, dear."

"Have you talked to him about it, Helen?"

"I tried, but he refuses to communicate other than the most basic necessities. This is so unlike him, Glenda. Maybe you can talk to him. You two were always close from the time he was young."

"I will be glad to. Is he home?"

"Oh yes, Richard can let him know you are here and wish to talk to him." She reached over and pressed a button on the table. Richard appeared almost instantly.

"Yes Madam, what can I do for you?"

"Be a dear and tell Marten Glenda is here and wishes to talk to him."

"Yes Madam, right away."

"I don't know how we would have managed without Richard and Emily. They have been a tower of strength throughout all this tragedy. I must do something extra special for them after the service, when all this has calmed down." She leaned over to pour Glenda and herself a cup of tea from a delicate tea service on a silver tray. "Where are my manners? I had asked Richard to bring us tea when I heard you were coming." She handed Glenda a cup.

"Thank you, Helen. This hits the spot. I have already had two cups of coffee this morning before I left the office." She didn't mention the tea was cold. It was good to be here and give comfort in any way she could.

Suddenly Marten stood in the door. He looked at her as if she was a stranger.

"Glenda, how good to see you." His voice was strangely cold.

"Marten, how are you, dear? Please, accept my condolences about your father. How are you coping?" She looked into his eyes. They were different, cold and distant.

"Richard says you want to talk to me?" He sounded reluctant.

"Yes dear. Can we go to the small library?"

"Of course, whatever you say." He turned without acknowledging his mother and walked out ahead of Glenda.

She turned to Helen and said, "I'll be back in a minute."

Marten walked to the window and stood with his back turned to her. He did not turn around when she sat down.

"Marten, you want to come and sit with me?"

Reluctantly, he sat in the chair opposite the table and looked at her with a strange, detached look.

"I'm concerned about you. You are not yourself. Do you want to talk? We have always been friends who could share about any and everything."

"I'm ok, Glenda, really."

"Are you sad about your father?"

"Of course I am. Why wouldn't I be?" He sounded defensive and she was surprised. "Do you have anyone you can talk to about what has happened, Marten? You don't seem to handle this tragedy well. That worries me."

"Please don't worry, I'm ok." He sounded annoyed now. "Everybody is asking me questions and I don't want to answer them anymore." His face showed signs of anger.

"I'm sorry. I won't ask you anything about your Dad. I will tell you that I'm helping the police to find out who killed your father. I was over at the precinct yesterday going through their data base about a woman who came to your dad's office the Friday before he was killed. He seemed to know her and talked to her for quite a while. The police call her a person of interest. She told me her name was Lora Weston. Have you ever seen or heard about her, Marten?"

She watched almost with fascination as his face showed signs of sudden anger.

"Did the police send you here to ask me about her?" He was almost shouting. "I told them I don't know her and that I don't want to talk about it anymore. Now you start on me." He jumped up and stood in front of her, filled with anger.

"Leave me alone, I never want to see you again." He turned and walked out.

Glenda stood, stunned and scared. What had happened to Marten? It was like there was something really wrong with him. Bob was right. This was not the same young man she knew only two weeks ago.

Slowly she got up and walked back to the morning room.

"That didn't take long, Glenda. He didn't want to talk, did he?"

Glenda looked at Helen. Should she tell her what happened or just let it go? Then she decided the woman was devastated enough.

"We talked for a little bit, but not much. You were right. He is taking all this very hard. Maybe he could go for counseling?"

"When all this is over and he isn't any better, I will suggest that to him. I don't know if he will agree. He stays very much to himself and doesn't want anyone to interfere in his life." Helen sighed deeply. "Thank goodness I still have Cassie. She is doing a wonderful job with the funeral service. There will be a lot of people there. We will hold it at New Life Church in Glenridge. I have spoken with our Pastor and he will do the service. Patrick and he were great friends as you know."

"Is there anything I can do to help?"

"You know Glenda, ask Cassie, she can tell you better than I can."

"Is she home now?"

"No, she's at the company actually to sign some papers. It looks like with Marten the way he is right now, she is the one to take over together with Mark Lenhart." Suddenly she sat up and looked at Glenda. "Maybe Cassie would like you to be her assistant? You know everything that has been going on." She perked up a little. "Do me a favor and go back to work and speak with her. Tell her I suggested it."

"It sounds wonderful, Helen. At least for now I could really be a great help."

She got up and hugged Helen. "I'm sure Cassie will let me know if this is to her liking. Goodbye Helen and take care. I will see myself out."

When she returned to her office she found a note from Cassie, saying she wanted to see her. She put on some lipstick and checked her hair before she walked down the hall to Cassie's office.

"Hi Cassie, you want to see me? I just came from your Mom. We had a nice talk."

"Glenda, I want to ask you a favor. I know it's not the same, but would you consider being my assistant? I really need your input and help. I feel totally overwhelmed and Mark is not helping. He still treats me like a kid." She looked at Glenda with pleading eyes.

"I thought you'd never ask," Glenda said with relief in her voice. "Before we go on let me tell you how sorry I am about your father. He was the best boss I ever had."

"Thank you Glenda. I have big shoes to fill." She walked around the desk and sat down on the chair in front of the desk. "Come and sit with me right here. There is something I want to ask you. Did you talk with Marten today?"

"Yes Cassie, I'm still in shock. What happened to him? He's not the same person he was two weeks ago before he went to the beach."

"I know. I'm really freaked out about him. He's rude and he almost bit my head off. I think he's lost it."

"I don't know. Don't tell your mother. The police are interested in him as a suspect, because of his weird behavior. He shows no signs of grief about your dad."

"How do you know that?"

"I talked with the Inspector at great length yesterday. He wanted me to ask Marten a certain question, which I did just a while ago. He got so angry he told me to leave, but it was more than that. His eyes looked crazy weird and I sensed a horrible anger that was way out of proportion."

"Who would he be angry at?" Cassie asked, puzzled.

"I don't know."

"What was the question the Inspector wanted you to ask him?"

"If he knew a woman named Lora Weston."

"That's strange, they asked me the same question, but I don't know anyone by that name. The thing is though, I spoke to my mother about it and she got really emotional and told me never to bring up that name in her presence again. Then she ran out of the room crying. That is weird," Cassie said. "Do you know anything about this woman, Glenda?"

"Like I told you, she was in your father's office last Friday. A real nasty piece of work she was, too. She acted like she had something over your father and was sure he would see her. The funny thing is, he did. He talked to her for almost half an hour and when he came out he was extremely upset and went home."

"You are kidding. My father knew this woman?"

"That is not all, Cassie. When I was at the police station I was invited to watch when they searched the data base from a sketch I made with the sketch artist. They used it and found her, but she was listed as dead."

"She was dead?" How can that be, you just saw her."

"That's right. She had a record of prostitution and was involved with a baby smuggling ring years ago. To top it all off, her name was listed as Camilla Preston."

Cassie sank into her chair. "Holy smokes. You have been a busy lady while I thought I had a lot to do. I'm amazed the police let you in on all the details."

Glenda moved uneasy in her seat. "Well, the Inspector took me out to dinner last night and we discussed the case."

Cassie looked at her in astonishment. "That handsome Inspector asked you out for a date?"

"Yes he did and I went." She smiled. "We had a wonderful time, too."

"Glenda Hinsley, do I have to get you a chaperone next time you talk to this man?" She got up and hugged her. "I'm happy for you."

"Now hold on, Cassie. It was only one date. He may not ask me again, although we did have a good time."

"My head is spinning with all this news." Cassie wiped her forehead.

"I meant to ask you if you need my assistance with the arrangements for the memorial service, Cassie."

"I definitely do. As a matter of fact, we will spend the rest of this afternoon going over what needs to be done. I will get Linda from HR to help us. She will be glad to get out from under old Mr. Pelosi's evil eyes." She moved behind her desk and sat down. "As a matter of fact, it is time Mr. Pelosi retires. He's getting worse every day."

"Don't you think that can wait until things are back to normal and you have gotten the hang of dealing with Mr. Lenhart?"

Cassie smiled. "You are a wise woman Glenda, and I'm glad to have you with me."

Chapter 10

Latimer returned from Anscott Laboratories discouraged. Greta had been a disappointment on all fronts. No gossip, no fresh lead, nothing. He was on his way to the Chief's office. The press conference was over and he had found nothing he objected to in what the Chief had said. It was telling though, the notes of the contents he had been promised arrived thirty minutes before it started. It was a subtle reminder by Carson not to make such a demand again.

"Come on in, Latimer." The voice filled the room completely. "Did I do ok?" Chief Carson smiled his crooked little smile.

"It was good, Chief. Nothing I would object to." Latimer sat down in the one chair in front of the desk.

"I thought you came because there are new developments, Inspector." The Chief's smile was replaced by a frown.

"There are, Sir. We finally found the woman we are looking for. Glenda Hinsley, Anscott's assistant, sat with the sketch artist and put a face to her. The computer identified her."

"That's great, Latimer!"

"Not so much, Chief. She is dead and her name is Camilla Preston."

"You are kidding. She is dead? Who the heck was that walking into Anscott's office last week?" He looked confused.

"We don't know, Sir. I interviewed the family again about this woman and two seemed to know who she is. One is Helen Anscott and the other the son, Marten. Both of them refused to talk about it after getting very emotional." Latimer stared at his hands. "Before I forget, the family lawyer knows about her, too, but was instructed by Mrs. Anscott not to say anything."

"So what you are saying is this, three people know who she is and none of them will talk?"

"That's right, Sir." He looked at the Chief. "I have a request to make. Remember what you said about resources and not to hesitate? I think we should have a surveillance team put on Marten Anscott. I can't shake the feeling he is somehow involved, even if his alibi looks pretty good."

"Do you have any idea what you are saying?" The Chief said in a raised voice. "First of all, what good legal reason do we have? Second, we are talking about the son of Patrick Anscott with a pretty good alibi, no priors or motive." He leaned forward. "Am I missing anything, Inspector?"

"I know all that, Chief. I still think it's necessary. Besides, there is no one else except a dead woman walking the streets of Glenridge who looks guilty." He held the Chief's gaze.

"I'm going to have to think about this." He reached for the telephone and motioned for Latimer to leave.

Latimer stopped by the lounge on the way back for coffee, hoping he wouldn't run into Brown. It was deserted and he took his time fixing his coffee. He looked at the donuts, but decided two yesterday was his quota for the week.

"A penny for your thoughts, Inspector," a female voice said behind him. It was Hattie Mansfield, one of the new recruits. "I heard about your case, everybody is talking about it." She looked very pretty in her new uniform. Her makeup was flawless.

That'll wear off in time, he thought, taken aback by his cynicism. No sense for him to dampen the spirits of a new face. "Good morning. Hattie, isn't it?"

"Yes Sir. I graduated from the academy a month ago and have been in the department for a week." She was completely awed by him. "I hope to do as well as you have, Inspector. I'm sure you will solve this latest crime real soon with all the experience you have," she said with confidence. "I'm going to work real hard to make it into the crime unit someday."

"I'm sure you will, Hattie. I wish you all the best." He took his cup and left for his office. *To be so young again.*

The phone started ringing as soon as he sat down behind his desk. It was the Chief.

"I don't know why, but I'm giving you the ok for limited surveillance. The only reason is I respect your instincts, Latimer. Just keep it under wraps for now, even in the office."

"Thank you, Sir. Who do you want on the detail?"

"I will let you know."

Latimer breathed a deep sigh of relief. He knew he was walking on thin ice with this. He actually doubted deep down anything would come of it. At the same time he couldn't get rid of a strong feeling there was something very wrong with Marten Anscott. All he knew was it had to do with the murder of his father.

The phone jarred him out of his deep thoughts. It was Glenda.

"How wonderful to hear from you," he said, his mood brightening considerably. "I was going to call you later to thank you again for the great dinner we had together."

"Funny, since you took me out and paid for it, I'm the one who should thank you. I had a wonderful time." She sounded cheerful. "This is not the only reason I called. "I went to the Estate and spoke with Helen and Marten. Helen was still pretty devastated, but I think she is going to be ok. She is relying on Cassie to make all the arrangements and asked me to help."

"What about Marten?" Latimer held his breath.

"You would not believe what happened, Bob. I tried to talk to him about how he was handling the death of his father and he insisted he was fine. When I asked him about Lora Weston he lost his temper and told me to stop asking him questions and to leave him alone. Then he ran out of the room."

"You are kidding. That is pretty strange, but it confirms that he is somehow involved with this woman, I just don't know how." He changed the phone over to the other ear. "Listen, this is not for public knowledge, but I just got permission from the Chief to put a surveillance team on him."

"I must say, two weeks ago I would have thought you would be dead wrong. Now I agree with you. On the other hand, I think Marten needs counseling with a reputable psychiatrist. Something is terribly out of sync with this young man. Could he have gotten involved in drugs?"

"No, there is something else. The fact that Helen Anscott knows this woman, as well as the family lawyer, speaks of some kind of secret from long ago." Latimer said.

"What would that have to do with Marten changing the way he has over the last two weeks?"

"I wish I knew. Nothing so far makes any sense. This is an extremely frustrating case," he added with a deep sigh.

"What do you hope to find out from following him? From what Helen said, he is staying holed up in his room and comes down just for meals."

"I wish I knew that, too. It's called fishing, Glenda, and I don't have to go to Florida for it either."

"Well Bob, I've got to run. As of today I'm Cassie's assistant and I have a funeral service to arrange. I hope you get some results, I really do. Take care, will talk to you soon, Bob."

"Thanks for calling Glenda. I will let you know if anything develops. Goodbye." He had so wanted to ask her for another date, but she sounded too busy.

"Inspector Latimer. I'm Mike Pollard with Patrol. I have been assigned to your office for surveillance duty, Sir." He was a young officer with a clean, fresh face and a tall, lanky frame. His curly, red hair was cut short, which gave him an even younger appearance. "This is my partner, Henry Miles." The two couldn't have been more opposite. Miles was African-American. He was short, a touch overweight and a tiny mustache gave his round face character and made him look older than he was.

"Come in officers and have a seat. I appreciate you helping out on this case. The way it looks, we need all the help we can get. My assistant Sgt. Brighton will fill you in on your assignment and what it is exactly I want you to do." He leaned forward and looked at them with an intimidating stare. "I'm sure you know how sensitive this matter is given the high profile of the victim. To top it off, the person of interest you are to shadow is the victim's son, Marten Anscott."

The officers did not comment but were clearly impressed.

"I hope I don't have to tell you that this assignment is not to be discussed with anyone and that includes your buddies at the precinct. It's a high profile case and if you mess it up your careers will suffer." He leaned forward as he spoke. "Do I make myself perfectly clear, gentlemen?"

"Yes Sir," they said in unison.

Latimer picked up the phone and dialed.

"Brighton, I want you up here right now on the double." He hung up.

"Sgt. Brighton will be here in a minute. It will take most of the afternoon to familiarize yourself with the case as far as you need to know it. Ask as many questions as pertain to your duty. A lot depends on you doing a good job. You will report to me at the end of your shift every day, is that understood?"

"Yes Sir."

"Here you are Brighton. These are officers Henry Miles and Mike Pollard. Take them into one of the interrogation rooms and brief them on the case. They are assigned to Marten Anscott for the time being. Come back to see me when you are done."

"Yes Sir." Brighton waved the two officers on to follow him.

"By the way, how is the file search going?' Latimer called after him.

"It is tedious Sir, and we haven't found anything so far." He noticed he didn't call him Kid just now.

"There is a Richard McAllister to see you, Sir," Ginny said shortly after they were gone. "Should I ask him to come in?"

"By all means Ginny, show him in." Latimer rushed around the desk to greet Richard at the door. "Richard, come on in."

The butler clearly felt uncomfortable.

"Inspector, I'm so sorry to come unannounced, but I had some errands in the area and thought I could prevail upon you to help me with something that really bothers me."

"Of course, Richard, please have a seat." He pointed to one of the chairs in front of his desk and then sat in the other.

"Inspector, I have come to respect you as a man of integrity and intelligence and I know you will keep what I have come to tell you to yourself."

"I will do my best unless it is necessary to help solve this murder. Otherwise, I will not say a word to anyone Richard."

"Thank you, Sir. It is with great difficulty I have to tell you that I misspoke the truth the last time I talked with you." He looked at Latimer with guilt written all over his face."

"What is it you said that wasn't true, Richard?"

"It has to do with that woman named Lora Weston and young Mr. Anscott."

"Go on, Richard," Latimer said with sudden interest.

"You see, I overheard Master Marten on the phone the day he returned from the beach. He was in his room and I was passing by."

"What did he say?"

"He asked someone to get Lora Weston on the phone. Since I had work to do in the adjoining room, I couldn't help but hear his side of the conversation. After a short time he addressed the other person as Camilla and then told her to leave matters alone and he could handle things just fine without her interference.

"What exactly did he say?"

"Let me see if I can remember. Yes, this is it. He said 'Why did you go there? You just couldn't wait, could you? Now it is up to me to make sure things don't get out of hand before I'm ready.' Then he listened for a while, then suddenly shouted, 'I do not want you to show your face around here again or I will have to do something you won't like. Just remember, I don't owe you anything, you owe me. Then he hung up."

Richard straightened his shoulders as if relieved to have unburdened himself. "I want you to know Inspector, I have been around young Master Marten since he was a boy. Never have I heard him be this disrespectful to anyone as he was to this person on the phone. I have no idea what he has gotten himself involved with, but it is not good."

"I agree with you, Richard," Latimer said. "You have no idea who this woman is or what Marten's dealings are with her?"

"No Sir."

"You are sure he called the woman Camilla?"

"Yes. At the time I thought it was a strange name."

"Richard, Helen Anscott knows who Lora Weston is but won't say. As a matter of fact, she got terribly upset when I asked her and left the room crying. Can you explain that?"

"No, I can't. I have never heard her mention that name in all the years. Whatever it is, it must have happened before my wife and I started working at the Estate."

"How about Emily, did you tell her what you overheard?"

"Yes I did."

"Did she ever hear anyone mention the name Lora Weston or Camilla?"

"No, Inspector, I asked her. She is as mystified as I am." He looked at Latimer with great sadness. "I hope I did the right thing talking about Master Marten. He has been behaving so strangely lately, I thought I better let you know. It would break my heart if I have hurt him with this in any way. He is such a dear young man and we all love him." He stared at his hands in his lap, a feeling of helplessness written all over him.

"Richard, you did the right thing. If he is innocent it will not hurt him. If he is guilty, it will have to come out one way or another." Latimer's voice was filled with compassion.

"I understand, Sir. I won't keep you any longer, you are a busy man." With that he got up and shook Latimer's hand. "Let me know if I can be of any help, Inspector. I truly hope you will figure out who did this horrible thing to the family I love."

"Thank you for stopping by Richard. You have done the right thing. Goodbye."

Latimer sat behind his desk for a long time after Richard left. There was no doubt now that Marten Anscott knew Lora Weston and Camilla. No matter how he took into account all the facts he had, he still had no idea what this relationship was all about. Let's face it, Marten was a rich, educated young man and Lora a low class street person. What in the world did these two have in common? What had she to do with Patrick Anscott that he would feel obligated to talk to her in his office? And why would Helen Anscott be so shook up just hearing her name? There had to be a thread to tie them all together. He couldn't see it, no matter how he racked his brain.

He hated it when he hit a dead end in an investigation. It happens in almost every case, but in the end he had always figured it out. Why did he have the feeling it would not be that certain with this one.

The phone rang.

"Latimer here."

"Sir, this is officer Latham. We found the file on Camilla Preston, but nothing so far on Lora Weston. Do you want us to bring it up?"

"Absolutely, bring it to my office, Latham."

He didn't care how long it took. He was going to go through that file with a fine tooth comb. He could smell it, something was going to give.

He jumped up when Officer Latham entered the office.

"Great, this is what I was waiting for. Good job. Continue to look for Lora Weston in the same year and location, I have a feeling they are somehow connected."

"Yes Sir." Latham's face beamed. He had heard about Latimer and how tough the old bird was. To be commended was worth all the boring hours he and Baker had spent in "the hole" as the file room in the basement was called. Everyone hated to be assigned down there.

Latimer went down to the lounge. This called for a celebration with a cup of coffee. It was his third today, but who cared.

He settled in for the long haul as he opened the medium size box sitting on his desk. Maybe here was the key to this whole blasted case. The contents smelled musty as he took the lid off. The box was filled with yellowed files neatly stacked. A picture stuck out of one of them half way down. He carefully pulled it out and looked at the face of the woman Glenda saw in her office. He slid it back into the folder on the bottom. He took the top folder out and pushed the box to the side of his large desk. As he immersed himself in the pitiful facts of this woman's life, he realized he was examining crimes from over thirty some years ago in the city of Glenridge. He had just graduated from the police academy and was as green as Hattie Mansfield, the girl from the lounge this morning.

Two hours had passed when he put the last folder back into the box. He felt he had been dumped on by a garbage truck reading the life story of a woman he was glad he never had to deal with. To sum it up, she was born into a family of five girls. The father was a hopeless drunk and the mother cleaned houses at first until she could make more money as a prostitute. Camilla was the oldest and had to take care of the other girls. At the age of twelve she followed in her mother's footsteps after she realized it didn't take much to make money pleasing men.

At the age of sixteen she was a seasoned prostitute in the streets of Glenridge and experienced her first arrest. Within two hours her pimp had posted bail. It became like a regular dance until she was twenty-three when she got involved in a large national baby smuggling ring. This was in 1984. The records were sparse on details about this time of her life until she was caught with a baby in a parking lot. Since she insisted it was her sister's baby, the police had to let her go. By the time they took out an arrest warrant, she had disappeared. This was in 1986. A year later, her body was washed up on the river bank east of Glenridge.

Latimer leaned back in his chair and rubbed his eyes. This was all very interesting. The big question still remained, who was Lora Weston?

Latimer had lost all track of time and realized it was an hour past quitting time. He suddenly felt hungry and decided to go to a drive-thru for some Chinese food. It would feel good to go home, sit on the couch and watch TV while he ate. Maybe he could find a crime drama and learn how the big boys solved every crime in one hour with time to spare for commercials.

Chapter 11

It was Thursday morning. Brighton was already waiting for Latimer in his office.

"Morning, Sir. I got you a cup of coffee. Cream, no sugar, just like you like it."

"Thanks, Kid. How did it go yesterday with the briefing of the surveillance team?"

"I think they will do ok. Both have done this before and helped solve a case as they tell it. They are starting this morning, Sir."

"Good. I hate to do it to you, Kid, but you have to go back to the hole one more day to find something on Lora Weston. I went over the files Latham brought up for Camilla Preston and found nothing to link those two together."

"So what's next?" He looked expectantly at Latimer.

"That is a good question. Five days into the investigation and I have come up with a suspect with no motive and a questionable alibi. A second suspect who has been dead for thirty years, but pays a visit to the victim three days before he gets killed. " He slumped in his chair. "You tell me Kid where to go from here."

"What kind of woman was this Camilla Preston?" Brighton looked eager.

"Exactly the way she looked; a common small time perp with lots of priors and a shady past all the way around. If Lora Weston is anything like her, I would be totally blown away if she turns out to be connected to the Anscott family."

"But she is, Sir."

"I know," he groaned. After a minute he looked at Brighton as if remembering something. "I didn't tell you, Richard McAllister came to see me yesterday," Latimer said.

"You are kidding! What did he want?" Brighton almost dropped his coffee.

"He wanted to tell me he lied about not knowing about Lora Weston. Overheard Marten on the phone with her three days before the murder and was yelling at her to stay out of his business or he would do her some harm. But that's not all, he called her Camilla."

"That is amazing, Sir. Are you going to question him about it?"

"I don't know. I've got to come up with something else on him first, something that ties him to the murder."

"Maybe Mike and Henry will have more luck during their surveillance today."

"Let's hope so, but so far Marten has been sticking close to home." Latimer had finished his coffee. "I've got to have another one of these to get me going this morning," he said and got up. "I will talk to you later, Kid. Try to find something for me in the hole, will you?"

"I will try real hard, Sir."

When he walked back into his office the phone was ringing.

"Latimer here."

"It's Glenda, Bob. Good morning." She sounded professional and yet cheerful. "Just want to let you know the funeral will be tomorrow at ten at New Life Church. I thought you might like to come."

"Absolutely. Thank you for letting me know. How are you, Glenda? Ready for another dinner with this frustrated old man?"

"I would love to Bob, but there is no way I can get away until this weekend when all this is over. I'm sorry. I'm sure we will talk tomorrow, got to go." She hesitated and then said, "I almost forgot, there will be a small gathering of friends, family and business people at the house after the service. I'm sure you are interested to meet them."

"When you say small, how small?"

"Oh, about two hundred or so." He knew she was smiling.

"I guess you call that an intimate gathering in your circles? What time should I get there?"

"A light lunch will be served from twelve to one. You can come any time during that hour." She hesitated for a second. "Just make sure to be discreet when you ask questions. Preferably don't make it obvious you are with the police."

"Glenda, I will try my best to blend in by searching my closet for the one and only black suit I own."

"Gotta run, Bob. See you tomorrow," she said and hung up.

Without putting down the receiver he dialed the Chief's office.

"Chief, Latimer here. You probably already know, but the Anscott funeral is tomorrow. I'm invited to attend not just the church service but a so called intimate gathering at the Estate afterwards. Any word on how you want me to proceed while I'm there?" He was sure the Chief would be there as well, but he wanted to make sure.

"We have a good number of units directing traffic at the church as well as at the gate to the Estate."

Latimer had to hold the phone away from his ear to escape the boom of the Chief's voice.

"Can't say I was invited to the shindig afterwards, but I'm sure the Commissioner will be there. How in the world did you get on the list, Inspector?"

"It's never what you know, but who you know, Chief." Latimer smiled when he heard the irritation in the Chief's voice.

"Maybe you can gather some useful insights since you're not doing much else that I can see."

Ah, pay back, Latimer thought and his smile got bigger. "I will try to make the best of it, Sir," he said in an even tone and hung up.

"Thank you, Glenda," he said out loud, still smiling.

The phone rang again. It was Henry Miles.

"Sir, we thought you ought to know we are following our man down the Parkway. He is turning on exit 35 toward the lower district and heading for the real rough section in that area."

"At least you can't lose him with that flashy car of his," Latimer said.

"No Sir, he is driving an older model Ford pickup truck. Wait a minute Sir, he is parking in front of a brownstone and getting out. We'll have to call back."

Well, well, our boy is finally doing something other than sitting in his room sulking, Latimer thought. This could lead to Lora Weston. From the looks of the woman she fit in this neighborhood. Right now there was nothing he could do but wait.

He picked up the phone and called Brighton.

"Anything?" he asked when the Kid answered.

"No Sir, nothing. I don't think she has a record. We searched every file box but her name does not come up.

"How about that baby smuggling ring, did you find anything on that?"

"Well, there is one box we found, but it is from several years later." Brighton said.

"Have Latham bring it up to my office."

"Yes Sir."

It was that same musty smell when he opened the box. There were only three files in it. It wouldn't take him long to go over it. The first thing he looked for were pictures of any kind. There were three arrest records of men he did not recognize. He read the names but none rang a bell. Apparently the case fell apart because two of the people involved were found murdered and one disappeared before he could be prosecuted.

Another dead end. Camilla Preston did not show up in the files because she had died the year before. Latimer sighed deeply and put the files back in the box. Why was it he couldn't shake the feeling they held the secret to this case? He was staring at the box on his desk in utter frustration when the phone rang.

"Officer Miles again, Sir. The suspect went inside a brownstone for quite a while and has now come out. He is driving off. Do you want us to check inside the building or follow him?"

"Go ahead and follow him, Miles. We can always go back later to find out who he visited."

"Yes Sir."

Latimer decided to drive down there himself and take a look around. He dialed Brighton and asked him to meet him at his car.

"This sounds interesting, Sir. What are we looking for?" He was happy to have escaped the hole.

"You tell me, Kid? What would you do if you were in the lead?"

"I would definitely check the building to see if we can find a name we know, Sir. Maybe even the name of Lora Weston."

"Very good, what else?"

Brighton thought for a minute. "Ask someone outside if they know who lives there if there are no names? But this is a high crime area. These people probably won't talk to us. We look too much like cops."

"True, so what can you do to get around that?" Latimer was smiling now.

"Let's see, check every floor and knock on every door?" He looked unsure of himself.

"That would not go over very well, would it, Kid?"

"No, I guess not, Sir."

"Watch what I'm going to do Brighton. Next time you'll know how," Latimer said as they drove up to the brownstone. He looked around and then walked up to a man who was in the middle of a small drug deal.

"How is business, gentlemen?" He flashed his ID.

One of the men bolted the moment Latimer had the words out. The other tried to follow but Latimer held him by the arm. "Not so fast, I just need some information, friend."

"I don't know nothing, man." He spoke in a high pitched voice.

"Of course you don't. Let's just say I ignore the drug deal you just made if you tell me who lives in this brownstone." Latimer said in a low voice.

The dealer thought it over for a moment and then relaxed.

"Ok, I'll tell you. I don't know all of them. There is one guy who lives by himself on the bottom floor. He sort of takes care of the place, not officially, but you know what I mean. They let him live there for less rent. Then on the other side of the hallway a man and a woman named Cosack have lived there for about six weeks. They fight all the time and you can hear it all over the place." He sounded a little more confident.

"Let me ask you something. By any chance does a woman named Lora Weston live there?" Latimer asked in a real friendly tone.

"Yeah man, she lives on the third floor by herself. Her son used to live with her but I guess he moved out about two or three weeks ago."

"What's the son's name?"

"I think it's Paul."

"Thanks friend, you have done well. If I had a lollipop I would give it to you. Scram and don't let me catch you again." He turned to Brighton with a triumphant smile. "Bingo. I feel like I'm in Florida already. Let's go upstairs and pay the lady a visit, Kid."

"That was smooth, Sir." Brighton said.

"Yes it was."

They climbed up to the third floor and Latimer hated to admit he was slightly out of breath when they got there. Maybe he should start exercising more. Brighton was waiting for him at the door at the top of the stairs. He knocked, there was no answer. He knocked again.

"Try the door on the other side," Latimer said.

After a second knock the door opened up a tiny slit.

"What do you want?"

"We are looking for Lora Weston." Latimer said.

"She lives across the hall." The door closed.

Latimer knocked again.

"Can we talk to you for a moment, Ma'am? We are with the police," he said and held up his ID when the door opened wider.

"I don't talk to cops."

"Just one or two questions about the lady across the hall, please." The old woman finally opened up.

"What do you want to know? I don't have nothing to do with her. She's mean." She pulled back a strand of her long gray hair and wrapped it around her ear. She was not nearly as old as he thought at first, just worn out.

"How long has she lived here with her son, Ma'am?"

"I don't know, they was here when I came two years ago. That son of hers is even meaner than she is. He moved out about three weeks ago and I haven't seen him since. Good riddance, he yelled at her all the time." She looked at Latimer suspiciously. "What's he done?"

"Nothing we know of. We just want to talk to him and his mother. Can you give us his name?"

"It's Paul Weston. I know because sometimes I see the mail lying around by the door."

"Did you see a man come up here a half hour ago?"

"No, I was busy watching a show."

"Do you know if Lora Weston is in, she is not answering the door," Latimer asked her.

"I told you, I was watching a show. What do you think? I stand in the hall and spy on everybody?"

"Thank you Ma'am, you have been very helpful. If anything out of the ordinary happens would you give me a call?" Latimer handed her a card.

"I told you I don't talk to cops." She took the card and closed the door.

"What do we do next, Sergeant?" Latimer asked as they got into the car.

"I would get a search warrant, Sir."

"Very good, let's do that. We need to get back to the precinct and I will talk to the Chief. This should not take long. I also think we are getting a little closer to what Marten Anscott is up to, don't you think?"

Brighton flashed him his best dimpled smile and pulled away from the curb.

"It looks like we are getting somewhere, Latimer." The Chief sounded pleased. "I will have my secretary initiate the search warrant. I'm certain my good friend Judge Harris will sign it without a problem." He reached for the phone and Latimer left for his office.

Things can change fast in this business, he thought. *There is finally a light at the end of the tunnel.*

Ginny handed him several messages. None of them pertained to the case and he ignored them. They could wait. He wondered if he should call Glenda and tell her about Marten. Maybe not, this was strictly police business and she might slip up talking to the family. Let's see first what we find at Lora Weston's place.

An hour later a courier brought the warrant to his office. It took a few minutes to get the team together and Brighton pulled out of the precinct parking lot for the lower district. The four men of the team followed right behind.

"I can't wait to see what we find, Sir." Brighton said as they drove up in front of the brownstone. They waited for the police van to park behind them before they got out of their car.

"Follow me, guys," Latimer said and waved them on.

There still was no answer when he knocked on the door upstairs.

"Go ahead Winston, break it down," he said after the third knock and several shouts. The door gave way easy and they entered. It was a dark place with tattered furniture. Latimer went through to the bedrooms and realized immediately Lora Weston had left. All her personal belongings were gone and the apartment had been left empty except for the furniture. After a thorough search they found nothing connected to the case or any personal information about the woman or her son. No pictures, no clothes or jewelry. All drawers were empty.

He did notice something that made him sick. The entire place had been wiped clean. Someone had erased all fingerprints! He groaned. Let the forensic guys worry about it.

Chapter 12

It was Friday, the day of the funeral. There was an air of sadness in the air. Emily and Lilly were busy in the kitchen. The caterers would be here soon. It was time to get breakfast for the family out of the way. They would eat in the kitchen this morning, because the dining room had been set up for the luncheon.

Cassie was the first to arrive. She was still in her dark blue satin robe and her hair was uncombed.

"Good morning, Emily and Lilly. It looks like the weather will be nice this morning. Is there any coffee?"

"Of course Miss Cassie, I'll fix you right up. Just have a seat over at the table in the corner." Emily handed her a cup of steaming coffee.

"Thanks Emily. You are wonderful as usual. Is Mom in the morning room?"

"No Miss, she has not come down yet. On a day like today that would not be unusual. Do you want Richard to go upstairs and check on her?"

"No, I guess not, she will be here in a minute, I'm sure."

At that moment the door opened and Helen walked in. She was already dressed. Her hair hung loosely around her drawn, pale face. She wore a simple black dress held with a wide black belt. A single strand of pearls matched by small earrings rounded out her perfect outfit.

"You are already dressed, Mom," Cassie said. "Dad would have told you how beautiful you look if he was here."

Helen smiled. "Emily, may I have some coffee and a dry piece of toast. That is all I want."

"Mrs. Anscott, I have a milk shake here for you with your favorite fruits and a little yogurt. It will hold you well till lunch. You need your strength today, Ma'am." Emily put the drink on the table and Helen sat down without protest and took a sip.

"It's delicious. You always know just what I need Emily. Thank you."

The door opened again and Marten walked in. He actually looked rested and in a good mood this morning.

"Hi everybody, I see breakfast is ready. I'm hungry. It's going to be a long day. Good morning, Mother. How are you holding up?" He leaned over and kissed Helen on the cheek. Morning, Sis."

"Well, it looks like you have come out of your hole and plan to join us today, Marten. That is nice, it's been a while." Cassie had a slight edge in her voice. She resented that he had left her with all the arrangements and now that it was done, he acted like it was a happy day.

"I'm ready to do whatever you need from me, Cassie. I'm sorry, but I just couldn't cope."

"I'm happy to see you are doing well, honey," Helen said and reached over to pat his arm. "We will get through this together. Your father would have wanted it that way."

"Do you want the usual, Master Marten?" Emily turned to him from the stove.

"Sure, give me the usual Emily. That sounds fine."

Within minutes she put a plate of scrambled eggs, toast and fruit in front of him.

"Is there any bacon?"

"Coming right up, Sir, I didn't know you wanted any. It's not what you usually have.

"Today is not a usual day Emily. We better eat enough to last us through the morning. I'm afraid it will be a three ring circus." He started eating.

"I would not want to refer to your father's funeral in those terms, dear," Helen said with a mild chiding. "He was a much loved icon in this city and there will be many people who are genuinely sad at his passing."

"Of course, Mother, I didn't mean it that way." A slight frown crossed his face and he said nothing for the rest of the breakfast.

The kitchen door opened and Richard came in.

"There are more flowers arriving, Madam. Where would you like me to put them?"

"Have the florist take them to the church, Richard. There is no more room here."

A moment later the doorbell rang. It was Glenda.

"Come have some breakfast, dear," Helen said and waved for her to sit with them at the table.

"That sounds wonderful. Good morning everybody," she looked around with a slight smile. "It will be a sunny day today."

"Is everything ready, Glenda?" Cassie sounded nervous.

"It is, Cassie, don't you worry about a thing. From here on I will handle all the little details. You just concentrate on your mother and the family and friends who will be here to talk to you. I checked at the Radisson. Most all the family from out of town arrived yesterday. Two or three are coming in right about now. I have arranged for them to be picked up at the airport. I arranged it so you will be able to spend time with them after the service here at the house. I hope that is alright, Helen?"

"That sounds wonderful."

Glenda glanced at Marten. He seemed to be his old self again. She was relieved because they didn't need his outbursts today. She took a deep breath. It would be a long, hard day for everyone.

It was a large church, modern in design with beautiful stain glass windows with contemporary biblical motives. The police had to direct the flow of endless numbers of cars pulling into the large parking lot. It was the event of the year without question.

Latimer was shown a seat well in the back. Brighton stayed to man the office. He saw the Police Commissioner and the Chief move toward the front. There were many familiar faces from all walks of life, including many well-known politicians and business leaders of the State. The Governor was ushered in through a side door and sat in the row right behind the family. Latimer noticed some security people coming in right behind him.

A hush fell over the crowd when the family came in. Latimer paid real close attention to Marten who walked beside his mother. He could not detect any sign of trouble in his demeanor.

Latimer enjoyed the solo in the beginning of the service. The minister walked slowly to the pulpit and cleared his throat.

"First of all, let me express my deepest condolences to this wonderful family. I was not just Patrick Anscott's Pastor. I was his and Helen's friend as well. The Bible says it is hard for a rich man to go to heaven, but I'm here to tell you that Patrick was one of the most generous people I have ever met, as many here can attest to. I realize you don't get to heaven by being generous alone. It has to come from a heart that is tuned in to God. Patrick Anscott was such a man. His kindness, generosity and respect he showed not just to his family, but to his friends and employees was the result of his Christian faith, his love of God and his Savior Jesus Christ. He was the genuine article. One of the first questions I will ask God when I arrive in heaven is why a man like that had to meet with such a terrible death. It is not for us to question, but to accept what happened.

As his Pastor, Patrick asked me to pass on a message to all of you who came to his funeral. The message is this or rather the question, 'Are you ready to meet that final day? Is your heart right with God if he took your life today? If not, look deep inside and then ask forgiveness for all the things you have done wrong and then ask Jesus to turn your life into something meaningful.'

The pastor looked out over the congregation with true conviction in his eyes. "I have done now what my friend Patrick had asked me to do. There is one more thing he wants you to know. Do not mourn for him, because he is with the Lord and he would like very much for you to join him when it is your time to face your day. It is your choice."

Into the silence a crystal clear voice sang "Amazing Grace."

Latimer had trouble finding a space to park at the Estate until a young man rushed up to his car. "I will park it for you Sir, just leave the keys in."

"Thank you, that helps," he said as he got out and walked through the open front door. There was no receiving line. The family stood in the drawing room to talk to anyone who wished to say a word to them. Latimer looked around the room carefully. There were many people he knew, but equally as many he didn't. Just as he wondered how he was going to get into a conversation with anyone, Glenda walked up to him.

"Bob, how good you could come. Please help yourself to food and a beverage in the dining room. There is seating available all through the house and out in the garden in the back. The close family is in the morning room to allow the other guests to speak to Helen, Marten and Cassie for now. Later on the entire family will meet in the morning room for a private gathering." She sounded very professional and looked quite stunning in her black dress with a silver gray jacket over it.

"You look great, Glenda," he whispered and felt like a school boy at the prom.

"Thank you, Bob. I will pass that on to Mrs. Anscott," she said in a loud voice as a group of people walked by. When they were gone, she whispered back, "Behave yourself Sir, or I must ask you to take me out to dinner again."

He couldn't help but laugh. "In that case let me make a huge scene if that's all it takes."

"Take care, Bob. I've got to go. Remember, no word about being a policeman." Before he could say any more she was lost in the crowd.

His main target for the day was Marten Anscott. He walked slowly into the drawing room and watched countless people shake hands with Helen and the children. Marten frowned slightly when he spotted him, but continued to be gracious to each person.

Something happened to make him feel better, he thought. Then it dawned on him. Lora Weston was gone. Marten had gone there yesterday to make sure she had left and the place was clean. Latimer had ordered a forensics team to comb the place. Surely they would find something, the one print that got away.

"Inspector Latimer, I'm surprised to see you here." It was the Police Commissioner.

"How are you, Sir? I'm actually on duty in a way. As you know this is my case."

"How is it coming, Inspector? Can we expect some results soon?"

Latimer cringed. He wasn't about to discuss the case right here, even if he was the Commissioner. "I will be glad to come to your office and give you a report, Sir, if you wish," he said as politely as possible.

"That sounds great, Latimer." The Commissioner turned and greeted someone else. Latimer was glad to be left standing. He spent the next hour and a half chatting with various people without gaining any insight into the case. Finally, he had enough and went back to the office. The whole thing was sort of a waste of time in his opinion, except of course for Glenda looking for another dinner date. He would call her tomorrow and set up something for Saturday. He was whistling a happy tune when he arrived at the office.

"How was the funeral, Sir?" Brighton was waiting for him.

"It was ok as funerals go."

"You look sharp in your black suit, Sir."

"Don't push it, Kid. You know how I hate to dress like this."

"Did you learn anything interesting at the wake?"

"Yes, I did. Our boy Marten seems to have gotten over his nervous spells. He seemed relaxed and even nice."

"Why the change, Sir?"

"He made sure yesterday Lora Weston was gone from the apartment and had time to clean up any kind of sign he or she had been there."

"There is no way he could have gotten everything, no matter how he or Lora tried."

"That is why I'm counting on forensics to help us out, Kid. They will find something, trust me. As a matter of fact, the team is on their way as we speak. It will take till Monday to have most of the results." He pointed to the file folder on his desk. "We have plenty to do checking out these names Pelosi gave me of the list of ex-employees at Anscott Laboratories."

"Are there a lot?"

"Let's first look into the ones locally and then spread out. Take Latham and get on it right now. It will take you guys a good long while to check priors and anything else suspicious you might find. Feel free to call Pelosi's office if you have questions even if he pitches a fit. The man may think he takes over when God takes a vacation, but this is a murder investigation and he better cooperate or we accuse him of hindering."

"I'm on it, Sir," Brighton said and left.

Latimer headed for the Chief's office for his daily report on the case, but not before he stopped by for a cup of coffee.

"Well, how are you doing with the case, Latimer, anything new?"

"As you know, surveillance followed Marten Anscott to Lora Weston's apartment and Brighton and I checked the place out with the search warrant. We found it empty except for the furniture which seems to be part of it," Latimer said. "I talked to the neighbor across the hall. She told me Weston's son moved out about three weeks ago. Said he was even meaner than his mother and yelled at her a lot."

"Get on with it, Latimer, I read your report. I asked for something new." Apparently the Chief was still ticked off for not having been invited to the wake at the Estate.

"I'm getting to it, Chief. I watched Marten Anscott real close at the luncheon and he seemed unusually cheerful, composed and totally in control unlike before. I could clearly sense a load had been lifted from his mind." Latimer took a sip of his coffee. "What I think, Sir, the reason he had gone to Weston's apartment was to make sure she was gone and every sign of evidence had gone with her."

"Do you think you should talk to him about this?"

"I would like to wait for the fingerprint results to come in if that is ok with you, Sir. They might come up with something more I can confront him with. This will take till Monday, though." Latimer started to get up. "I have Brighton and Latham going over files of ex-employees of Anscott Laboratories to see if there is someone who had reason to kill Anscott."

"In view of what you just told me, I doubt you will find anything, but you are right, we don't want to leave any stone unturned. Before you go, you still need surveillance on this guy?"

"Yes, I do, Sir."

"Ok, have a good weekend, Latimer, but remember the department is not made of money. I give you till Monday."

"Thank you, Sir."

Back at the office he picked up the phone and dialed Glenda's number, but she had put it on voice mail.

"Give me a call when you have a minute. I'm calling about that dinner date. Bye, Latimer." He would try again later in the evening. She probably went home and crashed after the kind of day she had.

Chapter 13

It was Monday morning and Latimer was in a foul mood. He never heard back from Glenda and spent the weekend mulling about it. He had even tried to call her again, but only her voice mail answered. Asking her for a date early Monday morning definitely would not look right.

Brighton walked in with two cups of coffee. "I thought you might need one of these, Sir. Anything new on the case?" He looked cheerful as usual.

"I'm waiting for the fingerprint guys to give me a call about the Weston apartment. They've had all weekend."

At that moment the phone rang. It was the fingerprint technician. "I have some results for you from the apartment in the lower district, Sir. Shall I bring them up?"

"We are waiting for them, Kelly. Get them up here on the double." He hung up and sat back, sipping his coffee.

After a few minutes a young man in a white coat came in and handed Latimer a folder. "Here they are, Inspector, pretty interesting stuff."

Latimer read in silence for a few minutes. "This is indeed pretty interesting, Kid. Guess whose prints they found? Camilla Preston's."

"What? The woman has been dead for thirty years!" Brighton almost shouted. "This is crazy, Sir!"

"There is only one explanation, Kid. Camilla Preston and Lora Weston are twins. The prints they found in the apartment, while not exact, are so similar, it is the only answer possible." He rubbed his beard. "This puts a new spin on this whole mess I should say."

"Are there any other prints, Sir?"

"Yes, they found some of Marten Anscott, which is no surprise since we know he was up there. None from Paul Weston. That's strange since he lived with the woman for several years. Maybe that is why the room had been wiped clean. He did not want to be found or is not in the system. None of the other prints they found were in the system either, which means Lora Weston did not associate with criminal elements, at least not in her apartment. On second thought, one of the many prints they found could be from her son, but we don't know since Paul Weston is not in the system. Latimer finished the last of his coffee. "You know, I remember from Camilla Preston's file, there were five girls in that family. We need to find where the other three are." He handed Brighton the file and said, "Here, take this and see if you can find out if any or all are still alive, Kid."

Brighton left with the file and headed to the data base section. He knew he would be busy for a while.

"Can you tell me more about the prints you found, Kelly?" Latimer asked after he got the technician on the line. "Are they exact or is there some discrepancy?"

"Funny you should mention that, Sir. The computer says they are too close to be from anyone else, yet not quite the same. This happens only with identical twins. Way back they didn't have the technology to differentiate between the two, but today we do."

"Kelly, keep checking the data base if you can find the exact match with another name attached to it. Look for a match from as far back as the computer will let you go."

"Ok Sir, I will keep on it."

Latimer sat deep in thought for a long time. This was a fascinating development. The question now was, which of them was the evil twin and which the good one, or were both of them evil?

Something suddenly occurred to him. What if Camilla Preston murdered her sister Lora many years ago to get the police off her back and then continued to live her life unhindered all these years as Lora Weston? It was perfect. No matter what Camilla had done with the baby smuggling ring, prostitution or even murder, no one came looking for her because to the authorities she was dead.

He let out a slow whistle. It was pure genius. They would have to find the other siblings to shed more light on which sister was dead and which was alive. Latimer felt a slight tingle down his spine with the new possibilities this opened up. How did this tie in with the Anscott family? In what way was Marten involved with this woman? Why did Helen and the lawyer know her and why was Patrick Anscott murdered?

He suddenly felt deflated, because true to form, nothing made any sense in this case in spite of this new information.

Sometime later he heard from Pollard and Miles, the surveillance team. They reported Marten Anscott had not left the Estate after the funeral all weekend and the Chief had ordered them off the assignment. Latimer thanked them and hung up. Well, at least they had found a solid connection with Lora Weston. The question now was, should he confront Marten with his visit to the apartment and his fingerprints inside? Other than arrest the guy, Latimer doubted he would give him any answers. What the heck, it wouldn't hurt to try. He dialed the Anscott Estate and got Richard on the line.

"Richard, this is Inspector Latimer. Can you tell me if Marten is home?"

"No Sir, he just left and I have no idea where he has gone. Can I leave him a message, Sir?"

"No Richard, but if you could give me a call when he gets back I would appreciate it. Don't tell him that I want to come by and talk to him."

"Very well, Sir."

"Richard, one other thing, has Mrs. Hinsley been at the house over the weekend?"

"Yes Sir, she has been here on and off working with Miss Cassie on company business."

"Thank you, Richard."

That explained it. He felt better. Maybe later on this week she would call him. He would just have to wait. It seemed he was on hold at every corner with Brighton checking on the employees and Kelly at fingerprints. Not to mention waiting for Marten to return and Glenda being too busy to call him. He hated when that happened.

The phone rang.

"Hi Bob, it's Glenda."

It was as if the sun had just come up. "Well, hello there. I heard you have been busy this weekend with Cassie. How are things at the Estate?" He tried to sound casual.

"Things have settled down somewhat. Some of the family from out of town is still here, but other than that everything is slowly getting back to normal, which cannot be said for the office. Cassie and I have been extremely busy trying to figure out who is in control at the company. Mark Lenhart is really throwing his weight around. I'm surprised because he used to be such a laid back guy."

"It's amazing what a little power can do to a guy," Latimer said. "I have some new developments which are quite amazing as well," he added.

"Oh really? Can we discuss those over dinner maybe this week sometime?" She sounded excited.

"Sure, when can you fit me into your busy schedule?"

"How about Wednesday evening, I have something every other day."

"Wednesday evening it is. Let's say I pick you up at around seven?"

"Great, you can meet me at the company. That would be the easiest for me. I'm looking forward to it, Bob. See you then." She hung up.

"Life is not all bad," he said with a smile.

It was not until later in the afternoon Richard called to say Marten was home. Latimer got in touch with Brighton and told him to meet him in the parking lot.

"This should prove to be interesting, Sir. Remember how emotional this guy got last time?"

"He seemed to have snapped out of it Friday when I watched him during the service and afterward at the house. Let's see how it will hold when we confront him with the facts we have."

Marten's red Lexus was the only car parked up front. Richard greeted them with a big smile and led them into the little library. "I will inform Master Marten you are here, Inspector."

It was a cheerful Marten who walked into the room a few minutes later.

"What can I do for the diligent crime fighters today?" He draped his slender body over one of the leather chairs in a lazy, relaxed manner.

"It is good of you to see us, Mr. Anscott," Latimer said. "I will come right to the point. There have been new developments and we are sure you can clear up some things we are looking into."

"Really, does that mean you are close to catching the killer?" There was no fear or apprehension in his voice.

"I wish I could say that, but unfortunately we have not been able to get that far." Latimer smiled at him with his most disarming smile. "We have two witnesses who saw you enter an apartment in the lower district occupied by Lora Weston, whom you told us you have never met. Can you explain that, Sir?"

The twitch on his cheek appeared again like the last time. His face was as if frozen in time. He tried hard to control his emotions and continued to stare at Latimer. Finally, he said in a thick voice, "Are your witnesses sure it was me and not someone else?"

"We are sure. Besides, we found your fingerprints in the apartment."

"Since I'm not a suspect and you have not arrested me, I see no reason why I should tell you where I go."

"What makes you so sure you are not a suspect?" Latimer said in a silky smooth voice.

"You are kidding, right? I'm Marten Anscott for heaven's sake and you can't touch me. My father is or rather was an influential man. For you to suggest I had anything to do with his murder is outrageous!" He was shaking visibly, yet kept his voice down.

"We are here to find out the reason why you have an association with a woman calling herself Lora Weston. She came to your father's office for what we believe was blackmail. Can you comment on that?" Latimer held his gaze firmly on Marten. His voice had a hint of steel in it.

"I don't know this woman you keep referring to and I have no idea how my fingerprints got into her apartment. You must be pretty desperate to use such underhanded methods to get me to confess to something I didn't do." He had more control now. "To think that I would murder my father is so far-fetched it isn't even in the realm of reality, Inspector. I loved him and have been trained from childhood to take over the company. Why would I murder him?" He sounded totally sure of himself by now.

"I didn't ask you if you murdered your father, Sir. I asked you what you were doing in Lora Weston's apartment." Latimer remained calm.

"And I told you I wasn't there."

"Sir, fingerprints don't lie and neither did the witnesses."

"Who are these witnesses anyway?" He was getting upset again.

"We put a surveillance team on you, Mr. Anscott. Two police officers followed you from your house to the brownstone in the lower district. So you see, there is no doubt it was you, Sir." Latimer said without emotion.

Marten looked at him for a long time without saying a word and then walked out of the room.

Latimer and Brighton had no choice but to leave.

"Now what, Sir?" Brighton said as they got into the car.

"We have two ways to go. One is to arrest him for failing to answer our questions. The other is to leave him alone until we find out more about Lora Weston, who I really think is Camilla Preston. Let's get back to the precinct and see what the boys at fingerprinting have come up with."

"Have you found anything with the files from Pelosi so far, Kid?"

"Nothing that stands out yet," Brighton looked at Latimer. "Have you ever considered we might be chasing the wrong guy in all this, Sir?"

"I have, but my instincts tell me we have the man in Marten Anscott. I don't know how yet, or why, but my nose tells me I'm on the right track."

"How can you be sure, Sir? You are in a lot of trouble if you're wrong."

"What can they do to me but give me early retirement, Kid." Latimer chuckled. "When you have been in this business as long as I have, your nose knows."

"Still Sir, the man has no reason to kill his father. He inherited everything and he already has a big chunk of change from the trust fund. I wish I had one of those," he added wistfully."

"Don't we all, Kid."

Chapter 14

He had trouble sleeping that night. Brighton's words stuck in his mind. What if he was chasing the wrong man? There was simply no one else so far who could have done it. There was no break-in, no footprints outside and no one heard anything in the house. Neither was there a visitor. The doorbell would have given it away unless Anscott let him in. On the other hand, there was the deal with Lora Weston or Camilla Preston. What the devil could Marten have in common with either woman?

Latimer's mind would not shut off and he finally got up and went to the living room to watch an old movie. He woke up at four in the morning in his chair, stiff all over and felt like a truck had run over him. The TV was still running. He turned on the news channel, but at that time of morning all they did was rehash the bad stuff from yesterday.

He staggered to the kitchen and put on a pot of coffee, extra strong, and headed for the shower. The hot water felt good and brought some of his stiff muscles back to life. He should get a TV in his bedroom so if he fell asleep he wouldn't have to sleep in his chair. He was probably the only person in Glenridge who didn't have a TV in the bedroom. He just had never gotten around to getting one.

When he got back to the kitchen the coffee was done. He sat at the small table and enjoyed it with a stale bagel from three days ago. He didn't even put it in the toaster but dunked it into his coffee. It was good. *It doesn't take much to make me happy these days,* he thought and tried to imagine if Glenda was here with him in the mornings. He even imagined she would fuss over him and fix him breakfast with orange juice, toast and anything else he asked her for. *Old man, you have it bad for this woman,* he thought.

That is when his cell went off. It was still on the coffee table in the living room and he rushed to get it. "Latimer."

"Inspector, this is Officer Cranston with dispatch. We have a murder. The Chief said to call you. The body of a woman has been found near the Lafayette Bridge in the lower district."

"I will be there in twenty minutes." He dialed Brighton's number on the way to the car and told him to meet him at the bridge. It was five thirty.

The place was already crawling with police, EMS vehicles and onlookers. He spotted Pat Christianson, the only female coroner in Glenridge, kneeling by the body.

"Good morning Pat, what have we here? Got an ID?" Latimer asked as he leaned over the body and then straightened up immediately. "I know who this woman is. Her name is Lora Weston slash Camilla Preston, whichever one you prefer."

The coroner looked at him with a strange expression. "You mean I get to pick and choose, Bob? That's a new one even for you." She was in her mid-fifties with short, gray hair. Her face was filled with deep wrinkles like she had been out in the sun too much. She was a large woman and wore jeans, a t-shirt and a pair of old leather boots.

"How did she die?" He asked her.

"That's easy. It was a gunshot wound to the chest, close range, with a Walther PK 380 is my guess. I will know more after the autopsy."

"Any guess how long she has been dead?"

"Roughly 15 to 20 hours judging from what I can see right off hand. I can tell you one thing, she was not killed here, there is hardly any blood around the body."

"Good morning, Sir, what's going on?" It was Brighton.

"It's Lora Weston, Kid."

"You mean Camilla Preston?"

"What is it with you two? You can't make up your mind about the name of this victim?" Pat Christianson asked.

"It's a long story, Ma'am," Brighton said.

"I believe you, honey."

"I want you to take extra care with the fingerprinting on this victim, Pat. It's extremely important," Latimer said.

"Sweetheart, I do everything with extra care with my bodies. They don't talk back to me or demand things like some people I know." She smiled up at him. "You know I will, handsome."

"You are the love of my life Pat, but your bodies have always come between us." Latimer's voice had taken on a melodramatic tone.

Brighton rolled his eyes. "Man, I think I'm going to be sick."

"Come on Kid, let's get to work and go over the crime scene. You realize we got too close to Marten Anscott yesterday, don't you? He took care of the problem he had with our victim by shutting her up permanently." He looked at Brighton. "You want to know something? I

105

spent a sleepless night worrying whether I was going after the right killer after what you said yesterday. Now I know I'm not."

"I agree with you, Sir."

They walked around in the vicinity of the body, looking for clues. The sun had come up in the meantime and made it much easier. Latimer looked up the steep bank and saw some branches broken off and a set of drag marks.

"This is where he dumped her over, Kid. Can you go around and climb up to the street? Make sure to stay away from the spot."

"Yes, Sir," Brighton said and walked a few feet before he made it up with very little effort. He walked back to the spot above the body, stepping carefully as not to disturb any possible evidence.

"Make sure the crime scene crew cordons off the spot," Latimer yelled up at him.

"I see nothing, Sir. There's no evidence of tire marks, but the grass is trampled down," Brighton yelled back.

He waved to the crew and pointed to the dump site. "Be careful guys," he shouted, "don't step any closer, this is a crime scene. They unrolled the yellow tape in a wide circle. "You want me to come back down, Sir?"

"No, you take a careful look around. Make sure the crime scene people don't miss anything."

It was over three hours before they returned to the office. There were several messages from the Chief on Latimer's desk to come see him in his office. He stopped by the lounge for coffee and headed down the hall.

"What the heck is going on, Latimer. The murders are piling up and we don't have a lead!" The Chief's voice thundered.

"We have a lead, Sir. I have no doubt the perp is Marten Anscott." Latimer said with conviction. "I wish we hadn't stopped the surveillance when we did, we might have prevented this."

The Chief looked at him and started to say something, but then just stared, his face getting red. "Are you saying I made a mistake?" he finally said.

"All I'm saying is I wish we had kept up the surveillance, Sir. It's hard to tell what to do in these cases and I realize resources are limited." Latimer's voice was casual. *I know the Chief made a mistake and so does the Chief,* he thought.

"What is the next step, Latimer? You want an arrest warrant?"

"No, not yet, Sir. Not until we have more evidence. I talked with Anscott yesterday. The guy denies everything about being in Weston's apartment or knowing her. We have to have more to go on. I'm really counting on forensics and ballistics to give me something solid. The coroner already told me it looks like the same gun was used here as with Patrick Anscott."

"Let me know when you need that warrant. We've got to stop any more murders. The media is going to fry us as it is, not to forget the Commissioner." He sounded a little subdued now.

"What I'm counting on Sir, is that Anscott is scared. He did not have time to plan this one the way he did the other one. I'm sure he made mistakes. As a matter of fact, I'm counting on it."

"Can I at least tell the press we have a person of interest to hold them off, Inspector?" He leaned toward Latimer almost with a look of desperation.

"I see no reason why not, Sir. I would appreciate it if you would not mention any names until there is an arrest. No need to start the media circus before I have more solid evidence." He looked at the Chief with confidence. "We'll get him, Sir. We just need a little bit more time. There is one more thing. Can I get a search warrant for the Anscott Estate, especially for Marten Anscott's room and the grounds around the house? That would include an old pickup truck or any other cars on the premises." Latimer said as he got up.

"I'll see to it," the Chief said as he reached for the phone.

It was early afternoon when they drove out to the Estate, search warrant in hand. Richard was surprised to see the group of four policemen standing behind Latimer and Brighton. "What is going on, Inspector?" he asked with concern in his voice.

"I'm sorry, Richard. We've come with a search warrant. Please allow these men to come in and show them Marten's room."

"May I show Mrs. Anscott the warrant first before they do that, Sir?"

"I'm afraid not Richard, but please notify her we are here. I will be glad to show it to her if she will see me upstairs. For now, can you show the men where Marten's room is?"

"He is not in at the moment. I think he's at the garden house out back."

107

"That is fine Richard, we don't need him for this," Latimer said as he followed the confused butler.

"Here it is, Sir," Richard said as he opened the door.

"Thank you Richard, we'll take it from here." Latimer walked in. It was a pretty large room with a king size bed, unmade, with pillows and clothes strewn all over the plush, beige carpet. In contrast, the papers on the good size desk were arranged in perfect order. The seating area around the fireplace appeared as if no one had ever sat there. Latimer peeked into the large walk-in closet and noticed the same neatness everywhere. He wondered why the bed was in such a mess in the midst of the rest of the order in the room.

The men were fanning out into the bathroom and the closet, opening drawers and cabinets wherever they found them.

"Is there anything in particular we are looking for, Inspector?" one of them asked.

"A gun would be nice, guys," Latimer said with a smile. "Make it a Walther PK 380 and I would really be happy," he added. "Look for clothes with blood on them as well as shoes. Don't forget to check for drugs in all the unlikely places."

It only took minutes for the entire room to take on the look of total chaos.

"My heavens, what are you doing, Inspector?" It was Helen Anscott. She stood in the door with a look of horror on her face. "Why are we treated like common criminals? Please explain to me what you hope to accomplish with this." She looked at Latimer with real anger. "I have called my lawyer, he is on his way."

"It is your right to do so Ma'am, but quite unnecessary. We have a search warrant." He handed it to her and she read it for only a minute.

"Is this really necessary, Inspector? You could have asked and I would have allowed you to look in Marten's room without all this." Her usual calm, kind demeanor was returning.

"I have tried to talk to your son several times, Mrs. Anscott, but he has refused to cooperate. I have even tried to speak with you about certain matters and you would not speak to me about Lora Weston. Now that she has been found murdered, I have no choice but to take these drastic measures to find out the truth." Latimer spoke in a very measured, polite tone.

There was a momentary silence and then she asked, "Does that mean you think I have murdered this woman, Inspector?"

"I don't think that at all, Ma'am, but I think your son did."

"What? That is ludicrous. Marten doesn't even know she exists," she said with great emphasis.

"On the contrary, Ma'am. He was overheard on the phone in this house talking to her and has been seen visiting her apartment in the lower district."

"You must be mistaken, I know my son. He would never be involved with someone like her." She sounded sure. "He would definitely not murder anyone."

"Then tell me how you know Lora Weston, Mrs. Anscott. From your reaction the other day, when I asked you, I know you do, and so does your lawyer. He didn't say he did, but I could tell when I spoke to him." Before she could say anything, he went on, "Why would you instruct him not to say anything? Mrs. Anscott, we are going to have a long talk about this now that this is a murder investigation. I will be back tomorrow, please make yourself available."

She stood there, unable to speak for what seemed a long time. She looked around helplessly as the men were methodically taking apart the room.

"I will have my lawyer present tomorrow Inspector, if you don't mind," she finally managed to say in a small voice before she started to go downstairs.

"I expect to interview you tomorrow afternoon Ma'am, around two. Please make sure you are home."

She did not answer him.

"Finding anything, guys?" He went into the bathroom.

"Nothing so far, Sir."

"Keep looking. When you are done here we are going over the grounds with a fine tooth comb. I'm looking for footprints in front of Patrick Anscott's study. After that we will walk over to the garden house a few hundred feet out back. There is a pickup truck I'm interested in." Latimer pulled his cell phone out and dialed his office. "Ginny, make sure you keep my schedule free tomorrow. I will be spending the time finishing up with the search warrant here and then interview the family."

"Ok, Sir. There was a call from a Clara Caskel for you. She didn't say what she wanted, but said she would call back."

"Did you get a number?"

"She wouldn't give it, but said she would call back. I dialed the number after she hung up. It was a pay phone somewhere in town."

"Thanks, Ginny. I have no idea who she is, but if she calls again give her my cell number. I have a feeling she knows something, especially after the press conference this morning."

"There have been many calls today, but the switch board routed them to the Chief's office. I'm sure his staff will fill you in if there was something interesting or important," Ginny said.

"See you when we finish up here for the day," Latimer said and hung up.

They found nothing in the room and Latimer asked Richard to point out the window to Patrick Anscott's study. It had rained two days in a row and he didn't think they would find footprints. What they did find was a broken twig off one of the bushes right underneath the window. It was small, but definitely had been broken off by something or someone.

Latimer told one of the men to take a picture before they put the twig into a plastic bag. "There was someone here looking in," he said, "very interesting."

He walked up close to the window and looked inside. He could see the desk and the cabinet with the safe in it quite clearly. Someone watched Patrick Anscott through this window. He was sure of it. It must have been Marten. It made sense, because he didn't need to ring the bell to get back in the house. He probably used a back door.

"Let's find a back door nearby," he said to Brighton, "then have it dusted for fingerprints."

It took quite some time to check the perimeter of the house, but they found nothing else. The big surprise was that the back door they were looking for had been wiped clean of prints.

It was close to three-thirty when they were done.

"We're impounding the truck," Latimer said. "Let's concentrate on the inside of the little house with your search," Latimer told the men.

"Does the warrant include taking the truck off the property?" Brighton asked.

"Get on the cell and have the Chief's office get permission before we leave here today, Latimer said. "It should not be a problem."

He was wondering why they had not run into Marten, but he must have left before they were finished with his room. His red Lexus

110

was gone from the front of the house. He remembered clearly seeing it when they arrived.

Before the day was over they had searched the garden house. It was a small building, about 200 feet in back of the main house. It looked like a miniature barn with a garage door and a small, regular door in the front. The house lay hidden behind a cluster of trees with a narrow paved road leading up to it. It consisted of only one room and held tools, equipment and other such things as needed for grounds maintenance. A police tow truck had hauled off the pickup parked in front of it.

Latimer was exhausted when he arrived at his office at five-thirty. He was glad his date with Glenda was tomorrow instead of today and looked forward to a quiet evening at home. He stopped by at a takeout place and got something for dinner.

Chapter 15

It was at four in the morning when he was roused from a deep sleep by his cell phone. "Latimer," he said in a sleepy voice.

"Bob, it's Glenda. I'm at the hospital with Cassie. Helen Anscott had a major stroke about two hours ago."

"Oh man, how is she?"

"Not good, Bob. They are doing everything they can. It's too soon to tell how much damage there is or if she will live. I'm here with Cassie. She's trying to get hold of Marten, who is nowhere to be found."

"What do you mean, he's nowhere to be found? Isn't he at home in bed?"

"No, he has not been home since yesterday and no one knows where he is. This is all so terrible. This whole family is being torn apart and there is nothing I can do to help. I will stay with Cassie for as long as it takes. Oh, by the way, I don't think I can make it tonight for our date. I will have to call you when things are better and we know more. Take care. I've got to go, the doctor is coming out. Bye."

Latimer's head sank back into the pillow. There went the two people who could have shed some light on the latest murder and with them went the interview this afternoon. He groaned. What was it about this case that drove him absolutely mad? Just as he thought he was getting somewhere and maybe obtain enough information to arrest Marten, the man disappears.

Poor Helen, he hoped she would not be paralyzed or even die. He felt frustrated that this couldn't have happened a day later. It wasn't nice thinking that way, but under the circumstances no one could blame him. He was sure she held the key to the mystery of who Lora Weston was.

Once again he felt he was at a dead end. In his office, he sat down at his desk with his first cup of coffee and growled at Brighton when the young man bounced in with his customary bright smile.

"We are in a bad mood and the day has not even begun." Brighton slumped into the chair in front of the desk. "Did something bad happen, Sir?"

"There are some days not worth getting up for, Kid," Latimer said and stared at Brighton with a gloomy expression on his face. "We were going to interview Marten and Helen Anscott today, right? Wrong! One is in the hospital with a stroke and the other disappeared."

"You are kidding me. That leaves us nowhere, Sir."

"You could not be more right, Kid. Nowhere is where we are with this case." Latimer emptied his cup. "Be nice to me this morning and get me another, Kid. I need something to drown my sorrow in."

"I will be right back, Sir." Brighton jumped up instantly as if glad to get away from the gloom and doom atmosphere in the office.

So, Marten had taken off for parts unknown. He would make sure and call Richard right now.

"Sir, I have not seen him this morning," Richard said, "I will go and knock on the door of his room if you will give me a minute. Maybe he came after poor Mrs. Anscott was taken to the hospital.

Latimer waited.

"No Sir, he is not in his room. Some of his clothes are gone and his computer is not on his desk. It looks like Master Marten has left."

"If you could guess Richard, where would he go if he was upset or wanted to get away from it all?" Latimer asked.

"The condo in West Palm Beach is the only place I can think of he would go to if something was bothering him, Sir."

"Thank you, Richard. Please call me immediately if he should show up."

"I will, Sir."

Brighton came in with the coffee.

"Where do we go from here, Sir?" he asked as he handed Latimer the coffee.

"All we can do is wait for the test results from the coroner's office, the fingerprint lab and for some evidence in the pickup truck. I'm afraid none of them will be ready till this afternoon." He leaned back in the chair. "You know what, we are going back to the Estate and check out that garden house some more. I have a feeling the guys yesterday were too eager to get home to do a thorough job of it. Let's go, Kid. We have nothing better to do."

They drove past the main house down the narrow road and parked in front of the little barn. Brighton opened the big garage doors almost before Latimer got out of the car. Every space inside was filled with all kinds of lawn and garden tools. There were two rider mowers and various tools and implements they had no idea what they were used for.

"Let's see what we can find, Kid. Our warrant is still good for today."

The interior had a faint gas smell from two large gas cans sitting on the side out of the way. Several large bags of fertilizer stood leaning against the wall. They were all sealed but one, which had been torn open. Shelves lined the upper part of the walls filled with all kinds of chemicals, cleaners and other things used with machinery. All in all, it was pretty neat the way it was arranged, given it was more or less a tool shed.

Latimer and Brighton rummaged around for at least an hour, but found nothing out of the ordinary and were ready to leave. Just before they stepped outside Latimer walked over to the fertilizer bags. He rolled up one sleeve and stuck his gloved hand in the open one.

"I got something." He pulled out a gun, a Walther PK 380 with a pearl handle.

"Bingo," he whispered as he slid it into a plastic bag. "I won the jack pot."

"It's literally the smoking gun, Sir," Brighton shouted. "We have the killer!"

"I wish we did, Kid. He's gone to parts unknown and we need to get to the precinct to put out an All-Points Bulletin on Marten Anscott."

Back at the office Brighton rushed the gun to ballistics.

"When you get back, check who it is registered to, Kid," Latimer yelled after him. Then he picked up the phone and called Glenda. "How is Helen Anscott, Glenda?"

"It is still too early to tell, Bob. Apparently the stroke was pretty bad and she cannot speak or move her right arm. The right side of her face is affected as well, but she is awake and that is a good thing the doctor says."

"Have you been able to get in touch with Marten?"

"No, I have tried everywhere, even at the company. I can't imagine what has happened to him. Cassie is steaming mad that he left without telling anyone where he was going."

"Glenda, don't tell Cassie or her mother. We found the gun that killed both Patrick Anscott and Lora Weston."

"Where?"

"It was hidden in a bag of fertilizer in the garden house at the Anscott Estate. Do you have any idea who in that family owns a Walther PK 380 with a pearl handle?"

"I don't. You think Marten is on the run, don't you, Bob?"

"Yes, and I have an APB out on him. When we find him he will be charged with murder."

"This can't get any worse for this family. I'm glad Mr. Anscott is not here to see this. Why on earth do you think Marten killed his father? What could his motive possibly be?"

"That I can't tell you," he said. I was going to interrogate Helen and Marten Anscott today. I guess that is not going to happen. Keep an eye and ear open. If you see or hear anything about Marten, let me know right away. Take care, I'll be in touch." Latimer hung up when he saw the Chief come in.

"I hear you found the gun at the Estate. It looks like it was Marten Anscott then, doesn't it?"

"Yes Sir, but he has left for parts unknown."

"I have scheduled another press conference with the media. I will let them know we have identified the killer. That should satisfy a few people in higher places." The Chief sounded positive.

"I don't know how satisfied they will stay when you have to tell them that the killer has also escaped, Sir."

"Well, there is that. I have to try to put a positive spin on things and try to bury that fact somehow. I'm relying on you Latimer, to find him soon," he added and left.

That afternoon the coroner's office called. It was Pat Christianson.

"Hi handsome, I got some interesting results for you. I thought I would tell you myself." Her voice sounded deep and raspy. "First of all, the victim was indeed shot at close range with a Walther PK 380. I have the bullet. Secondly, and this is what you wanted me to be so careful about, her fingerprints are not in our data base. There are some who are real close, but not the same. Now I understand how you couldn't make up your mind about which name to use. This woman was the twin of Camilla Preston wasn't she?"

"You are not going to believe this Pat, but this is not Lora Weston. It is Camilla Preston." Latimer interrupted.

"Now there you go again. I'm glad you have it all figured out. I go by what my data base tells me. Now let me finish. Third, she never had any children because of scar tissues in her fallopian tubes. Since you told me she lived with her son, whoever she lived with is not her son."

"Any drugs in her system?"

"None, she is clean. What she did have was advanced diabetes and some arthritis. She was also underweight for what seems to have been from lack of nutrition. In other words, the woman did not have enough to eat. First thing in the morning I will send you the details of my report."

"Thank you, gorgeous, you are fabulous as usual," Latimer said with a big grin.

"I bet you say that to all the female coroners, you handsome devil." She was laughing as she hung up.

There was nothing new there. It seems Lora Weston, who died so many years ago, did not have a record at all, but her sister Camilla made up for it. That is when Latimer remembered he had told Brighton to look for the rest of the siblings in that family. Since the Kid had not mentioned anything, he must have struck out. Latimer knew they had to pursue finding at least one of them to figure out how Camilla was connected to the Anscott's since Helen could not talk at the moment. He would try to get her to agree for her lawyer to talk when she was able to receive visitors.

"Ginny, did that woman Clara Caskel call again by any chance?"

"No, but the fingerprint lab did. They have the results of the prints they took in Anscott's office at the Estate. I had him bring them over. Here they are." She handed him the folder.

"Great, let's see what we have here."

There were prints of all the family members, the staff and several not found in the data base. Marten's were there. The team had gotten samples from every member of the household that first day they covered the crime scene. There was no unusual person or anyone with a record found among the remaining prints at the crime scene. Marten's prints did not show up in the criminal data base. It meant he had no record, which was no surprise.

Latimer stopped. Why would a guy who was normal, wealthy and living in a good family suddenly murder two people in cold blood? It made no sense. Why had he changed into a sullen, emotional person from a likable, easy going young man? Latimer realized he may have the killer, but there were still a tremendous number of unanswered questions.

What if he had the wrong man? What if Marten Anscott was just distraught and was framed by someone else? Latimer felt a nagging feeling of doubt deep inside. It was like a puzzle, but none of the pieces fit. They should, but they didn't.

He sat at his desk and his thoughts swirled around in a circle. He did not feel good about this case. Something was either not right or missing. If he could just talk to Helen Anscott, he was sure it would all come together.

Brighton interrupted his thoughts and he was almost relieved.

"I have the ballistics report from the Anscott murder, Sir."

"Is it the gun we found?"

"I don't know, but it was a Walther PK 380, so it probably was. They will test the one we brought and let us know by tomorrow." Brighton sat down and took a deep breath. "This was a good day, wouldn't you say, Sir?"

"We'll see, Kid. Did you ever find any of the sisters of Camilla and Lora?"

"No, I didn't. Do you have any idea how hard that is? All these women probably changed their names when they got married and we don't even know their parents' name or where they lived. It boggles the mind. I don't even know where to start."

"Did you check the old records? Was there any mention of a maiden name?" Latimer asked.

"I did Sir, and there wasn't. I guess they didn't ask that in those days or the page was missing or something." Brighton sounded frustrated. "I didn't get anywhere Sir, I'm sorry."

"We have to keep digging. We may think we have the killer, but there are too many loose ends concerning these two women. We need to know what they have to do with Marten Anscott and why he murdered Camilla Preston, formerly Lora Weston."

"Maybe we have to wait and ask him when we catch up with him," Brighton said, almost relieved. "It would certainly help me out." He smiled.

Latimer's cell phone rang. It was Glenda.

"Bob, Helen Anscott died an hour ago."

"You are kidding. I'm so sorry. Please give my condolences to Miss Anscott.

He hung up.

"She died?" Brighton asked, totally shocked.

"Yes." Latimer was silent for a long time. "She was a great lady. In a way I'm glad she did not have to live with her son's disgrace. I have a feeling that is why she did not fight to live. Her husband's death and her son's possible crime made it impossible for her to go on." He leaned over the desk, tired. "Who I really feel sorry for is Cassie. When all this is said and done, she will have lost her entire family in the span of two weeks."

"That is hard to imagine, Sir." For once, there was no smile on Brighton's face.

The phone rang again. It was the Chief.

"Latimer, I want you to do the press conference with me late this afternoon. As the detective on the case you should get some of the credit."

"I would rather not, Sir. There are yet too many loose ends for me to declare victory. I'm having some serious doubts as to the killer and why he did it." He cleared his throat. "There is something else, Glenda Hinsley just called me. Helen Anscott died an hour or so ago of a massive stroke."

"You are kidding me! This is terrible. We can't have a press conference with that going on. We'll have to delay it till further notice." His voice changed into a positive tone. "Maybe this will give us enough time to find Marten Anscott, right?"

"Right Sir, that sounds good to me." He hung up.

Latimer was truly disgusted. That's why he had never wanted to be Chief. When you get that high, it is all politics with very little room for human kindness.

"Kid, did you ever check who the gun was registered to?"

"I forgot to tell you. It's a guy named Peter Richman from Kansas City. He reported it stolen five years ago."

"That means it was probably bought illegally." Latimer said. "Another dead end."

"That makes me wonder," he said almost to himself. "If Camilla Preston couldn't have children, who then is the man she called her son?"

"Could it have been her sister Lora's baby she took in after she killed her, Sir?"

"No, remember, she sold it." "

"Oh, that's right. The man who goes by the name Paul Weston, I wonder why we haven't heard from him? After all, he should have reported her missing by now," Brighton said.

"People in the lower district go missing all the time and no one cares. Those two did not seem to be on the best of terms," Latimer said. "He may have even heard she's dead from the news reports and doesn't want to get involved with the police."

"This case is like an onion and we are the ones peeling it back layer by layer. It's a very painstaking process. I'm absolutely sure we will get to the center of it after a while." Latimer sounded more optimistic than he felt.

"I heard you tell the Chief you were not so sure about the killer," Brighton said. "Did you say that because you didn't want to do the press conference, or did you really mean it, Sir?"

"I have been having a nagging doubt. Not necessarily about the killer, but about the circumstances, and especially the motive. There is still no good reason why Marten Anscott should suddenly turn into a cold blooded killer. He has no priors, no history of violence according to the people close to him, and no reason to kill his father. This all has to do with Lora Weston and her sister." Latimer's voice had a hint of frustration in it. "We just have to keep peeling that onion, Kid."

"What's next, Sir?"

"We need to find Paul Weston and one or all three of the sisters."

"Good luck with that." Brighton said, thinking about the hours he might have to spend scanning the data base.

The phone rang.

"Glenda, how are you?"

"Bob, I'm home at the moment. It has been a horrible night. I simply need some sleep this afternoon. I just wanted to call you before I go to bed. I would like to get with you to discuss something. Maybe we could have that date later tonight?"

"Absolutely, call me back when you wake up and we'll arrange a time and place." Before he hung up he added, "Make sure you turn your cell off. The world can get along without you for a few hours."

"Another date, Sir?" Brighton asked.

"Bite your tongue, Kid. She wants to discuss something about the case. I wonder what it is."

"Maybe she heard from Marten?"

"She would have said that. No, this has something to do with the family. I guarantee it is a sad house over there. The funeral and running the company, all fall on Cassie's shoulders. When the Chief has the press conference, the media attention about her brother will add to it."

"Maybe it's not all a bed of roses when you're rich and powerful like they are, Sir."

"Life is the great equalizer, Kid. In the end we all have to deal with problems. It really doesn't make that much difference, whether we are rich or poor, but how well we handle them. What does matter, is whether we have the inner strength to go on or give up. Look at Helen, she gave up and she looked like a very strong woman from the few times I talked to her. In the end she could not face life any longer. It will be interesting to see what her daughter Cassie is made of."

Latimer had formed a certain attachment with the people at Anscott Estate. He realized the personal insight he had gotten had come through Glenda. How many times over the years had he preached to the new recruits? Do not get personally involved in your cases. This was his last case and here he was personally involved!

Ginny rang on the intercom.

"What's up?" Latimer had trouble getting back into the presence.

"There is a man named Mark Lenhart on the phone wanting a word with you. He says he is with Anscott Laboratories. You want to talk to him?"

"Absolutely, put him through."

"What can I do for you, Mr. Lenhart? I'm sorry to hear about Mrs. Anscott. I'm sure things are in an uproar from where you sit." Latimer thought he could have found better words for this situation. He stopped talking before he made matters worse.

"Inspector, I told you I want to help in this case. Something has come up and I'm at a loss as how to deal with it. It has to do with Marten Anscott." He cleared his throat and Latimer knew he was uncomfortable talking about this. "I spoke with our man in finance this morning and he informed me there are certain inconsistencies with Mr. Anscott's trust fund. You must understand, it's really not my business what Mr. Anscott does with his money, but since he is missing, this seems to be important. We are even considering this could be a kidnapping, but there has been no ransom demand."

"It is definitely not that, Mr. Lenhart. However, something is going on."

"Oh, my goodness, is there any way you could stop by and talk to Kevin Rathbone? He's the one in charge of this matter."

"Please notify Mr. Rathbone I will be there within the hour, Mr. Lenhart. Thank you, I have a feeling this will definitely help our case."

"Do you have any idea where Mr. Anscott is? I was astonished to hear from Cassie he has disappeared."

"We are looking for him, Sir. Since this is an open case, this is all I can tell you at the moment."

"I understand, Inspector. I'm glad I can be of help."

Chapter 16

Walter Rathbone's office turned out to be on the seventh floor. A secretary announced their arrival. Latimer and Brighton were ushered in without delay. The man who greeted them reminded Latimer of Abraham Lincoln without the beard. He was every bit as tall and lanky, in his fifties, with coal black hair. It was definitely a dye job Latimer decided.

"Inspector Latimer, I presume. I'm Walter Rathbone. Mr. Lenhart said you would be coming by."

"It is good to meet you, Sir. This is Sgt. Brighton. How good you could see us right away."

"Have a seat, Gentlemen." He pointed to the two chairs in front of his large desk. Latimer was glad the man was tall, otherwise he would have disappeared behind the numerous high stacks of papers and piles of folders. The rest of the office was in equal disarray with files covering every surface.

With all this mess I don't know if I would trust him with my finances, Latimer thought.

"Don't worry Inspector, I know where everything is," Rathbone said, as if reading his thoughts.

"Of course Sir, I have no doubt." Latimer hoped his face hadn't betrayed him. "Let's get right to the point. What is it exactly you have for us that pertains to Mr. Anscott? Mr. Lenhart said it has to do with Marten Anscott's trust."

"Yes, it does." He took a file in front of him and opened it. "You see, Marten Anscott has a very large trust fund at his disposal. I would never presume to tell him how to spend his money. However, when large sums are taken out suddenly without notice or warning, that is alarming. Especially since I have been made aware he is missing." He shuffled through several pages. "Is this a case of kidnapping, Inspector?"

"I don't believe so, but it is true, he is missing. We are looking for him since he seems to be unaware what has happened to his mother."

"Oh my goodness, that is terrible." The man seemed genuinely upset.

"Do you know Mr. Anscott very well, Sir?" Latimer asked.

"Well, we have frequent dealings when it comes to investments and other money matters. I like the young man. He is amiable, sensible with money and in every way a responsible person at his young age. In the past he has always notified me if he had extra expenses, so I can make the necessary transfers of funds for him."

"What has changed, Mr. Rathbone?" Latimer said to keep him on track.

"Last Friday he withdrew a very large sum of money from his bank account without notifying me."

"How large?"

"Five thousand dollars in cash. The bank did not notify me until yesterday, because they had a second request for fifty thousand."

"Fifty thousand? That's a large sum, even for Mr. Anscott, I presume," Latimer asked. "Which bank are we dealing with?"

"It's Continental Trust Bank in downtown on Main Street, right here in Glenridge."

"Did the bank say it was Marten Anscott who made the withdrawals?" Latimer asked.

"I questioned the teller about that and she said it was definitely him. He told her he was taking an extended trip overseas and that is why he needed the cash. When she told him she would have to contact my office before she could give him the money, he left." Rathbone closed the file. "That is all I can tell you."

"One more question. The bank teller asked for an ID from Mr. Anscott, right?"

"I don't know. I imagine with this kind of amount, they would."

"Thank you, Mr. Rathbone. We will make a trip downtown and stop by the bank. "Would you be so kind as to call them and let them know we are coming? It makes things easier." Latimer smiled at him with an expression of sincere gratitude. It worked. Mr. Rathbone reached for the phone and started dialing.

Melody Kessler, a shy, quiet young woman, remembered Anscott very well. She had dealt with him on many occasions, but still insisted to check his driver license. When she found it to be in order, there was no reason for her to withhold the funds the first time he came by. She remembered him smiling at her and even flirting a little.

When he returned the second time and asked for fifty thousand, he seemed very stressed and nervous.

"That's when I told him we had to contact Mr. Rathbone's office for verification," she told Latimer. "I hope I didn't do anything wrong, Inspector. I simply did my job," she said, unsure of herself.

123

"You did absolutely nothing wrong, Ms. Kessler." Latimer pulled out one of his cards. "Do me a favor. If Mr. Anscott comes again for any reason, give me a call immediately, but don't let him know."

"I certainly will, Sir."

"It looks like our boy got in a hurry." Latimer said, once outside the building. He has five thousand dollars in cash, a new car and seems to be in no hurry to leave town."

"I bet he has had the car painted by now with a more neutral color and found an apartment somewhere, "Brighton said. "For the life of me, why would he stay here in Glenridge when he knows the police are looking for him?"

"Five thousand dollars isn't going to last him very long. Especially since he is used to spending money without worrying where it comes from," Latimer said. He groaned. Once again, nothing made sense. None of the pieces of the puzzle were coming together. Nothing was sure, except the fact that people were dropping dead, whether from natural or unnatural causes.

"Florida sounds good again, Kid," he said when they got into the car.

At the office he found the report from the pickup truck. Before he read it he headed for the lounge. "Can I bring you a cup of coffee, Kid?"

"I can get it, Sir." Brighton jumped up from the chair.

"No, it's my turn. Besides, you are not here to serve me tea and crumpets, Sergeant," he said on the way out.

This is what Brighton liked about the old man. He treated him right, like he was an equal. Well, maybe not quite, but nice.

"Let's take a look at the report," Latimer said when he came back with two steaming cups of wonderful smelling coffee. "Someone just made a fresh pot."

He opened the file and read for a long while. "This is interesting," he finally said. "They found a lot of blood in the bed of the truck. It belongs to Camilla Preston, which means Anscott killed her and then transported her to the river."

"He made no attempt to clean it up?" Brighton asked.

"Apparently not, which is strange. It's almost like he wanted to get caught." Latimer said with irritation in his voice. "Either this guy is stupid or he didn't care. Even the shell casing was found in the front seat."

"He had to be high on drugs to do something like that, Sir," Brighton said. "Nobody is that stupid, stone cold sober."

"The only prints they found were Marten Anscott's and Camilla Preston's and the two men who take care of the grounds. So why do I still have doubts in my gut about all this?"

"You are kidding Sir, right?"

"No, I'm not. It's all too easy and too convenient for us to find the evidence. For the life of me, I can't figure out who else would go to this length to make Marten look guilty."

"You are never going to convince the Chief he's innocent, Sir. He'll be chomping at the bit to hold that press conference with you right there up front with him."

"I'm afraid you are right, Kid." Latimer leaned back in his chair with a heavy sigh. "I should be happy. I figured out who the killer is. So why am I not happy?"

"I don't know, Sir. I sure would be." Brighton's face had that happy smile all over it.

The phone rang. Sure enough, it was the Chief, telling Latimer to be there for the press conference at three this afternoon. He had already gotten the report from the pickup truck and was rearing to go.

The media was out in force. The Chief had set up a microphone on the steps in front of the precinct building. Cameras were everywhere. Latimer stood behind him to the side.

"Good afternoon, Ladies and Gentlemen! I'm Chief Carson. Standing next to me is the man responsible for identifying the killer of Patrick Anscott and Lora Weston. There will be time for questions after I read a statement first." He put down a piece of paper in front of him on the small podium.

"Before I give you information on the case, let me share something with you first. Helen Anscott, the wife of Patrick Anscott, the victim of last week's shooting incident, died of a massive stroke early this morning at a local hospital. Our prayers and condolences go out to the bereaved family." He took time for a dramatic pause.

"To add to the tragedy, Marten Henry Anscott, the son and heir of Anscott Laboratories has been positively identified in these two murders. He has been reported missing for two days and is presumed to have fled the area. We have put out an APB and expect to apprehend him shortly." He looked up from his paper and pointed to Latimer. "Inspector Latimer will now answer your questions."

The session dragged on endlessly. Finally, after an hour the Chief put a stop to it. Latimer remained calm throughout and managed to add a few words of caution into the mix that all the facts were not clear as of now. He stressed the point, the investigation would continue until the arrest of the perpetrator, whoever he may be. He was sure no one paid any attention to his warnings. It would come out on every TV station and newspaper that the crime had been solved. The mere fact the murderer was not yet in custody, was but a blip in the reporters' minds and seemingly of no importance.

The Chief was happy. The wolves were fed a bunch of scraps and his superiors were satisfied he had done a good job. Life was great again.

No one seemed to care that Latimer did not look happy at all.

His office was inundated with phone calls from well-wishers and people who reported having seen Marten Anscott. A phone bank had been established to sort out the nut jobs from any credible sounding informants. Latimer was in a foul mood and went home promptly at five. He had a date to keep. Glenda had called him on his cell phone. They had arranged to meet at seven o'clock at a small restaurant, just outside of town, called "The Wishing Well."

Latimer took great care dressing. Not too much and not too casual. He felt a little overwhelmed with Glenda's highbrow background as personal assistant to a business tycoon. He was sure she had been to all the swanky places in town in line of her duties. He had let her pick the place, just to make sure he would not make a blunder in selecting a restaurant that was not to her liking. He had never been to The Wishing Well and had called ahead to find out about the dress code. Casual was the answer, whatever that meant.

He stood in front of the mirror in the bathroom. Well, this would have to do. His nicest shirt was light blue, matching the color of his eyes. His best dress pants looked pretty good. He chose a dark, conservative tie with barely visible red stripes, which went well with his dark blue jacket.

Latimer still had no idea what she wanted to talk to him about. It may be a business meeting for her, but for him it was an honest-to-goodness date. When he tried to suggest he pick her up at her place, she insisted to meet him at the restaurant instead. Who knows, maybe she got burnt before and had trust issues. Although, what he had seen of her so far, she seemed like a well put together woman emotionally and in every other way.

He was fifteen minutes early when he arrived at The Wishing Well and sat in the car for a few minutes. When he finally went in, the waiter showed him to his reserved table. Glenda had not arrived yet. Darn it, he really was nervous. It was a feeling he had not experienced for many years. He took a sip of the water the waiter had put in front of him.

"Hi Bob, I hope I'm not late." She looked like she came straight from the office, wearing a dark gray business suit. It matched her silver gray hair perfectly.

"No, you are exactly on time." He got up and pulled out a chair out for her. "Thanks, it's been a horrible day in every way, as you can imagine." She looked at him and a smile appeared slowly on her face. "You look nice, Inspector."

"Thanks, this is my outfit for taking gorgeous women out on a second date. How is it working for me so far?"

She leaned back and studied him with a mock critical look. "How did you do with them?"

"I had to fight them off every time," he said, trying hard not to smile.

"Humility is not one of your faults, is it?" She was teasing.

"I tried it once and it didn't work."

She laughed and reached for the menu lying on the table.

"You are just what I need, Bob." Looking over the menu she said, "You can't go wrong with the steaks here. They really know how to fix them just the way you like. Patrick and Helen Anscott loved this place and brought me here many times." She was suddenly sad. "I'm going to miss them terribly."

After they had ordered, he asked her about Cassie.

"How is she holding up? This must be a nightmare for her."

"She amazes me. The girl has a lot more strength than I ever gave her credit for. As a matter of fact, she will do just great running Anscott Laboratories someday. It won't be near as far in the future as Mark Lenhart might imagine."

"You said you wanted to talk to me about something." He waited.

"I found an old diary in Helen's room. Cassie had asked me to go through her stuff to look for it and bring to the hospital. Helen managed to communicate to Cassie that she wanted it. She actually was able to say a few words. They were slurred, but Cassie could make them out. Helen was very agitated about the whole thing until Cassie assured her she would look for it."

Latimer hung on to her every word. "Did you read it?"

"No, not yet. I knew you wanted to know certain things that had to do with Lora Weston, but Helen wouldn't tell you. I asked Cassie if I could take it and show it to you. She was fine with it."

"Did you bring it?" Latimer held his breath.

"No, I left it at the office. You will have to send someone to pick it up tomorrow. It seemed of great importance to Helen."

"Does Cassie have any idea what is in it?" he asked.

"I don't think so. She just told me she wanted it back when you are done with it. Of course, Helen was still alive when all this happened. I have a feeling she did not want anyone to read it," Glenda went on.

"What makes you say that?"

"It was the worry and agitation in her voice and her body language when she tried to communicate with Cassie about this."

"I will definitely have someone pick it up first thing in the morning, Glenda. I'm really counting on finding out the secret of the relationship between Camilla Preston and the Anscott family." Then he leaned over and put his hand on her arm. "We have talked business long enough, don't you think?"

"You are right, Bob. I know nothing about you, except that you are a detective and your wife died ten years ago. There must be lots more to tell." She smiled at him with such warmth, it made him feel almost giddy.

"That about sums my life. My wife and my job have been all I have ever really cared about."

"You must have loved her a lot."

"I did, but ten years is a long time to be alone." He fumbled with his tie. "Seriously, I never thought I would ever meet someone I would even consider going out with, until I saw you that day in your office."

She pretended to be busy with the food on her plate and didn't answer.

He felt awkward and couldn't think of anything else to say.

At that moment the waiter walked up to their table.

"Is there anything else I can get for you?"

Latimer was glad for the interruption.

"We will have some wine, please. Red, if that is ok with you, Glenda?"

"That sounds great."

He knew he was smitten when he looked into her eyes as they lifted their glasses to each other. They were blue with gray specs in them. He tried to act "cool", a term Brighton would use under these circumstances. *Better not push things too fast,* he thought.

"To a better day tomorrow for both of us," Glenda said.

"Ditto."

"By the way, how did the press conference go? I watched most of it. People at the company are in total shock about all these terrible things. The worst seems to be the fact that Marten murdered his father. A lot of employees knew and liked the young man and watched him grow up over the years. Everyone finds it hard to imagine he could do something like that." Glenda took another sip of wine.

"So do I," Latimer said quietly.

"You are kidding, right?"

"I can't explain it, but there is that vague feeling something is not right about this case. I don't know that Marten is innocent, but there is more to it than him murdering two people in cold blood after a totally normal life for twenty-eight years." He put down the silverware and pushed back his plate. "This was delicious."

"Wait a minute, you are telling me that someone else might have done it?"

"I don't know. I'm telling you, I have many more questions than answers about this case."

"I'm afraid I don't understand. If Marten didn't do it, who did? There is so much evidence in your own words you spoke about at the press conference. Plus there is no other suspect, is there?"

"No, there isn't."

"So what you are really saying is, this case isn't over?"

"Not by a long shot, even if and when we find Marten."

"This is incredible. Do you mind if I tell Cassie? I'm certain it would give her some hope that she still has a brother in her future." Glenda sounded excited.

"Sure, go ahead. Just make sure you impress on her not to say anything to anybody."

They spent the rest of the evening talking about the case and Latimer was sad when Glenda looked at her watch and told him she had to go.

"It's going to be another long day, Bob." She leaned over and kissed him on the cheek when they got to the car. "I cannot tell you when I spent a more pleasant evening. Thank you, Bob."

He stood for quite a while in deep thought after she drove off.

The next morning Latimer told Brighton to get the diary the minute the Sergeant walked in the door. "Make sure you bring it straight to my office."

He knew something was wrong when the Kid returned.

"The diary is gone, Sir. They couldn't find it anywhere. I talked with Glenda Hinsley and Cassie Anscott as well as several secretaries. "It's gone."

"You have got to be kidding me!" Latimer took his empty coffee cup and threw it against the wall. It was the first time Brighton had ever heard the Inspector shout. A long silence filled the room. Latimer just sat there and stared into thin space. He was so angry his hands were shaking.

Finally he called Glenda.

"What happened to the diary?" he asked without so much as introducing himself.

"I have no idea Bob, but we are looking into it. I talked with the janitor who cleans the offices at night. He told me a man came in, walked into my office and after a few minutes walked back out to the elevator."

"Did the janitor call the police?"

"No, the place was sparsely lit and he assumed it was Marten. He hadn't heard the news since he works nights and sleeps during the day. He had no idea the police were looking for Marten, until I called him at home a while ago. When I asked him if he was sure it was Marten, he said there was no way he could be sure. He was too far away to be positive."

"What made him think it was him?"

"I asked him that. He said Marten would sometimes come in at that time of night. He just assumed it was him."

"Thanks, Glenda."

This was brazen. First of all, the guy doesn't even leave town. Then walks into his own company and takes the diary without anyone stopping him. That janitor was probably the only person in the country who didn't know the police were after Marten. But then, what if it wasn't Marten who the janitor saw? How did the guy know about the diary, whoever he was?

Latimer groaned. He felt like the good Lord had run out of breaks. He needed one badly.

By the time Friday afternoon came there were no new leads on Marten Anscott, no new developments and no diary. Latimer was glad to be able to leave for the weekend and try to clear his mind for two days. He was at a complete dead end and had no idea where to go from here. He had gone over all the reports about this case with a fine tooth comb for most of the day.

Before he went home, he called Glenda. She told him she was extremely busy with funeral arrangements and helping Cassie make the transition in the company. What that entailed was her doing all the transitioning and Cassie coming in for a few hours to get an update. That didn't leave much time for her to see him.

Chapter 17

The man sat and stared at the TV. The news conference had been over for hours. Everything had gone wrong. All his careful planning had come to nothing because of one stupid woman who couldn't wait. Because of her he had to kill Anscott. He didn't want to, but what choice did he have? The guy was going to stir things up from way back when and he couldn't let him do that.

To build a silencer was easy. All he had to do was go on the internet and get some ideas and then do what they showed him in living color. All he really needed was a D cell flashlight, freeze plugs and other small, ordinary items from the local auto parts store.

He didn't enjoy killing the man. Neither did it bother him when he killed the other one on the boat. He had finally gotten over the nightmares and had done ok with all the changes since then.

Killing Camilla had been a moment of revenge. It had felt good and she deserved it. He couldn't help what happened to him. It was his destiny to set things straight.

He would have to be careful, though. This Inspector was pretty smart. Thank goodness he got the diary in time. He was glad Helen Anscott died when she did. There was no way he was going to let her mess everything up.

He had spent many hours sitting in his car. He had fallen asleep just down from the Estate entrance. Suddenly, the lights and sounds of the ambulance jarred him awake. He had no idea why he had decided to park there, watching. It had paid off. He followed the EMS vehicle to the hospital.

It was easy to find her room number the next day. After hanging around, pretending to search for a name on different doors, he saw Cassie and Glenda come out of Helen's room. They headed for the small waiting area, just down the hall. He took a seat in the corner and overheard them talking about the diary. They never knew it was him.

He was beginning to get one of those headaches again and reached for his medicine. His mind was not very clear. What good had it all done? Everything had gone wrong and his great plan had failed. He had failed and now he was nobody again.

Chapter 18

Latimer sat in his favorite chair with a good book. He loved to read historical novels, especially about WWII. He was totally engrossed when the phone rang. It was Sunday afternoon, who could that be?

"Glenda, I did not expect to hear from you. What a wonderful surprise. I hope the reason you called is, you figured out you can't live without me and must hear my voice, or your heart will stop beating."

"Bob Latimer, you are an incorrigible flirt." She sounded delighted. "You are not all wrong. I have decided I need a break from all this madness."

His face lit up even more.

"There is a harvest festival in one of the smaller communities south of Glenridge today, called Pinehill. I went some years ago and really enjoyed it." She paused for a moment. "Want to go with me?"

"I would be delighted, especially since I find nothing but empty space on my calendar at the moment. Can I pick you up at your place?"

She gave him her address and he put it in his GPS. It showed it would only take about half an hour to get there.

She met him in front of an upscale condominium in the East section of town. It came with valet parking and a uniformed door man. He didn't recognize her at first with her casual yet elegant white pants and a blue, flowing floral top. A stylish white bag hanging down her side and matching white shoes put the finishing touches on the sharp looking outfit. She looked younger without the business suit and there was a spring in her step as she walked up to his car.

"Hi Bob, I'm looking forward to this, thanks for taking me. I simply need a break from all this tragedy."

"You look absolutely smashing, lady." Admiration clearly showed in his eyes. "Let's go and have some fun today."

Pinehill was a medium size bedroom community outside of Glenridge, situated in the midst of rolling hills and green pastures. The road was packed with cars as they got closer.

"We better find a place to park. We might have to walk for quite a ways," she said," I'm wearing my walking shoes."

It took ten minutes to reach downtown from their parking space, which was in an open field. Main Street was filled with artistic items under big, white tents, food vans and vegetable stands. A big crowd mingled casually in both directions.

"Are you up for bratwurst and sauerkraut?" he asked her as the smell of the delicious delicacy drifted their way.

"I'm much more in the mood for pizza today," she said. "If I'm going to get off my diet, I might as well get something I haven't had in forever and dream about every day. There is a pizzeria, let's go and have a beer with a pepperoni and mushroom pizza."

They even found a tiny table outside.

"This is great, it reminds me of when I was a kid and the circus came to town," he said while munching on his second slice. My wife loved to go to this kind of stuff and would drag me with her whether I wanted to go or not."

"Like I'm doing today?" she asked.

"You have no idea how much I wanted to do something other than work this weekend. I wouldn't tell this to anyone else, but I'm stumped. I had counted on that diary more than you can imagine."

"Ok, let's make a deal, Bob. No talk about work today. We are here to have fun and getting away from it all, remember?"

"It's a deal. So what do you want to talk about?"

"Do you have any kids?"

"No, Mary couldn't have any. We thought about adopting, but somehow never got around to it. I was involved with my job and she was real active in her church and in many charities. She even met Helen Anscott at one of them."

"You go to church?"

"Not anymore. I got out of the habit after she died. You know how it is. How about you, you have children?"

"I have a daughter and a son. Both live in Denver, are married and have five children between them."

"So you're a grandmother?"

"I am. Unfortunately, I don't see them very often because of the distance and my work. I usually try to fly there for Christmas and Thanksgiving." She took a sip of her beer. "That's why the Anscott's are so close to me, they're more or less my family here in Glenridge. This tragedy has hit me much more than just losing an employer and his wife. Helen and I were close friends in many ways. We confided in each other about a lot of things. I wasn't as close to Patrick for obvious reasons, but all three of us did a lot together. We even went to the same church."

"The one where the funeral was?"

"Yes, New Life. I really like the pastor. He is a wonderful speaker and a very nice man. Maybe we can go together sometime?" She smiled.

"I wouldn't mind. Changing the subject, did Helen ever talk to you about what was in the diary?" He couldn't resist.

"No, I didn't even know she kept one."

"This is not about the case, but growing up did Marten ever show signs of the kind of behavior he displayed in the last few weeks? What I mean, was he prone to lose his temper or show violence when angry?"

"Never. He was a most easygoing, friendly and outgoing boy, loved by everyone, even the staff. As a matter of fact, they spoiled him behind his parents' back on many occasions."

"So what do you think made him change the way he did?" he asked.

"I don't know. It was as if he became another person."

"Maybe he did because nothing else makes sense." Latimer finished his beer and waved the waiter over. "You want another one, Glenda?"

"No thanks, one is my limit. You don't really think he's another person, do you?"

"Of course not, I'm just grasping at straws."

"Let's get back to you. How long were you and Mary married?"

"Almost 25 years."

"That is amazing. My husband and I split up after thirty. Well it was more like he split because he found a younger version. It devastated me and I still have issues with trusting men." A touch of sadness had crept into her voice.

"I'm sorry. It must have been hard."

"It was eight years ago and I'm totally over him. It's just that I've never been able to form any kind of attachment to a man since then."

"Are you saying you would not be able to go steady with me?" He smiled. "I sound like a teenager."

"I must confess, I have thought about this and do not feel the usual reluctance with you as I have when a guy tried to get close before."

"Does that mean there is hope for me?"

"Let's just say, it's not hopeless." She looked at him with a warm smile.

"All I can say, if you cannot trust a well-respected Inspector of the Glenridge Major Crime Unit, who can you trust?" He had a big smile on his face.

"That is pushing it a bit, isn't it, Inspector?"

"In my line of work I have to use all the ammunition I can."

She laughed. "There is one thing I really like about you, Bob Latimer. It is your sense of humor.

"There really is hope for me if that is all it'll take to win you over."

When they got back to her condo he got out and opened the car door for her. "Glenda, I had a wonderful time today," he said and then leaned over and brushed her lips with a kiss.

"Thank you for taking me, Bob. I had a great time, too," she said and stood on her toes and kissed him. Then she turned, walked to the door and waved to him before she went inside.

He whistled a happy tune all the way back to his place.

Chapter 19

What was it about Monday mornings that produced pandemonium at the precinct? It was as if the problems took the weekend off and waited to descend on the place on Monday. Latimer was still in a pretty good mood when he walked into his office. Brighton was waiting for him.

"Got your coffee, Sir."

"Thanks Kid, anything new this morning?"

"The Chief is really ticked off from what I've heard, because there is no sign of Marten Anscott. After that press conference and all the hype about solving the case, I think he's in trouble again with the brass."

"I knew that was going to happen. I tried to tell him to take it easy, but as usual he wouldn't listen. We have a long way to figure out all the unanswered questions of this case. I'm not even certain we ever will, unless something gives."

Ginny stood in the door.

"Sir, that lady Clara Caskel is here to see you. Remember, she called once before, but hung up when you weren't in? You want to see her now?"

"That's what I'm talking about, Kid. We've got a break." Latimer jumped up from his chair and almost ran to the door. "Show her in, Ginny."

Both Brighton and Latimer stared at the woman who entered the office. She was the spitting image of Camilla Preston. Her face had that same pinched look, the same big nose, pronounced chin and stringy gray hair. The only difference was, she was about forty or fifty pounds heavier. She wore jeans and a t-shirt with a brown sweater over it and presented an overall look of sadness and poverty.

"Won't you come in, Ma'am," Latimer said and introduced himself and Brighton. "I was hoping you would get in touch with me again after your call last week. What can I do for you Mrs. Caskel?" He pointed to one of the chairs.

"I don't like to talk to cops," she said as she sat down with her hands folded in her lap, like a child about to be scolded.

"I understand, Mrs. Caskel," Latimer said and waited for her to go on.

"I wasn't going to call back, but then I heard that stuff about Lora on TV and I knew I had to come."

"What about Lora, Mrs. Caskel?" His voice was gentle as he smiled at her with his most benevolent smile.

"Lora Weston was my sister and she died thirty years ago. That woman who was murdered the other day was my other sister Camilla. They was twins." She fumbled with her sweater as she spoke.

"Can you tell us about your twin sisters, Ma'am?"

"It's been so long ago, but I do remember. Lora was always a good girl and never did nothing wrong. It was Camilla who was the bad one." She looked up at Latimer. "I didn't live here then. My husband and I moved to North Carolina, so I don't know what all happened." She fidgeted in her seat.

"Go on, Mrs. Caskel," Latimer said in a soothing voice.

"One day, Lora called me and said she was in trouble with Dad. He wanted to kick her out because she got herself pregnant. Dad told her he didn't need another mouth to feed. I said she could come up and stay with me and my husband, but she didn't have the money for the bus ticket. After that I didn't hear nothing more, until Camilla called and said Lora had given her baby up for adoption." She started to sniffle and Brighton handed her a tissue.

"But something was wrong. I called Lora and she was screaming and crying, saying Camilla stole her baby and sold it to some rich folks in Glenridge for a lot of money. Before I could ask her more, someone took the phone away from her and hung up.

Two weeks later Lora was dead. Everybody said it was Camilla who died, but it wasn't. I know better. Camilla killed her and told everybody she was Lora. You see, they looked exactly alike. When the papers wrote about Camilla being dead, I knew it was Lora. Camilla was the one being part of that baby smuggling ring. She was the one who done sold Lora's baby."

"Did you ever find out who the rich people were who bought the baby?"

"No, all I know, they lived here in Glenridge."

"Mrs. Caskel, Camilla told the neighbors her son lived with her. Do you know anything about that?" Latimer asked.

"I didn't know she had a son, but that doesn't mean nothing. After what happened, I never wanted to talk to her again."

"Was Camilla married?"

"I think she did get married. Well, she must have, because her name was Preston. I know nothing about that."

"Are your other two sisters still living, Ma'am?"

"No, they both died near two years ago with cancer. It seems I'm the only one left."

"Are their husbands or children still living?"

"They both married no good bums who didn't stick around for long." She thought for a moment. "I think Mettie had a girl, but she moved away a long time ago. Alice didn't have kids."

"Is there anything you can tell us about Lora's baby, any distinguishing marks or abnormalities?"

"I remember my sister Alice telling me she saw the little boy only once. He had a dark mark on his leg, way up where nobody would ever see it. My Daddy had it and so did his Daddy. Camilla snatched the baby away from her and told her to leave the house or she would do something bad to her."

"Is there anything you can tell us, anything at all about the baby, Camilla or Lora?" Latimer didn't know exactly what he was looking for.

"I can't think of nothing. I just came here to tell you the dead woman by the bridge last week was my sister Camilla Preston. Not Lora Weston like you people said on the TV."

"One more thing, your maiden name then was Weston?"

"Yes it was."

"Thank you so much, Mrs. Caskel. My secretary Ginny will take down your address and phone number. If we have any more questions we can contact you."

"I didn't do nothing wrong, did I?" She looked frightened.

"Of course you didn't. We appreciate you coming by and talking to us." Latimer walked around his desk and escorted her to Ginny's desk.

When he came back into the office he looked at Brighton thoughtfully.

"Wouldn't it be something if Marten Anscott has a birth mark on his upper thigh? It sure would explain a lot of things." He picked up the phone and dialed Glenda's number.

"Hi Glenda, this is your favorite Inspector calling. I have a question for you. By any chance, do you know if Marten has a birth mark on his upper thigh?"

"Bob, I know Marten well, but I don't quite know him that well. Hold on, let me ask Cassie, she's right here."

Latimer tapped his fingers on the desk impatiently.

"Bob, Cassie doesn't ever recall seeing anything like that on her brother. Neither Marten nor his parents ever mentioned a birth mark. That doesn't mean it isn't there, it's just nobody has ever said anything about it to Cassie or me. What is this all about?"

"I can't go into it right now. I will talk to you later. Thanks, Glenda, I'll be in touch."

"It would have been nice, Sir, but I guess he's not Lora's baby." Brighton said, disappointed.

"Darn it, it sure would fit right in and solve that part of the puzzle. I swear to you Kid, I've never had a case where none of the pieces fit. They just look like they should."

"That woman Camilla Preston sure was a piece of work, selling her own nephew for money and then killing her sister to cover it up. It makes me wonder why one of the twins was good and the other bad. Do you think this kind of thing is in the genes, Sir?"

"That is a million dollar question even scientists have not figured out."

"I would like to check out the birth certificate of Marten Anscott. Why don't you look into that Kid, while I meet with the Chief in a few minutes. He wants an update."

"Will do, Sir."

"If you don't get anywhere with that, check the blood type and DNA of Patrick and Helen Anscott to make sure they are Marten's parents."

"That should be much easier. Do you mind if I do that first, Sir?"

"It makes no difference to me, just get it done. I have a feeling we are going to find something there," he added with great emphasis.

The meeting with the Chief was what he expected. Get results and get them now, because the brass was getting impatient. When Latimer told him about the visit from Clara Caskel and the whole sordid story about Camilla's part in it, Chief Carson's ears perked up.

"That is quite a can of worms, Latimer. What does it mean to our case, though?" he added.

"I want to pursue this lead, Chief, because of the connection between the Anscott family and Camilla Preston. I'm having Brighton look into blood type and DNA of Marten and his parents. I know the sister doesn't know about any birth mark, but that doesn't mean it isn't there. What I mean, even siblings don't discuss something that is in a sensitive area of the body."

"Sounds good to me, Latimer. What a bomb shell it would be if the son of this prominent family was adopted. It might even explain why he murdered Patrick. Technically speaking, he wouldn't be his real father. Maybe he found out and got real mad about not having been told."

"It would be a reason for Camilla to blackmail Anscott that day in the office. It would definitely answer a lot of questions I still have about this case, Sir."

"This all sounds good, Latimer. I knew I could depend on you." The Chief suddenly sounded upbeat.

"Let's not jump to conclusions Sir, nothing has been proven." Latimer was getting concerned. Once again the Chief took possibilities and treated them as facts in order to placate his superiors.

The rest of the morning was spent writing reports. Latimer had been lax about that. He needed to update and fill in more details he had left out because of time restraints. It also gave him a good chance to go over the finer points of this case.

The biggest question he had in all this was, why did Marten change so drastically in the span of two weeks? Like Glenda told him yesterday, all his life the man had been easy going, kind and a real gentleman. Only to turn into a mean, rude and almost psychotic guy, driven by fits of overwhelming anger. Not to mention turning into a double murderer. Could it have been he somehow found out he was adopted and felt so distressed, he lost it? That would be pretty extreme and could only happen with an already unstable personality. According to everyone who knew him, that was definitely not the case. Rather the opposite was true.

Latimer was sure there had to be facts he had either missed or didn't know. What were they and why couldn't he think of anything he might have missed? He leaned back in his chair and rubbed his beard. Maybe the Kid would come up with something.

The morning went by without hearing anything from Brighton. Finally, he couldn't stand it any longer and dialed his number.

"Well? Did you find anything yet?"

"I'm on my way to your office, Sir. You're not going to believe what I found." He sounded excited.

"What is it?"

"I'll be there in two minutes and show you, if you don't mind, Sir."

"Hurry up, Kid. I'm getting old while we speak."

Brighton walked in with a folder and sat down with one of his brightest smiles. "We struck gold, Sir!" He almost shouted. "Look at the DNA and blood type results. Marten Anscott was adopted!"

"You are kidding! Good job, Kid."

"But that's not all, Sir. According to the blood type he could have been either Camilla's or Lora's son. They didn't do DNA in those days so we can't verify that part." His face was beaming. "I think we are getting close to answering a lot of questions, Sir."

"Yes we are, Kid. Yes we are." Latimer took the folder and studied the results in greater detail. "We know he wasn't Camilla's son, because the coroner told us she couldn't have children," he said after a while. A sudden thought struck him. "Do you realize I can go back to that lawyer and confront him with these facts?" he said as he put the folder down. "Since both of his clients are dead and I already know all this, he will probably talk to me this time and maybe fill in a few blanks."

"Ginny, get the Anscott lawyer on the phone and make an appointment for me to see him," he shouted out to her. "Tell him it's urgent. If he objects, tell him I'm aware of Marten's birth record and just want him to verify the facts, without violating his professional obligations."

"Will do, Sir," she shouted back.

Latimer and Brighton were made to wait over twenty minutes at Connor Mathews office. Whether done on purpose or not was hard to say. When he finally came out he led them into his office without any effort of an apology. His face showed he was not a happy person.

"I really thought we had discussed everything about this matter, Inspector. I made it clear to you I could not say any more than I did."

"Mr. Mathews, thank you for seeing us. To make one thing clear, you did not say anything at all in this matter, as I recall. I want you to know I found out Marten Anscott is the son of Lora Weston and was adopted thirty years ago by the Anscotts. We have DNA and blood tests to prove he is not their son. We also have testimony by Lora Weston's sister, Clara Caskel, that he was sold by Lora's sister Camilla to a rich couple in Glenridge." Latimer leaned forward a little as he continued. "Mr. Mathews, it doesn't take a rocket scientist to put two and two together in this matter. By your reaction the last time I was here, I surmised you were involved in this adoption. I would like for you to fill in the details. It seems both of your clients are dead and their son is accused of murdering two people, one is his father and the other his aunt."

Connor Mathew's face became a stony mask the longer Latimer talked. After a moment of silence he cleared his throat.

"Are you telling me, the woman who claimed to be Marten's mother was someone else?"

"She was Lora Weston's twin sister. She was also part of a baby smuggling ring and took Lora's baby, sold it and then murdered her sister to cover up her crime."

"Good heavens have mercy. This is terrible. I had no idea. You must believe me, Inspector."

"I'm not here to accuse you of anything, Mr. Mathews. I just want to find out how the Anscotts came by their son."

He settled back in his chair and began to talk, slowly at first, then with more confidence.

"It was years ago and I was a close friend of Patrick's from college, as you recall me telling you. When he got married he chose me for his best man. I got along well with Helen. When I married my wife, all of us became good friends and remained so over all these many years.

After five years of marriage, when they failed to have any children, Helen and Patrick approached me about the possibility of adoption. This is where the situation gets sticky. I called an old friend from Stanford, also a lawyer, who specialized in finding suitable children for couples like the Anscotts, for a price, of course. Since money was no object, I did not question him where the children he found came from. It was much later when I found out he was part of a nationwide baby smuggling ring. When he told me he found a boy, I didn't question where he got him. I was astounded when he charged a fee of thirty-five thousand dollars. That was a lot of money, even in those days.

However, the Anscotts didn't care and the adoption went through. I never questioned the legality of the transaction since I trusted my friend. He handled all the paper work and I was only there for moral support, more or less. The only stipulation he made was, it would be a closed adoption and the child would never be told. Of course now I know why." He sounded tired and then went on.

"Ten years later a woman named Lora Weston, came to see Patrick at his office. She told him she was Marten's real mother and if he did not give her ten thousand dollars, she would tell Marten who he really was. She threatened to let him and the world know his adoption was illegal, because he had been stolen. Patrick came to me. There was nothing I could do but explain that legally, she had a case. If nothing else, it would be a nasty, public court battle. The choice was his and he paid her. Over the years, Lora Weston blackmailed Patrick regularly. He kept her at bay with whatever amount she demanded." He leaned back in his chair and wiped his forehead with a tissue. "That's the whole sordid story, Inspector."

"Do you think Marten found out he was adopted and killed Mr. Anscott and the woman who sold him?" Latimer asked.

"I don't know. I definitely never told anyone," he said emphatically.

"What became of your friend who handled the adoption?"

"He died in a car crash under mysterious circumstances shortly after the police began to look into the smuggling ring and before he could be arrested."

"I appreciate you being honest with us, Mr. Mathews. Except for Marten, all the parties involved are dead and he is missing."

"I'm sort of glad this is out in the open. It has always bothered me there was nothing I could do for Patrick. I certainly did not want him to lose his son."

"Were you close to Marten?"

"No, my friendship was with his parents. I met him at family occasions of course, but never talked to him at great length. From what I observed, he seemed a very nice young man, unlike his birth mother."

"Are you the lawyer for the company as well, Mr. Mathews?" Latimer asked.

"No, at my age I don't work full time any longer. I have turned that account over to my younger associates, one of which is my daughter."

"Well Sir, thank you again for your candid account of what happened. I hope we do not have to bother you again." Latimer got up and then stopped. "When we catch Marten, and we will, will you or someone in your firm represent him?"

"Heavens no, we do not practice criminal law, but I'm sure Miss Cassie will want me to advise her as to which firm to choose."

"Finally some of the pieces to this puzzle are starting to fit, Kid. All we need now is a murderer," Latimer said as they got in the car.

Chapter 20

The next morning Latimer called Cassie Anscott's office and requested an appointment. He was told she would not be in for the rest of the week because of the funeral. When he asked for Glenda, she was not in the office either. His next call was to the Estate. Richard sounded pleased to hear his voice and informed him both Cassie and Glenda were having a breakfast meeting in the morning room.

"Could you inform the ladies I wish to speak with both of them, please? I would like to come over in thirty minutes, Richard."

He did not look forward to informing Cassie that her brother was adopted, but the Chief was chomping at the bit to release that information. Besides, with the number of people who were aware of these facts at the precinct by now, there was no way to keep it under wraps much longer. There was no choice, it had to be done today. The funeral had been yesterday, a quiet dignified event attended by a small, intimate crowd, Glenda had told him. Everyone was overwhelmed with shock and grief over the tragic events of the last few days. The fact the son and heir of Anscott Laboratories was on the run for two murders was almost too much for family and friends to comprehend.

Glenda told him she was astounded with the composure and dignity with which Cassie had conducted herself through all this. There was a lot of her mother in her after all, she thought. As a matter of fact, Glenda had taken on the place of her mother in some aspects during this time. The two of them spent a lot of time together trying to make some sense out of it all. She had spoken to Latimer over the phone last evening after he got home from work. He did not share the latest news about Marten, because he felt Cassie should be told first. Finding them both here was convenient.

"Inspector, it is always good to see you," Richard said with a sad smile, nodding to Brighton as well. "This is a sad place these days. I hope you bring good news for a change."

"I don't know if it is good or not, Richard, but at least it isn't bad," Latimer answered as the butler showed them to the morning room.

"I have taken the liberty to set up a place for you to join the ladies for breakfast," Richard said before he showed them in.

"Thank you. That would be wonderful Richard," Brighton said before Latimer could decline. He would love some eggs and bacon and all the rest of the good stuff. It would sure beat the dried bagel with a slice of cheese he had at his place before he rushed off to work this morning.

Latimer threw him a disapproving look, but didn't say anything.

"Inspector, Sgt. Brighton, do come in," Glenda came toward them with a faint smile, "how good to see you both."

"Gentlemen, join us for breakfast. Richard set a place for you. The food is over there. Help yourselves." Cassie pointed to a small heated food bar against the wall. "Do you have news of Marten?" she asked when they were both seated.

"Yes I do, Miss Anscott," Latimer said. "It is not bad as such but it will shock you."

"Please, call me Cassie, Inspector," she said with such sadness in her voice, it made Latimer cringe. "Thank you, Cassie."

"So, what is this news you have for us? I don't know if I can stand any more, good or bad." Her eyes began to tear up, but then she composed herself.

"It is quite a story I have come to tell you. It is about your parents and your brother Marten." Latimer searched for the right words to make this as easy as possible. "Yesterday morning a woman named Clara Caskel walked into my office. She had tried to talk to me last week on the phone, but when I was not there she hung up without leaving a number. She had heard the press conference and came to tell us a tale we would not have believed had we not already figured out most of the facts." He continued without interruption and without leaving out anything, including what Connor Mathews had shared. When he was finished, a heavy silence filled the room. Cassie sat frozen, unable to say anything.

"What you are telling me is so astounding, it's almost ridiculous, Inspector. I guess I have no choice but to believe you," she finally managed to whisper in a thick voice. Then she started to sob uncontrollably. Glenda reached over and put her arms around her shoulders.

"Go ahead and cry, honey, it will do you good," she said in a soothing tone.

Latimer and Brighton felt helpless and just sat there quietly. Like most men, they had no idea what to do when women cried. Brighton finished the last of his breakfast. He wasn't going to let this good food go to waste. Latimer took a sip of his coffee in spite of it being cold by now. He hated cold coffee.

It had started to rain outside. The weather matched the mood in the room perfectly. The once vibrant colors of the flowers in the fall garden outside the big window had taken on a subdued hue and the usually bright morning room looked almost gloomy.

"What you are saying is that my brother isn't really my brother," Cassie finally managed to say without emotion. "What I want to know is how he found out about this. It must be the reason why he changed so much and then committed those horrible murders." She was almost talking to herself. "It also means I'm the only one left of my family." She started to cry again.

Richard had come into the room quietly and heard what Cassie had said. He stood motionless by the door, his face filled with a grim determination to keep his feelings under control.

Cassie looked up at him and said with a childlike voice. "Please Richard, don't leave me. You and Emily are the only family I have now."

The big man walked over slowly to her and stood, still every inch the butler, and said, "Miss Cassie, be assured Emily and I will be here for you for as long as you want us." Then, probably for the first time since she had known him, he put his hand on her shoulder and held it there for a few seconds. "We will never leave you, no matter what happens."

Latimer felt clearly uncomfortable. Darn it, he had no idea what to do next.

"Are you sure there is no mistake about any of this, Inspector?" It was Glenda. "I know you have blood tests and DNA and all that." Her voice trailed off.

"We are very sure, Glenda. What we don't know is how Marten knew unless Camilla told him at some point. It must have been within the last few weeks, because that is when his behavior changed so dramatically. When and how he met her we have no idea. I guess we will find out when we apprehend him."

Cassie had stopped crying and tried to compose herself.

"Richard, could you bring us some fresh coffee, I think we can all use some." She managed to give him a faint smile.

"Right away, Miss Cassie."

She turned to Latimer. "What does all this mean legally? He is still my brother under the law, right?"

"Yes, he is. However, in view of his being a murder suspect on the run, we have requested that all of his accounts be frozen. I spoke with Mr. Rathbone and he said he would see to it. What you have to decide is if you want to support him by providing him with a legal team when we catch him. He is going to need it."

"Will the press be informed about Marten being adopted?" Glenda asked.

"Yes, that will probably happen today in a press conference the Chief has already scheduled," Latimer answered. "He is waiting until I have talked to you, Cassie."

"Good heavens, that means the media will be on our door steps again, doesn't it?" Cassie said with a sigh of resignation. "I will have to inform management, especially Mark Lenhart, right away." She turned to Glenda. "Could you handle that for me?"

"I will get right on it, Cassie," Glenda said as she got up from the table. "May I use your father's study?"

"Sure, go ahead, that would be the best place."

"There is something I would like to suggest Miss Anscott, if I may," Latimer said. "Your family lawyer, Mr. Mathews, can probably tell you more of the details about the adoption as well as suggest the best legal representation your brother needs."

"You mean I have to pay for it after what he has done?" There was anger in her voice.

"That is entirely up to you, Ma'am. Remember, legally he is still your brother." Latimer sounded neutral. "One way to know what to do is to ask yourself, what would your parents do?"

"I know one thing, they always treated Marten as if he was their real son. They really wanted him to take over the company when Dad retired. That fact alone shows they loved him as much as they loved me." She looked at Latimer with a look of despair. "I can't say now I love him at all, because he killed my father and caused the death of my mother. How am I supposed to feel anything but hatred for him?" She tried hard not to cry again. "I was raised a Christian, but I don't feel I can ever forgive Marten. He took everything that was dear to me and left me an orphan with a huge company to run." She blew her nose. "I'm only 26 years old, for heaven's sake. I don't have the knowledge, understanding or experience how to do that."

Latimer didn't feel she wanted him to say anything. Anyway, what was there to say?

Chapter 21

Two weeks had gone by and still no sign of Marten Anscott. It was as if he had disappeared into thin air. The media frenzy had died down as other news dominated the headlines. In spite of a statewide APB, the number of officers actively involved in the search was scaled back because of financial restraints. Marten Henry Anscott was added to the ten most wanted list in the State.

Latimer had called the precinct in West Palm Beach and asked them to send a unit to the condo to check if Marten Anscott was there. After looking through the place with Cassie's permission and inquiring if the neighbors had seen any activity, they reported back that no one had been there since Helen and Cassie had left.

Cassie had returned to the office and together with Glenda tried to put the pieces of her life back together by submerging herself in work. It turned out the two worked well together and there was no question Glenda would remain as her personal assistant.

The probate of Patrick Anscott's estate would take years to untangle with one of the heirs not just a murder suspect, but missing as well. With Mark Lenhart at the helm and a board of directors to manage the company, Anscott Laboratories continued to function without major problems. Cassie joined the board as a simple member with one vote, but without any special powers or privileges. She would, however, be a major player in the future since she now theoretically owned two thirds of the shares, the rest still belonging to Marten. The final outcome would have to wait until her brother Marten was apprehended and if found guilty, convicted. It presented a legal tangle that would keep a team of lawyers busy and financially prosperous for a long time.

Cassie was in her office with Glenda when the call came on her cell phone.

"Sis, this is Marten."

"Marten? Oh my goodness where are you?"

"I need some money. They have frozen my accounts, can you help me?" His voice was pleading.

"After what you did you want me to help you? Are you crazy?"

"I didn't do it, Cassie. You've got to believe me." He sounded like he was almost in tears. "I was framed."

"So why don't you turn yourself in if you are innocent. Then maybe I would believe you." Cassie was trembling and she sounded cold and matter of fact.

"They won't believe me and I don't want to go to prison for the rest of my life. All I need is a few thousand dollars and I will disappear forever, I promise." He sounded desperate.

"Are you kidding me? Do I look like I want to aid a fugitive and then we can both sit and rot in jail? Marten, you have no choice, you have to turn yourself in, please."

"Go to hell, Cassie."

The line went dead.

Glenda was dialing Latimer before Cassie hung up.

"Bob, Cassie just had a call on her cell from Marten. What do you want her to do?" she said without introduction.

"Marten Anscott called his sister?" He was almost shouting.

"She just hung up with him."

"Brighton and I will be over there as fast as we can. Don't let her go anywhere, Glenda. Tell her not to use her phone until we get there, maybe we can make out where the call came from."

Cassie sat in shock. Her hands were shaking and she tried hard not to cry.

"Glenda, it was him. He sounded so desperate and scared and I was so harsh with him. Maybe I should have been nicer and said I would help him so I could have found out where he is."

"That would have probably been a good thing, but what is done is done. You were too shocked to think clearly," Glenda said reassuringly. "He will call back because he needs the money. Besides, Inspector Latimer will let you know how to handle it from here on."

Latimer and Brighton arrived in record time and were shown in without delay by a secretary.

"Tell me what happened, Cassie," Latimer came right to the point. "You are sure it was Marten?"

"Yes, he was nice at first, but then when I told him I wasn't going to help him and urged him instead to turn himself in, he got really mad and hung up." She was still shaking. "He did insist that he was innocent, Inspector. What if that is true and I didn't help him? I would never forgive myself." She was crying now.

"Cassie, if he was innocent he would not have tried to run off with fifty thousand dollars. With that kind of money he could have left the country and disappeared safely for quite a while. Did he give any kind of a hint where he called from, any suggestion whether he was still in Glenridge?"

"No, I was so stunned I got mad at him because he murdered my father and now he wanted money on top of that. I should have thought to try to find out where he was instead," she said.

"Let me have your cell phone. We will let the lab check it out and see if they can trace where the call was made from." He took it and put it in a plastic bag. "I will get this back to you. For now we will leave it turned off so he will be forced to call the office or your home phone if he wants to get in touch with you."

"What do I say if he does? He will know by my voice that I'm not honest with him," Cassie said.

"We will teach you what to do and say between now and then, Cassie," Latimer said with reassurance. "Another thing we need to do is put a trace on your home phone and one line here at the office, with your permission of course."

"That is fine with me, Inspector. I just don't know if I'm a good enough actress to pull this off," she said with a deep sigh.

"You will do fine, Cassie, we'll help you all the way," Latimer said with confidence. "This is our only hope, because we have been totally unsuccessful in finding even a trace of him in spite of all our efforts. We are counting on you, Cassie."

Latimer got on his cell and ordered a team of technicians to come to the office as well as the Estate to set up the trace equipment. He also asked for an officer who specializes in negotiating techniques to come and teach Cassie what she could or should say if her brother called back.

"We will have to inform your secretary to be on the alert to put his call through to you without delay, no matter where you are, Cassie. There will be two or three technicians here to set it all up," Latimer told her. "Please make sure they have access to your office and anything else they ask for."

"What if he calls me at home late at night?" she asked.

"Once again, there will be technicians in a van outside your home to monitor your phones at the Estate. Don't worry. When they get here they will show you exactly how it works and what is expected of you." He got up. "Brighton and I will go back to the precinct with your phone. We will be in touch, Cassie."

"Do you really think Marten will call back, Sir?" Brighton sounded skeptical.

"If he needs money he will Kid, and he does. What this can also mean, he is still in the area. As a matter of fact, that is probably the only reason he hasn't left, because he thinks Cassie will get him some cash. He can't use a credit card or any other paper trail, so he has to be here to pick it up in person."

"He did say he was innocent. What if he really is?"

"I really vacillate on that issue day by day," Latimer said thoughtfully. "There are still so many issues I don't understand about this case. Motive is the biggest issue for me and the fact that a nice person doesn't turn into a raging killer just because he was adopted. There has to be something else."

"What if we never find out, Sir?"

"This is my last case and I will not give up, even if I have to keep on digging after I'm retired," Latimer said with grim determination. "There is a missing angle we have not found or have overlooked. I'm absolutely tired of not being able to find it, Kid."

Three days went by and the Chief was having a fit about the expense for the equipment and manpower for the phone trace. Latimer stood his ground. If he could have had another day of surveillance before, they could have avoided the murder of Camilla Preston. He knew Marten Anscott was going to call Cassie, because by now he really must be low on cash.

They had traced the call to Cassie's cell phone from a pay phone in Landsburg, a town twenty miles north of Glenridge. Latimer asked Cassie if she knew anyone there Marten might be staying with, but she was sure there was no one. At least they found out Marten was still in the area.

Latimer instructed Brighton and Latham to call all the motels and hotels in Landsburg to find out if he was staying there, but found nothing. The two were then sent to canvas the town with a picture of Anscott. They spent two days asking around if anyone had seen him, but with no results.

The Chief even agreed to an increase in manpower for another day or two, but even that didn't produce even the smallest lead. He raged at Latimer every day with comments laced with a good amount of embarrassing accusations. His superiors were not pleased and the Commissioner had called to ask in a terse language what the Glenridge Major Crime Unit was doing about this situation.

Latimer could only sit there and let the Chief's loud complaints wash over him. There was nothing he could do but agree with the man, but he kept that part to himself. He almost admired Anscott for his cunning ability to evade the police. The man was smart. He had to give him that. The whole thing put him in a bad mood every day. Brighton and Ginny tried to stay out of his way as much as possible. The many trips to the lounge for coffee had produced a bout with acid reflux and he was forced to cut down on his intake. In his estimation, that was worse than not finding Anscott, but he kept that to himself, too.

He had called Glenda several times to make sure everything was set up at the office and the Estate. Each time she sounded friendly, but stressed to the point he didn't dare ask her out for dinner. According to Glenda, Cassie was doing well under the circumstances and didn't jump any more each time the phone rang.

His world had pretty well come to a standstill. He seriously wondered if this case was going to be the one to end his career with a failure. Thank goodness he had not run into Brown lately, because he had the feeling he would lose his temper with the man's snide remarks.

Brighton still managed to smile and find something good to say every day he walked into the office. Latimer truly appreciated his positive attitude in spite of the lack of progress on all fronts. Together, they had spent the days checking every one of the many leads of sightings they got of Anscott in the area, but every one of them turned up nothing.

"I've made up my mind that there are a bunch of crazies out there who have nothing better to do than to make up stuff to get their seconds in the limelight," Brighton said. He discovered the man who reported this last one was almost blind and hadn't been out of the house in many months. When they questioned him where he might have seen the fugitive, he admitted it may have been on the internet.

"Just think, Kid, I could be laying on the beach in Florida having a good time doing nothing," Latimer said when they got to the office.

"Well, all that's missing now is the beach, Sir. We're already doing nothing."

Chapter 22

It was midnight when the call came. Cassie was sound asleep and she answered with a groggy voice.

"Cassie, it's Marten."

She snapped awake instantly. Would she remember everything they had taught her to say?

"Hi Marten, give me a minute until I'm awake. It's pretty late you know. How are you? I've been worried about you since you called last. I'm sorry I yelled at you, but I've been under a lot of stress with all that's been going on." She tried to sound casual as if nothing was wrong and to put to use her training in how to talk to him. The most important thing was to stretch out the conversation for as long as possible to give the police outside in the van time to trace the call.

"You think you have been under stress? What about me?"

She had never heard him whine like that before.

"I know. It has been terrible for both of us, Marten. I missed you at Mom's funeral, it was nice. Not too many people were there, mostly family and close friends. They all asked where you were." She tried to sound genuine. "I wish you'd come home, Marten, I miss you."

"You know I can't, Sis. I have to lie low for a while to get the cops off my back. So far I've been lucky. I almost got caught several times, but they didn't recognize me." He sounded more confident. "I'm in a safe place where no one will ever find me."

"Maybe I can come see you Marten, just to make sure you have everything you need."

"You said before you didn't want to help me."

"That was before when I was still too upset to think clearly. I thought about it. I really think you are innocent. That's why I want to help you." Cassie felt terrible lying to him.

"Does that mean you'll get me the money, Sis? It's my money from my trust fund, so it won't cost you anything." He sounded hopeful.

"How would I get that much cash, Marten? The bank would notify the police and they would know. Have you thought about that?" She pretended to sound helpless.

"Don't you run the company now?" he said with a touch of sarcasm. "Nobody will notice if you skim off some cash gradually. Just get old Mr. Rathbone to transfer some money into your personal account. Tell him you need it for things now that you are in charge."

Cassie was astounded. With a master's degree in business, he sounded rather simplistic in his approach about her role in the company or how to get cash. Could it be he was on drugs?

"I tell you what, Marten. You let me know where I can meet you and I will have as much cash for you as I can get without anyone getting suspicious."

"You really mean it?" He sounded excited.

"I really mean it. Give me till this afternoon and I will call you when I'm ready with it."

"I can't give you a number, Sis, you know that. Also, you are going to have to leave it somewhere and I will pick it up."

She could tell he was thinking.

"I'm really counting on seeing you, Marten. I'll meet you anywhere you say, just tell me where." She was pleading with him now.

"Let me think about it and I'll call you back in the morning. I got to go. Bye, Sis."

Cassie was shaking when she put on her robe and hurried downstairs and outside to where the police van was.

"How did I do, Officer Graham?" she said, trying to catch her breath.

"You did great, Ma'am."

"Did you get a trace on him?"

"Yes, we did, we'll let you know more later," he said through the van window. "We'll be back early, around six in the morning."

Before she could ask any more questions, the van took off racing down the driveway back to the precinct.

Latimer got the call at two in the morning.

"What have we got, Nolan?" he asked the officer in charge.

"We have a lead to a phone in the lower district, Sir. It's not at the apartment we searched before, but not far away from there. We are in the process of getting a search warrant."

"Give me the address and I will meet you guys there. Wait for me."

He was in the car within five minutes. There was hardly any traffic at that time of morning. It only took another fifteen to get to the house, located on a side street of Maple Avenue, the notorious red light area in the lower district. The police were there in full force and had already surrounded the house when he arrived.

Latimer stood back when one of the officers knocked on the door. An old man in a thread bare robe finally opened up. His eyes looked sleepy and his white hair was matted down on one side.

"What do you want?"

"I'm Inspector Latimer with the Glenridge Major Crime Unit. We are looking for a man called Marten Anscott who made a phone call from this location. May we come in?"

"I don't let cops in my house," he said and slammed the door shut.

"We have a search warrant Sir, and will break down the door if you don't open up right this minute!" Latimer shouted.

Slowly, very slowly, the door moved a few inches. Latimer stepped aside. Several officers, dressed in heavy protective armor, guns held in front of them, pushed in and passed by the old man.

"Stay out of the way Sir, or you will get hurt," one of the officers barked at him.

"There's nobody here but me," the man said meekly as Latimer stood in front of him. He told the man to step outside.

"Do you know a man named Marten Anscott, Sir?"

"I don't know nobody like that."

"Did anybody use your phone about two hours ago?"

"I don't know, I was asleep."

"Do you know a young man about thirty with brown hair, brown eyes, tall and slender who drives a red Lexus?"

"You must be talking about Paul, but he drives a gray old car. I don't know what make. He hasn't been here in a long while."

"How long?"

"About four or five weeks, I'd say."

"What is your name, Sir," Latimer asked.

"I'm Mat Lansky."

"And what is Paul's last name?"

"I don't know. He never said and I didn't ask." The old man pulled on his robe.

"What is your connection with this Paul?"

"He sometimes comes to visit me and stays a few hours. He brings me a bottle of hard stuff and I don't ask no questions."

"Was he here last night?"

"No, but sometimes he comes in late and I don't even know he's here. I just find a bottle for me on the counter when I get up in the morning."

"Have you seen a bottle anywhere this morning?"

"I don't know. I've been asleep until you knocked on the door. If there is one it would be in the kitchen, Sir. I'll go look." He shuffled down the hallway.

"All clear," Latimer heard one of the officers shout from the back. "There's no one else here, Sir," he said as he came down the hall toward Latimer. "We looked everywhere, no sign of Anscott."

Latimer nodded and continued to follow Mat Lansky into the small kitchen. It was a mess with dishes piled up in the sink and dried-on food on several plates on top of the tiny wooden table. No liquor bottle anywhere and no sign that anybody else had been here.

"He hasn't been here Inspector, or else he didn't leave nothing this time." The old man sounded disappointed.

"I want the phone dusted for fingerprints," Latimer shouted to no one in particular as he found the phone at the far end of the kitchen counter.

A technician appeared seemingly out of nowhere and started the dusting process.

"It's been wiped clean, Sir," he said after a minute. "There are no prints on here whatsoever, Inspector."

Latimer felt anger rising in his chest. He had a deep frown on his face when Brighton walked in, looking very sleepy, his clothes rumpled as if he had slept in them.

"It's nice of you to join us, Kid. Once again, he got away with no leads. Do me a favor and show Mat Lansky a picture of Anscott. Here." Latimer took a crumpled sheet of paper out of his coat pocket and handed it to Brighton.

"No, I don't know that man. He looks a little like him, but no, that's not Paul." He sounded certain.

"You are sure?" Brighton asked.

"Yes, I'm sure." He shook his head. "This ain't Paul."

After encouraging the technicians to take their time and go over everything carefully, Latimer and Brighton went home. There was nothing more to do here. It was four in the morning and there was just enough time to get cleaned up, have breakfast and be back in the office in time for another day of dead end leads. The only thing to do now was to wait for Anscott to call Cassie back to set a time and place for the money exchange. If Marten had watched the police arrive at the house last night, he would know the line was tapped to the Estate. Latimer was too tired and disgusted to try to figure out who the heck this Paul was the old man was talking about. All he wanted to do was go back to sleep.

Latimer spent the morning waiting for preliminary reports from the crime lab. He was still reeling from coming up empty last night. He sat at his desk, bone tired. He tried to go over the events once again, but nothing made sense. If the technicians were correct and the phone call to Cassie came from that house, why had the old man not heard anything? Unless he had lied. Anscott could have paid him or threatened him before he left just before they got there. It was the only possible answer.

"Brighton, we need to bring Mat Lansky in for questioning. Ask him if he will come willingly. If not, let me know and we will get an arrest warrant. Take Latham with you."

"Right away, Sir."

An hour later Brighton called Latimer. Mat Lansky was in the interrogation room. He had come without complaint and seemed in no way upset to be questioned. After checking phone records, it was definitely established that the call from Marten to Cassie had come from Lansky's phone.

"Mr. Lansky, we have proof that Marten Anscott made a call from your house to the Anscott Estate. What do you say to that?" Latimer asked in a kind tone.

"Inspector, I don't know nobody with that name. If he came into my house early this morning, he must have done it while I was asleep." The old man sounded sincere.

"Can you tell me more about this Paul who comes to visit you occasionally?"

"There is nothing to tell. We met two years ago in front of my house and he asked if he could help me with carrying in my groceries when I had a broken leg. You see, I was on crutches. After that he would come by sometimes and we would have a cup of coffee."

"What did you talk about?"

"He liked sports and we would watch a ball game together. We never talked about nothing personal. He acted unhappy on some days and then we would have a drink together. He never said nothing about what bothered him, and I'm not one to pry." Mat Lansky looked at Latimer with a smile. "He was always nice to me and I hope he's not in any trouble. It's a rough neighborhood, you know. In my younger days it wasn't bad then, everybody was right neighborly."

"I'm sure it was, Mr. Lansky. Do you mind looking at some pictures to see if you know anybody in our data base?" Latimer asked and spread out several sheets with different mug shots of known criminals, including one of Marten Anscott.

The man looked at all of them very carefully and then shook his head.

"I can't see too well without my glasses, Inspector, but I can see well enough to tell you I don't know nobody on them pictures."

"Are you sure, Mr. Lansky?" Latimer urged him to look again.

There was no sign of recognition on the man's face. Latimer pointed to the picture of Anscott and said, "Sir, if that man ever comes back to your house, will you give me a call? Here is my card."

"I sure will, Inspector. I'll keep a lookout for him."

"Thank you, Sir. Sgt. Brighton will take you home now. You have been very helpful."

I wish that was true, Latimer thought as he got up and left to return to his office, but not before he stopped to get a cup of coffee.

The phone was ringing when he got back. It was Glenda.

"Bob, have you found out anything? Cassie and I are pretty anxious," she said.

"We found the house from which Marten made the phone call, but that is all. It is occupied by an old man who was asleep upstairs in his bed when Marten called. We have just finished interrogating him and he has never seen Marten before." Latimer sounded disgusted.

"I'm so sorry, I know you are frustrated. Why don't I meet you at the precinct and we go get a bite to eat after you finish up at work tonight?" she said.

"That is the nicest offer I've had all day. It's a deal. Can I call you when I'm done? I still have to have a meeting with the Chief for my daily barrage of insults of why I haven't found Marten Anscott. For that reason alone, I'm going to kill the guy when I finally find him," he said with a tiny smile.

"Well, at least you will solve this case in no time at all then, won't you?"

"Ok, Mrs. Hinsley. That is enough smart stuff from you. I expect nothing but sympathy, empathy and tender loving care this evening from you."

"Yes, Mr. Inspector, I will give it my best shot. Oops!" She chuckled. "See you later, Bob."

They went to a Chinese buffet. Latimer felt like drowning his frustration in the large selection of wonderful smelling dishes. He had no idea what some of them were.

Glenda was more selective and stayed away from breaded foods and fried items. As usual, she was watching her weight.

"This was a great idea, Glenda," Latimer said. "It has been a rough week of new leads and dashed hopes. Your boy Marten is a genius at evading the police," he said once they sat down.

"I was sure you had him last night from what Cassie told me."

"She was very good with him on the phone and held his attention until we had a trace on him. She even convinced him to meet with her to give him the money. Let's just hope he didn't find out we were at Mat Lansky's house. If he does, we will never see him there again." Latimer looked at Glenda as if seeing her for the first time. "You look wonderful and I missed you."

"It has been quite a while, but I've simply been too busy. Things are settling down somewhat and I feel I can live my own life again." She smiled at him. "That's when I realized I hadn't seen you for two weeks." She reached over and put her hand on his arm. "Let's not wait that long again, what do you think?"

He took it and held it in his. "I've been alone for ten years, but until I met you I was never lonely. It scares me a little, what if you don't feel the same way about me?" His smile had a question mark in it.

"I think we are on the same wave length, Bob. I do want to make some things very clear before we go any further with this relationship." She took her hand away and went on. "I'm a person who lives by certain principles. I'm a Christian and when I say that I mean it. I also know it's a lot to live up to in today's world, especially when it comes to having a relationship with a man. I will never agree to sleep with you unless we are married. Please understand, this is not a marriage proposal, but a line in the sand which I will not cross, not even for you, Bob." She looked him square in the eyes as she continued. "If you can live with that, I would be very happy to start dating you on a regular basis. If this does not sit well with you, it has been nice knowing you." Now it was her turn to smile at him questioningly.

"First of all, I admire you for your convictions, Glenda. Second, what choice do I have but to abide by them if I want to date the prettiest girl in Glenridge?" He took her hand back. "I do want to have a relationship with you and see what the future holds for us after we get to know each other better." He leaned over and kissed her and was delighted when she blushed. "I think this calls for a toast, sweetheart. They don't have wine here, but what do you say we have a delightfully sinful dessert instead?"

"I think that sounds wonderful."

Chapter 23

Cassie was in the morning room. It was filled with memories of her mother and she could still smell the faint, wonderful fragrance of her perfume. Or was it her imagination? Richard had brought breakfast and she sat deep in thought when the phone rang. It was Marten.

"Hi Sis, it's me."

"Marten, how wonderful to hear from you. Maybe you can come over and we can talk before I give you the money." *How easy it is to lie after a while,* she thought.

"You got the money?" His voice sounded animated.

"I do. It wasn't easy, but with all the changes and adjustments at the company, nobody paid much attention when I withdrew it from my account."

"How much?"

"Five thousand."

"That's not enough, Sis. I can't live on that, darn it!" The cordial tone had suddenly changed into one of frustration. "I have expenses, you know. When can you get me more?"

"Marten, are you sure you don't want to turn yourself in? I will pay your legal fees and we can fight this thing together." She was being honest now. "I know we can work this out. The police will find the real killer and your life will be back to normal." She was pleading. "I want my brother back. We only have each other, Marten. Please come home."

"You don't understand anything, Cassie. Nothing will ever be the same. I have to get away for a while until all this blows over. I want you to know I didn't do it, but the police won't believe me. They don't understand either."

"Can you explain to me what it is we don't understand, Marten? You can tell me, I will listen and I will understand, I promise."

"I wish I could, but it's too late. There is nothing anybody can do now. The only thing left is for me to leave." He sounded deeply saddened. "Please, Cassie, I need at least fifty thousand dollars to go somewhere far away for a time. I promise I will come back when they give up looking for me or find the real killer."

She realized she had to get back into her role playing if she wanted to meet with him.

"Marten, how about me giving you the money I have for now and then we go from there. Where do you want me to meet you?"

"I want you to put it in a locker at the Glenridge bus depot this afternoon at two. Leave the key in an envelope. Then throw it into the green trash bin to the left of the row of lockers. I will find it. Make sure it's the green one and not the huge black one further down."

"Are you sure I can't give it to you instead, Marten? I want to see you and talk to you. It's been so long."

"No, this is the way it has to be done. Just make sure you don't tell anyone or you will never see me again, Sis." The phone went dead.

Within a few minutes an officer from the van outside was shown in by Richard.

"Sgt. Bender is here to see you, Miss Cassie."

"Good morning, Sgt. Bender. How did it go?"

"Miss Anscott, the call was made from a public phone at the Glenridge Mall."

She motioned for him to take a seat.

"Thank you, Ma'am, there is no need to send anyone out there. Your brother will be long gone. Two of my men will spend the morning informing you on how this is going down. We will also discreetly check out the locker area of the bus station so we can cover all the escape routes in that vicinity. The manager of the bus depot will be notified of course and will have the locker area cleared of the general public at that time. They will be replaced with police in civilian clothes. When you go there with the money, any people you see will be ours." He looked at her reassuringly.

"I hope I don't mess up. He sounded so desperate and pitiful. Are you absolutely certain he is guilty, Sergeant? I'm beginning to have doubts and feel terrible to lead him on like this." She cleared her throat. "I don't know how long I can continue, he is my brother after all. I will never forgive myself if he gets hurt and I'm to blame by leading him into a trap."

"Miss Anscott, you have done great so far, please don't give up on us now. We know what we are doing and have no intention of hurting him unless of course he uses a weapon. Please remember, he has killed your father and Camilla Preston. Our officers are aware of that fact and will shoot in self-defense, should the need arise."

"Of course, Sergeant. It's just every time I talk to him all I can hear is the brother I grew up with, who was a wonderful person." She leaned back in her seat. "I just wish I was sure he was guilty, it would make this easier for me."

"I can understand, Ma'am. With any luck it will all be over today."

The door opened and Glenda walked in.

"Cassie, I heard. I'm going to stay with you today." She took Cassie's hand. "We are going to get through this together."

"I'm so glad you are here. I'm so scared and unsure about all this." She looked at Glenda with tears in her eyes. "What if he's innocent? He told me again today he was."

"Why don't you let the police sort this out, dear? All you do is what they tell you to do and that takes away any guilt on your part. Remember, they are the professionals."

"Yes, but I'm his sister."

"Richard, is there a chance for some fresh coffee for all of us?" Glenda asked when she saw the butler walking in quietly.

"Of course, Miss Glenda, I will get right on it."

Glenda was sure it would be a long, stressful morning.

Latimer and Brighton sat in the office waiting for a detailed report from Captain Graham, the officer in charge of surveillance. Both were on edge. Would this be the day?

"I will feel a lot better when this is over, Sir," Brighton said into the silence.

"Remember that part about the fat lady singing, Kid?"

"I know, but maybe she took the day off or joined the church choir." Brighton smiled. "I have a good feeling about today, Sir. I think we'll get him."

"Wouldn't it be nice if the world ran on your good feelings, Kid? It would definitely be a better place." Latimer tried hard not to sound cynical. Before he could say any more the phone rang.

"Graham here, Inspector. Could you join us in the conference room for a briefing and planning session about the Anscott case?"

"We'll be right there," Latimer said as he walked around the desk toward the door.

The conference room was used for occasions like this and was furnished with a large, oblong table and about twenty chairs placed around it. A chalk board was at the far end and a white, rollup screen next to it. Extra chairs lined one wall and the other had two large, closed windows with blinds broken in several places. Not exactly the Ritz, but it served its purpose well.

Captain Graham was standing at the head of the table with the Chief on one side and a chair held for Latimer on the other. The rest of the table was filling up with technicians, plain clothes officers and any other personnel needed for this afternoon's event at the bus station. Brighton found a chair way down at the far end.

There was a lot of nervous tension in the room and Graham was chewing on his lip. The Chief's face looked subdued as if he was not going to allow himself to be positive until the perp was in custody. Latimer sat with a stoic expression, trying hard not to give away his feelings of a mixture between nervousness and excitement. He refused to look at the Chief. There was no need to encourage the man to berate him in front of everyone about this case, with his favorite rant about how it was time things started going right. The bad part was, everybody felt that way, including Latimer.

"Chief, Inspector Latimer, ladies and gentlemen," the Captain said after clearing his throat several times. "We are here this morning to brief you on what has happened so far in the Anscott case over the last few days. This is also a planning session about how we will proceed to apprehend the suspect this afternoon at the Glenridge bus depot." He cleared his throat again before he went on. "We don't have much time and I have asked the manager of the depot to join us this morning." He turned to a man in a gray suit at the far end of the table. "Welcome, Mr. Cranston. Please feel free to make suggestions and ask questions during our planning session, Sir."

Lance Cranston was a heavy set, short man with a gray mustache and a bald head. His face broke into a friendly smile and he nodded all around after the introduction.

"Chief, would you care to say anything before we get started?" Graham asked.

Here it comes, Latimer thought and cringed.

"No, we have much to discuss, Graham. Let's get this over with and finally get this guy."

Latimer let out a silent sigh of relief and saw Brighton look at him with a slight smile.

Captain Graham turned to Latimer and asked him to give a run down on the surveillance efforts and the raid on Mr. Lansky's house in the lower district. After he was done, Graham finished by giving a report on the phone tapping details and the content of the phone conversations with Cassie Anscott and the suspect.

"Are there any questions so far?" he asked when he finished. No one spoke.

"Ok, that being done, we will now discuss the plan for apprehending the suspect at the bus depot. I had someone take pictures of the locker area real early this morning." He turned to the screen. "Larry, will you show them to us now, please. Mr. Cranston, if you could come up front and explain to us in detail what these pictures show."

The rather overweight man came up front with amazing agility in his step. He pointed out the most advantageous places to put officers and suggested several things which proved helpful in laying out the best plan to get close enough to Anscott, but not too close so he would get suspicious.

The meeting went on for two hours. By the time they left there was no doubt what everyone's job was. By order of the Chief, Latimer and Brighton were relegated to staying in the car a block away since Anscott knew their faces. Someone would let him know immediately when Marten Anscott was apprehended. He felt frustrated about that, but knew there was no other way.

Cassie Anscott walked in with Glenda right after the meeting. Latimer and Graham greeted her and spent another hour going over her part in the operation. She seemed calm, but Latimer knew better. She had brought the money in a medium size brown leather bag Mr. Rathbone had given her, together with a long, white envelope for the key. She seemed to get more tense as the time drew closer and refused lunch altogether.

"What if I can't find the locker?" she suddenly asked Latimer. "Shouldn't I have gone over there before today to check out where it is?"

"No, it will seem more natural if you have to search for it if he is watching. Don't worry, if you can't find it, just ask one of the people milling around. Remember, they are all police officers and will show you where it is." Latimer sounded reassuring.

Finally, when it was time, she got into her car alone and drove to the bus depot. An unmarked police car drove in front of her to show her the way and turned away just before she got to the parking area. Cassie leaned back into the car seat and said a silent prayer. She felt terribly nervous and almost forgot to take the bag with the money before she finally got out. She looked around. There was no one who paid any attention to her as she walked toward the building a few hundred feet away.

She was amazed how normal everything and everyone looked when she stepped through the big, double glass doors. There were all kinds of people walking and talking and even laughing. She couldn't believe all of them were police officers. She followed the sign to the locker area and opened up the door with a number 26 on it. She put the bag inside, locked it and took the key out. Carefully, she sealed it in the white envelope and looked for the trash bin. There it was. She dropped it in and looked around to see if she could spot Marten before she walked back outside.

What she didn't see was a young teenage boy walking up to the bin and taking the envelope out. He opened it, took the key and walked up to number 26 and slid the key in the key hole. He looked around carefully before he took out the bag to see if anyone was watching. When he was sure no one paid any attention to him, he carefully lifted it out of the locker and headed for the glass doors. No one stopped him as he walked down the street for a few hundred feet. He stopped at the corner of an abandoned building as if waiting for someone.

A car parked several hundred feet away, and several cars drove by, but he didn't notice anything special about them. Thirty minutes went by and the boy still stood waiting. He was getting restless and it looked like he was going to leave.

That is when the parked car drove up closer and a van coming from the other direction stopped suddenly in front of him. Four officers with guns jumped out.

"Stop, police, don't move!"

The boy dropped the bag and started to run, but was immediately overtaken by one of the officers and handcuffed.

"I didn't do nothing!" he shouted. "I was just standing here."

Latimer and Brighton drove up and heard the last of the Miranda rights read to him.

"We'll meet you back at the precinct," Latimer said to the arresting officer.

"Ok, kid, tell us what you were doing taking a bag with five thousand dollars out of a locker at the bus depot?" Latimer's voice was filled with anger and frustration.

"I didn't know what was in it, honest." He was whining.

"So you say your name is Tom Brewer from the lower district area. "Who told you to pick up the bag?"

"He was just a man in the neighborhood. I have never seen him before. He said he would give me a hundred dollars if I go to the bus depot and look for an envelope in a trash can by the lockers. After that I was supposed to take the key in it and bring him what's in the locker." He was almost crying. "Honest, that's all I know."

"Where were you supposed to deliver it to?"

"Right at that corner where your goons arrested me, but the guy never showed."

A middle aged woman opened the door to the interrogation room.

"He has one prior, a minor theft at a liquor store, Sir. He got off with probation."

"Thanks, Wendy."

"Now, Tom, can you give me a description of the man who asked you to do this thing?"

"He was wearing a hoody and I really couldn't see much of his face. He was old, though."

"How old?"

"At least thirty."

"And that's old?" Latimer wiped his forehead with a deep sigh. "That means I must belong to the dinosaur age, right kid?"

"You said it, man." He relaxed a little.

"Had you ever seen this guy around?"

"I told you no, I know everybody in my neighborhood."

Latimer leaned back in his chair and looked at the young man. He knew the kid spoke the truth. He also knew, once again, Anscott had given him the slip.

"I'm going to let you go, Tom, but if you ever get in trouble again, it won't go easy with you. Now scram. Make sure you stop at the front desk to pick up your stuff."

"Yes Sir, thanks."

"If you ever see that old guy again, call me." With a smile he handed him a business card.

Not even a cup of coffee on the way back to his office could do much to cheer him up. He was sure, if Brown would have shown up, he would have done him real harm. Latimer picked up the phone and called Glenda.

"He slipped right through our fingers again and I may be on my way to Florida on an early retirement vacation any day now," he said when she picked up the phone.

"I heard, Bob. I'm so sorry. I was with Cassie when the call from Captain Graham came. She didn't know whether to be sad or relieved. Do you think Marten will call again?"

"I doubt that very much. He must have somehow found out the police were there in force and didn't show up at the meeting place with the kid and the money. We had to let the youngster go. He didn't know anything and couldn't even describe Marten. I tell you one thing, this guy is smart and I'm tired." Latimer sighed deeply.

"Would dinner at my place make you feel better tonight?"

"That is about the only thing that would come close. Just say when and I'll be there with a bottle of good wine."

"Let's make it eight because I have a lot to do at the office. Since I have to play housewife as well, that will take some time." She sounded cheery.

"Eight it is. Prepare yourself for a grumpy old man tonight who needs a lot of cheering up."

"I think I can handle that. See you then."

"Wow, we are dating now are we?" Brighton had walked in while Latimer was talking.

"Zip it Kid, you are not old enough for those kinds of conversations."

Brighton saw the twinkle in his eyes.

"I wish I had a date. My luck with the ladies has not been the greatest lately. Maybe I need to go to charm school or something."

"Have you noticed Mattie Hansfield down the hallway? She looks very pretty and very available, Kid."

"Oh, I have noticed, but have not had the nerve to ask her out. You think I should, Sir? She is awfully pretty if you ask me."

"If an old man like me is not too shy to try his luck with a good looking woman, I would thing a young man like you should not have any problems. Since Mattie is not in the same department, there is nothing to stop you."

"Can I tell her you told me to do it, Sir?"

"You do and I'll skin you bald headed."

Chapter 24

Cassie sat in her office with her head in her hands. She was going over the events of the day and couldn't make up her mind how she felt about Marten. If he was truly innocent she had tried to lead him into a trap. She could only imagine if he had done something like that to her how she would feel. The hurt would be unbearable. The confusing part was that he was adopted and therefore not really her brother. Did she feel about him the same way she had before? She felt confused. How do you turn off loving someone who you thought was your brother and then suddenly he wasn't. Do you love a person because they are a blood relative or they were a part of your life for 26 years?

What if he was guilty and murdered her father? Hate was the only feeling that made any sense, especially since he was not her real brother. This would really come to the forefront if she had to pay for his legal fees. Why should she do that? He deserved to rot in prison if he murdered two people and caused Mom's stroke and eventual death.

Her body tensed up as feelings of anger and resentment took over her mind. She was alone now. All her family was gone in the span of two weeks, and for what purpose? Why would Marten have done such a horrible thing?

Then he said on the phone he was innocent. Her mind was spinning in circles as she stared at the picture of her mother on the desk, still left there from when the office belonged to her father. She would have to find a picture of Dad to put next to it, or better, one with both of them together. The thought of having a family picture of all of them caused her to cringe, because Marten would be included.

She wished she could just curl up into a ball and go to sleep and when she woke up all this would have been a dream.

The phone rang.

"You betrayed me! How could you do that? I told you I didn't do it and you still told the police. I hate you, you know that? I hate you!" He was screaming uncontrollably.

Cassie couldn't say a word. She sat in silence and listened.

"I will get even with you, you'll see. I'll kill you!"

"Just like you killed Dad?" she finally managed to say.

"I told you I didn't do it. How many times do I have to say it? Why don't you believe me?" He started to sob. "I need that money, please give it to me." He suddenly sounded like a little boy. I don't have anything left to live on. What am I supposed to do, Sis?"

She felt torn between guilt and fear.

"Marten, listen to me, you have to turn yourself in. I told you I will get you the best lawyers in town, but you have to do what I tell you."

There was a moment of silence.

"I saw that Inspector and the Sergeant in the car two streets over from the bus depot and I knew you had called the police." His tone was suddenly calm. "Why did you do that? What are five thousand dollars to you, you own everything." There was a menacing tone in his voice now. "If you don't get me the money you will never get to enjoy what you have. I will never allow you to be in charge of the whole company, I will make sure of that. If I can't have any of it, neither will you." His voice was low and menacing. "You better look over your shoulders from now on, I'll be watching. I'll never do what you tell me to do."

The line went dead.

She sat perfectly still. It was as if her mind could not comprehend what had just happened. Marten was threatening her life. Finally, she picked up the phone and dialed Latimer's number.

"He called me again, Inspector. More than that, he said if I don't give him the money, he will make sure I don't get it either. Those were his words."

"You realize we no longer have surveillance on your phone, Cassie." Latimer stated. "We thought we'd already have him in custody."

"I know, but there is one thing, I'm now convinced he's guilty." She took a deep breath as anger and hatred washed over her. "It's time you find him Inspector, before he kills me, too."

"I'm aware of that, Cassie. Please tell me, did he say how he knew the police were watching?"

"Yes, he did. He saw you and Sgt. Brighton sitting in a car several blocks from the depot and that's how he knew I had called the police."

"I can't believe this!" Latimer was almost shouting. *Just wait till the Chief hears about this,* he thought. "I'll talk with the Chief, Cassie, and ask for a protective detail for you for a few days. Please stay in your office until you hear from me."

"Latimer, this is the first case I've known you to bungle since I've been here." The Chief's voice was strangely low key. "I'm beginning to agree with some of the higher ups that maybe you are getting a little tired these days."

Latimer knew this was the latest phrase to use when discussing old age without getting in trouble about age discrimination. He almost agreed with the Chief at the moment and couldn't find anything to say in answer to that accusation. He felt tired and worn out from the adrenalin rush this afternoon. Let's face it, all he had to show was failure again.

"What are you saying, Chief?"

"I didn't say I agreed with them exactly, but you will admit this case has not gone as well as it should up to now. Everyone is worried about it dragging on for so long. It leaves a bad impression on the department."

"Are you saying I'm too old for the job, Sir?"

"Of course not, I'm still confident you will solve this case. It's just we could use a break and find this guy." The Chief was almost mumbling.

"Do you have any suggestions where we should go from here, Sir?" Latimer's voice was silky smooth. He knew he had him.

The Chief looked at him and then a grin crept over his face.

"You are still a sly fox Latimer. I know when I've been had. And no, I don't know where to go from here, but I'm sure you will come up with something." He leaned forward and looked straight into Latimer's eyes. "You still have my full confidence, Inspector, no matter what the brass thinks."

"Thank you, Sir. I will try my best not to disappoint you before I retire. By the way, Anscott called his sister a few moments ago and threatened to kill her if she didn't come up with some money for him."

"You are kidding, that man has a lot of nerve." The Chief's voice was back to its normal volume again.

"He also told her he saw me and Brighton sitting in the car several blocks from the depot. That's how he knew we were on to him."

"I can't believe it. We had everything so well planned and then it takes one small incident to foil the whole thing."

Latimer remembered it was the Chief who ordered them to that spot at the meeting this morning. *And so did the Chief!*

"Since we discontinued the electronic surveillance, there is no telling where he called from. He told Cassie Anscott he is out of money.

That means he's getting desperate and might very well carry out this threat. I told her we would have a protective detail assigned to her for a few days. I hope that meets with your approval, Sir. There is no need for another killing."

"That's fine. Contact Meltzer, he will give you two men from his team."

"Thank you, Sir." Latimer stood up and headed for the door.

"Don't give up Bob, we'll get him," the Chief shouted before he was out of earshot.

He hadn't called him Bob in a long time. Latimer smiled.

He bought red roses and a bottle of wine on his way to Glenda's apartment. In spite of the bad day, it had been many years since he felt this young, energetic and happy. To think he found a woman he could love at his age was a miracle.

She was totally different from his wife Mary, who had been a home maker, confidant and friend through the years. Mary had not been pretty as such when he married her. It was her genuine outgoing love and sparkly, warm personality that had attracted him to her. Over the years they grew together in a strong, solid relationship. It lasted through the many tough trials of everyday living and a job that demanded patience and understanding on her part.

The doorman greeted him with a tip of the hat and asked him where he was going.

"Mrs. Hinsley is expecting you, Sir," he said with a knowing look at the roses and the wine. "It's on the second floor, apartment four."

I bet that man could tell many tales with this job, Latimer thought as he walked passed him.

Even the elevator was elegant with mirrored tiles on one side, which Latimer used to carefully check his appearance. His hair was in place and he straightened the open collar of his light blue shirt one more time. The dark blue jacket fit nice over the gray pants. "This is as good as it gets," he said out loud. He hated to admit it, but he was excited.

Glenda looked completely different with a colorful apron over a comfortable pants suit. Her face was slightly flushed from standing over the stove.

"Come on in, Bob," she said with a warm smile. "If those roses are not for me I will be very unhappy."

"I thought about giving them to the doorman, but he wasn't as pretty as you," he said with a serious expression on his face. He handed them to her together with the bottle of wine and a kiss on the cheek.

"Thank you, you are incorrigible as usual, Bob. Come on in and say 'hello' to Cassie.

"Hi Inspector, I'm sorry to intrude on your evening. I was such a basket case that Glenda took pity on me and invited me to join you for dinner. I hope you don't mind." Cassie held out her hand to him with an apologetic smile.

"I'm delighted to see you, Cassie," Latimer said as he took it. "This is perfectly fine and the three of us will get to enjoy Glenda's fabulous cooking." He looked at Glenda. "Although this is the first time I've been here to taste it."

"Oh no, I didn't know that, now I feel even worse." Cassie sounded truly uncomfortable.

"Cassie, honey, Bob and I are not two teenagers on a date, given our age. You're not intruding at all. We love to have you, don't we Bob?" She threw him a telling look.

Speak for yourself, woman, he thought.

"Of course we are, Cassie," he said out loud. "With what you've been through today, I'm glad you're not alone at home." He gave her his best comforting smile. "By the way, have they arranged for a protective detail yet?"

"I told them since I'm coming here tonight, we could start with that tomorrow morning," she said.

"You are spending the night here then?"

"Yes, I was too scared to go home after what happened. With you being here I feel even safer." She looked young and vulnerable with a faint touch of fear in her eyes.

Latimer put his arm around her shoulders.

"I'm truly glad you are here, Cassie, and if a crusty old guy like me makes you feel safer, that's even better." He smiled at her with sincere warmth. By the way, please call me Bob."

"Dinner is served," Glenda tried her best to imitate Richard as she pointed to the dining room table.

"Don't give up your day job." Latimer grinned as he leaned over and kissed her slightly on the cheek. "My having dinner with two ladies instead of one is turning out to be much better than I first thought," he said as he pulled out a chair for each of them. "All these hugs and kisses are making me realize what I've been missing for the last ten years."

"In that case, you might go all the way and do the dishes afterwards while we ladies go into the parlor, Sir." Glenda passed him the platter filled with three big steaks. "Here you go, Bob, this will give you the energy to do a good job of it."

"Thank you, sweetheart, where are yours?" he said as he took it.

After dinner they had cheesecake for dessert in the living room. Latimer made sure he found a place next to Glenda on the couch. Cassie chose a chair on the other side of the round coffee table. Each had a glass of wine in front of them. There was a momentary silence until Glenda turned to Latimer.

"Bob, do you mind if we talk about what happened today? Also, Cassie and I would really like to know where we go from here. Let's face it, Marten is a real threat and the police won't be able to protect her forever."

"I understand how you feel." He looked at Cassie. "I wish I could see into the future and tell you we will catch him and put him away for good tomorrow, but I can't. It has been astounding how he has managed to escape us so far. With him running out of money, the situation has intensified, not just for him, but for you as well. Short of robbing a bank, he will have to try to reach out to you again, Cassie. Whether that is by peaceful means or violence is anybody's guess. All we can do for you now is to provide a detail for your personal protection."

"What if I went away for a while?"

"That sounds like a great idea. Where would you go?" Latimer sounded interested.

"I could go to the condo in West Palm Beach. He doesn't have the money to fly down there and so couldn't follow me." She was getting really excited about the idea as she was talking, "and I would feel safe."

"You shouldn't go by yourself, Cassie," Glenda said.

"I know, but you could go with me."

"Honey, I have a ton of work to do here which no one else can do with the transition still in full swing. I truly don't think Mark Lenhart would allow me to leave right now."

"Who is more important right now, Mark or me? I'm the one in danger. You can do a lot of the work over the computer and by telephone from down there." She sounded determined. "And by the way, who owns the place, Mark or me?"

"Cassie, right now he's in charge and what he says goes." Glenda tried to be diplomatic. "There is no reason you can't bring this up in the morning as soon as we get to the office. If he agrees, I'll be glad to go with you."

Latimer groaned. "It would be a tough job, but someone's got to do it." He was thinking of being away from Glenda as well, just when he had found her. "How long are we talking about?" He asked no one in particular.

"Hopefully until you catch him," Glenda said, "which should not be too long now that he is desperate and without funds."

Latimer leaned back and put his arm around Glenda's shoulders.

"You better start praying, because so far we have not been doing too well and could use a break." He smiled at her. "But seriously, the fact that he is without money is bound to cause him to make mistakes. He will have to rely on other people to do things for him and that is always risky if he wants them to keep silent." He rubbed his beard. "Cassie, would you be willing to put up a pretty good amount of money for a reward? The people he is forced to deal with are poor and always ready to make some extra cash."

"That sounds like a great idea, Bob. How much are you thinking about?"

"How about a hundred thousand dollars?"

"Consider it done." She jumped up and walked to the window. "I have a good feeling for the first time that this will get results." She was smiling at him. "Bob, get in touch with Mark Lenhart in the morning and have him arrange for the money. I will talk to him first thing when I get there. I know there won't be a problem." She reached for her glass and held it up in a toast, "To success, guys."

After she put it down she smiled at both of them and said, "I'm going to turn in. It has been a long day and you two can spend some time alone. It was a wonderful evening and a delicious dinner, Glenda. Thank you for putting up with me, Bob. Good night." Without waiting for an answer she left.

Latimer looked at Glenda and emptied his glass.

"Well, sweetheart, I have been waiting all evening for this." He pulled her close and kissed her gently at first, but with much more passion when she responded to him. "You are beautiful and I think I'm falling hopelessly in love with you."

"We have known each other for only four weeks," she whispered as she snuggled up to him. "You sound like a reckless teenager."

"I feel like a reckless teenager." He kissed her again until she pushed him away.

"One of us has to be the adult here." She was smiling. "I'm going to make us a cup of coffee. You had wine and I would feel better if we make sure it is safe for you to drive home."

She came back with one cup of coffee and another with herbal tea.

"Here you go, I can't drink coffee this late. It would keep me awake the rest of the night."

He took the cup and leaned back into his seat.

"I'm really not happy about you leaving for West Palm Beach just as we are getting to know each other." He looked at her with frustration. "Can't someone else go with Cassie?"

"Bob, she needs me right now. She is only 26 years old and has been through a terrific nightmare on so many fronts. It will take someone who she is comfortable with to help her get through this." She took his face in her hands. "We can talk on the phone as many times as you want, day or night, my big, tough crime fighter." She leaned back and started to giggle. "Just think, if the guys at the precinct could hear you now."

His face crinkled in a sheepish grin as he took another sip of coffee.

"See what you do to me, woman? I'm down to a mere shadow of my tough former self after only four weeks."

Chapter 25

"This is your local Fox News Channel with the latest headlines. I'm Ken Windham. This is a new development in the sensational double murder of the owner and CEO of Anscott Laboratories and a woman named Camilla Preston. The family is offering a hundred thousand dollar reward for the capture of the suspect, their own son and heir Marten Henry Anscott. It was revealed by the Chief of the Glenridge Major Crime Unit that Marten Anscott was adopted as a baby and raised as their own son by Patrick and Helen Anscott. After several weeks on the run and a failed attempt to apprehend him by the Glenridge Police Department yesterday during a sting operation, Anscott managed again to elude all attempts at capture. It has nearly been four weeks since the murders were committed and it does not look like Glenridge law enforcement is any closer to capturing this dangerous criminal. We are showing you a picture of the suspect. If you have seen this man, please call the special hotline at the Major Crime Unit immediately at 555-3894. In other news…"

And so the circus begins, Latimer thought after he turned the TV off. It would take a lot of manpower to sort through the maze of calls coming in from around the State with every weirdo and crazy finally getting their chance to report a sighting. The Chief had instructed the switchboard to concentrate more on local calls than from around the State. It was at the urging of the Governor's office they released the news bulletin and created a hotline. Many saw it as a sure sign of the dissatisfaction with the Glenridge Major Crime Unit at the highest level. Needless to say, the Chief was in a total frenzy.

Cassie and Glenda had arrived at West Palm Beach in the afternoon on the company jet, since a commercial flight was considered too risky at this point. Richard and Emily accompanied them and were getting the condo ready for a prolonged stay. The woman, who was usually hired when the family came down, was not available at such short notice. It was decided to bring Richard and Emily. Lilly was charged with looking after the Estate together with the two groundskeepers.

Richard was sent immediately to get groceries and such things as were needed while Emily prepared the bedrooms and the rest of the house. There was not that much to do since they had just been there four weeks ago. It seemed a lifetime had passed since then.

Latimer had notified the West Palm Beach police department to alert them to the presence of Cassie Anscott and asked they check on the condo as often as they could. Since they were well acquainted with the case, they promised to send a patrol car by the place at regular intervals. He spoke with a Sgt. Hollister who seemed to have taken a special interest in the case and took some time to discuss it with Latimer.

Since it was September, one of the hottest months in Florida, Glenda regretted she could not sit out on the veranda facing the ocean, but had to settle behind the large window in the living room. She had always enjoyed watching the people on the beach. Only a few hardy souls had the stamina to brave the late afternoon heat at the moment.

The family usually came down in early spring or the end of November when the temperature was more tolerable and a walk on the beach in the evening an enjoyable experience.

She had brought her computer and used Patrick's office to hook up to the company's system. It made it like an office away from the office, a well-established way to do business in today's world. She would have to share it with Cassie, but there was plenty of space for both of them to work.

She reached for her cell phone and called Latimer.

"We got here ok, Bob. I could get used to the private jet. How are things at your end?"

"Hi Glenda, it's a circus here. We had the broadcast with a picture of Marten and a phone number to call, plus the reward money, of course. I will probably not get home till real late if at all today. In a way I'm glad you ladies are not here. Try not to enjoy the beach more than I can stand to hear, will you?"

She laughed.

"I promise I won't tell you I'm sitting in front of a large window overlooking the ocean."

He groaned.

"Neither will I describe the sunrise I usually watch in the early morning hours. It will be breathtaking."

"That does it. I demand you return immediately to the rest of us working stiffs who have a window with the blinds closed so we don't have to stare at a parking lot." He let out a deep sigh as if suffering.

"Poor thing, I'm thinking of you, though. Just remember, I also have to work tomorrow all day. Can I help it if my office is at the beach?" She tried hard not to gloat. "Seriously Bob, I hope our stay won't be too long, because I really miss you."

"Have a wonderful time, sweetheart. I'm glad you and Cassie are out of harm's way. This will pass, but please pray we'll get him soon. I have to go, and before I hang up, I love you." He smiled as he could almost sense her blushing.

It was amazing, but Emily managed to put a wonderful meal on the table that evening. Cassie and Glenda sat in the living room and watched the darkness swallow up the ocean. They turned on a low light inside which allowed them to watch the waves.

"How are you doing, dear?" Glenda asked in a gentle voice.

"I feel I'm going to be in shock for the rest of my life. My mind somehow refuses to believe all the terrible things that have happened." Cassie sounded as if she was going to cry.

"I think you'll need counseling to get over this, Cassie. Don't wait too long, it only makes it harder."

"I don't know any counselors, Glenda. Let's face it, I never had the need for one before."

"Can you tell me what the hardest thing is about all this other than the death of your parents?" Glenda was careful not to push.

"I feel so desperately lonely, like I'm the only one left on earth." She looked at Glenda with utter sadness in her eyes. "That is not the worst, though. It's the hatred I feel for Marten. I now believe he is guilty. If I could just understand why he did those horrible things, it would make it easier. Maybe I wouldn't hate him so much."

"It's understandable you feel that way, dear. You realize you cannot live with that kind of turmoil in your heart for a long time. It will destroy you in the end." She took Cassie's hand in hers. "The first step in this process is to feel shock. That is where you are right now for the most part. The shock over the loss of your parents and what Marten has done is the mind's way to shield you from facing these facts as reality. The next step will be disbelief, then anger and hatred. Our mind uses hatred for a defense mechanism as a first reaction when something so bad happens it would destroy us if we faced it as stark reality. The next step will be the desire for revenge, which usually gives way to sadness. After that should follow understanding and forgiveness if we process it in the way the good Lord has designed it. These steps and feelings are a part of our human mind to deal with trauma. However, in the end the true healing process cannot begin until there is forgiveness. It is the ultimate ointment for the soul."

"I really don't need a counselor if I have you to talk to, do I Glenda?" Cassie managed to give her a tiny smile. "I cannot imagine right now I will ever be able to forgive Marten for what he has done. I want him caught and put in prison for the rest of his miserable life. Something else, I'm glad he's not my real brother. He would have never killed Dad, not in a million years if he was." She was shaking. "He deserves to die if there is justice in this world."

Glenda remained silent and allowed her to vent.

They sat in silence for a long time as darkness descended over the ocean.

Into the stillness Cassie said in a low voice, "All I know is that I don't want to become an emotional cripple because of this. I'm afraid I have a long road to travel until I feel normal again. Finding Marten would definitely be a good beginning."

"I have no doubt you will get through this, dear. Give yourself some time and ask God to help you." She smiled. "He has an amazing way to do that."

After a while the sliver of a moon came into view and created a beautiful picture of white foam dancing on the waves.

Cassie stood and walked up to the window.

"Do you love Bob?"

Glenda was completely startled at the turn of the conversation. After a moment she said, "I think it's a little early to be sure."

"He loves you."

"I know."

"He's nice, Glenda, don't let him get away." Cassie suddenly started to cry. "That's another thing about my life. I wish I had a man who loved me and would hold me right now so I could feel safe." She reached for a tissue on the small table and wiped her face. "Listen to me, the poor little rich girl."

"In the end it's not money that counts, but the love of someone special in our lives. That will happen for you, too, Cassie, you wait and see. I plan to be at your wedding someday." Glenda smiled at Cassie and filled her glass again. "Have some more wine and then we'll go to bed.

We can't solve all the problems in one evening. It will be a busy day tomorrow."

That same night, sixty miles north of West Palm Beach, in the beach town of Lake Worth, parts of a human body washed on to the shore.

Chapter 26

The man stayed in the shadows. He watched the main gate of the Estate from across the street. He felt the first chill of autumn in the air and pulled his hoody tight around his body. He was tempted to climb the high wall to the side, but it was impossible to get a foothold on the smooth surface. He really wanted to get in and see if he could find a way to steal some of that high priced stuff in the house. It was a shame he couldn't have taken it before, but then he didn't know he needed it. He would have to now, there was no choice.

He was not afraid to get caught. Nobody knew who he was. The police had no clue he was right there in plain sight under their noses. His mother had always told him cops were stupid. He believed her now. He had watched the news today. They can show all the pictures they want on TV, it won't do them any good. They will never find him. He felt good about that. He was the invisible man. He remembered watching an old show about that and now he was living it. He chuckled. Funny, they wouldn't find Marten either.

Poor Marten, he had no idea what real life was like, living in that big mansion with his big trust fund. Imagine, having all that money. He got what he deserved and so did his father. He had made sure of that. There was justice after all, even if things didn't turn out perfect. Revenge still felt good. Or maybe it was justice.

He felt the headache coming back and he was out of medicine. Maybe he would stop at the free clinic tomorrow. They wanted to put him in the hospital, but he wouldn't let them. He didn't trust doctors. When it came down to it, he didn't trust anybody.

He walked across the street to the main gate and looked through the wrought iron bars. Too bad, Marten, you lost all this and I did it to you. If I can't have it, neither will you. That's the trouble with rich people, they think they deserve their money and look down on the poor as if they were dirt. He showed them all he wasn't dirt.

The man laughed a quiet little laugh and turned around and walked off into the night at a leisurely pace just out of sight of a police car driving down the road.

When he got to his apartment he took out the diary he stole from Glenda's office. Slowly he opened it and laid it on the single simmering log in the old fireplace and watched it burn until nothing was left but black ashes.

Chapter 27

It was midnight before Latimer got home. It had been exactly as he feared. Among the hundreds of calls not one was of any use. One man swore he saw Marten Anscott at a meeting place for aliens. A woman reported her daughter's boyfriend was him. When asked how old the boyfriend was she said he had just had his fifteenth birthday. And so it went. The crew manning the phones tried their best to be friendly, patient and courteous with each caller. However, by midnight their nerves were at a breaking point. The Chief finally suspended the hotline until morning and told everyone to go home.

By the next morning the circus started all over again. Latimer, by the time he had his third cup of coffee, was ready to kill the first person who told him they saw Marten Anscott. He had even dreamed he saw the man and couldn't arrest him because he was an alien made of smoke.

Brighton had lost his smile when he was told he had been assigned to help man the phone bank. There were maybe five legitimate calls which were passed on to Latimer, but each turned out to be nothing. By the end of the day the Chief decided to call it quits and discontinued the operation.

Latimer had never been so discouraged about a case in all his thirty years. He had tried everything he knew to do and had run out of options, he told the Chief when he met with him at the end of the day. The two men looked at each other, defeated, tired and ready to call it not only a day, but a case ready to join the dead files.

"You know, Latimer, I'm not a drinking man, but today I feel like I want to get stone drunk and then drink some more," the Chief said into the silence.

"You couldn't have put it better, Sir. I'm going home and I may never come back. This sounds like a good day to retire."

"You are kidding, right?"

"Maybe I am and maybe I'm not, Chief. This is not the time to ask me. Good night, Sir."

His apartment felt cold, lonely and sad. He imagined Glenda coming to greet him at the door and slumped into his chair, too tired and depressed to get himself something out of the fridge. He remembered the terrific steak dinner at her house and simply couldn't face a bologna sandwich with mustard and no mayonnaise. He was out of mayonnaise.

It was two in the morning when he woke up in his chair, stiff as a board. Without getting undressed he stumbled into bed and went right back to sleep. He didn't wake up till eight o'clock. He would be late for work!

Brighton walked in looking tired and depressed.

"I hope I don't ever have to answer a phone again, Sir. I'm convinced the entire population of this State belongs in a nut house, except us, of course." A tiny smile crossed his face for a second.

"After the last two days, I'm not so sure about us either, Kid." Latimer drank his coffee like it was the only thing able to keep him alive. "That reminds me, did you ever ask Mattie Hattfield out?"

"I did, Sir, but she turned me down, said she was too busy with work, being new on the job and all."

"Give her another month and try again. At least she didn't flat out say no, did she?"

"I thought that was a flat out no, Sir." Brighton looked confused.

"That's what's wrong with this new generation. If it doesn't happen in thirty minutes like in a sitcom on TV it isn't happening. Like I said, Kid, ask her again in a month. In the meantime, shower her with compliments and pour her a cup of coffee in the lounge every time she walks in. Then hand her a donut." He had a twinkle in his eyes. "She wants to know if you really mean it. Women are that way. If that doesn't do it, tell her you will not give up unless she goes out with you at least once." He took the last sip of coffee. "If that doesn't do it, kill yourself. At least then she'll know you loved her." His face was one big grin.

"I will keep that in mind, Sir," Brighton said, laughing.

At that moment the phone rang. It was Glenda.

"Hello, sunshine lady," Latimer said. "You are just what the doctor ordered after the horrible ordeal we've gone through with the statewide TV campaign for the reward money."

"Oh, I'm so sorry, no luck at all?"

"We dug up every nut job in this State and then some. I'm totally convinced aliens kidnapped our boy and he is gone forever to another planet."

"You sound giddy about it, Bob."

"I am. I'm also fed up, disgusted and ready to pack it in. The only thing that'll save me from total despair is hearing your lovely voice."

"I don't think I've ever heard you like this, Bob."

"It's called slap happy. It's a state of mind that comes with continued, consistent and absolute failure in a hopeless situation. That should sum it up in a nutshell."

"I'm truly sorry, what can I do to make it better?" she said in baby talk.

"You can come home, woman, that's what you can do. I'm in need of some TLC, a nice steak dinner and anything else you and I can think of to do given half a chance."

"Is that an order, Inspector?" She was laughing.

"The trouble with women these days is they don't obey like they used to. I think there should be a law against it."

"You could write your congressman, but I'm pretty sure she is a woman in our State." Glenda was really laughing now. I'm sorry you feel so terrible, Bob, but it will be a while before I can come home. Cassie needs a lot of care and counseling right now and I believe I can help her. Besides, Marten is still on the loose, isn't he?"

"Did you have to bring that up, sweetheart?" He wasn't really serious.

"I'm glad you are doing well. Keep up the good work and don't forget me."

He felt better after he hung up and wished he was retired and in Florida.

Latimer spent the rest of the afternoon going over some of the phone calls the hotline had received. A technician helped him weed out the ones who really were of no value. Some were made clearly because of the money involved. Others hoped to get their two minutes of fame. In the end no one who called had seen Marten Anscott in or near Glenridge. After three hours of listening he decided it was enough and left the rest for other people to evaluate.

He decided to call it a day and went to a grocery store on the way home. He bought some meat and vegetables and salad material. It was time he got back on his regular diet instead of the fast food he had eaten lately.

He felt lonely. How ridiculous, for ten years he didn't mind coming home alone until he met Glenda. Now the place felt empty and cold. Well, it was cold. A first hint of fall was in the air and it was time to get out the blanket for his chair. He made a note to get a technician to come out tomorrow and hook up TV reception in his bedroom. The twinges in his back reminded him of it. His friendly old neighbor, Malcolm, would let them in and have it done by the time he got back from work tomorrow. He called Malcolm and then started on his dinner.

Later that evening he had a wonderful conversation with Glenda. The ladies were doing well and Cassie was starting to relax a little bit more each day. She was sure the beautiful surroundings of the beach and the splendid view of the ocean helped.

"Cassie is asking if you could go by and check on Lilly to see if she's doing ok at the Estate. It's the first time they've left her there alone. It's a big house and with all that's been going on it might be a little scary for her," Glenda said.

Latimer promised to call in the morning and send a patrol car by to see if everything was well. He told her they were keeping an eye out for any kind of suspicious activity in the vicinity of the front gate at night anyway.

It was ten by the time they said good night and Latimer called it a night and went to bed.

The phone rang at three in the morning. At first he had a hard time hearing anything. A woman was screaming and crying.

"Ma'am, calm down and talk slow so I can understand you."

After a lot of sniffling and sobbing he finally figured out it was Lilly. Before he asked her any more questions he jumped out of bed and told her he would be at the front gate in half an hour. He made sure she would let him in when he rang the doorbell before he hung up.

From what he could make out from her slurred speech in between crying and sniffling was that someone had broken into the house. They had threatened her with a gun and taken stuff, as she put it. On his way over there he called the precinct for back up on his cell phone.

It had to be Marten Anscott. He needed money and had finally resorted to breaking into the Estate. There were enough valuable items to keep him going if he sold them to the many fences in the lower district. He had to hand it to the guy, he was smart and cunning to do all this in spite of the increase in police attention.

The gate was open by the time he arrived and an officer waved him in when he showed his ID. Two patrol cars were parked in front of the entrance and he walked inside without anyone stopping him. It was strange not to see Richard standing there.

He found Lilly and three officers in the drawing room. She ran up to him as if to hug him, but stopped when she saw him stiffening up.

"He held a gun to my head, Inspector. I could have been killed."

"Calm down Lilly, and tell me exactly what happened," Latimer said in a firm voice.

He motioned her to sit down on the love seat and he took a seat in a chair next to it. He had remembered to bring his tape recorder with him and turned it on.

"It was really late, about midnight, when I heard a noise downstairs. I slept in the room to the left right up on the first landing." She wiped her eyes nervously. I knew I was alone in the house. The groundskeeper Peter Redden had stayed till eleven and then drove home. His wife called to say she was sick. He had me open the gate and that is when the guy must have gotten inside. I had the security alarm system on in the house, but it didn't go off. I don't know why not." She looked confused. "Why would it not have worked? I turned it on myself."

"Then what happened?" Latimer asked. Brighton had come in and he waved him to work the recorder.

"When I heard the noise I went downstairs and looked around. I was scared to death, but I was sure nobody could get in because of the alarm system. There he was, standing in the hallway down by the morning room. When he saw me coming he pulled out a gun and pointed it at me." She started to cry again. "I was so scared and started begging him not to kill me. He just stood there and didn't say anything."

"Could you see who it was, Lilly?"

"No, he wore a dark hoody and sun glasses. He had a beard. Then he held out a piece of paper. It said on there for me to give him all the money in the house and the jewelry. I told him I didn't have any money and Miss Cassie was out of town with Richard and Emily. That's when he laughed. I know it's crazy, but he laughed, not loud or anything, just a little laugh." She blew her nose. It was red from crying. "Then he waved the gun for me to go upstairs and he made me go to Mrs. Anscott's room.

"Did you see his face when he turned the lights on?"

"He had a flashlight and didn't turn any big lights on. He always made sure I walked in front of him. One time I tried to turn around so I could see him, but he stuck his gun in my back and I didn't do it anymore.

When we walked into Mrs. Anscott's room he held up the paper again. I looked for her jewelry, but Richard had put all of it in a safe downstairs. When I couldn't find it, he acted real mad and then waved me on to go to Miss Cassie's room. There he found some of her stuff she hadn't taken to the beach. He had brought a bag and put it in there. Then he went into Mr. Marten's room and waved the gun for me to turn around so I couldn't see what he was doing. I heard him open some drawers and he went into the closet.

After that we walked all over the house. He took many things from the shelves and the book cases and put them in his bag. Then he broke open the gun cabinet and took out Mr. Anscott's 1911 Colt 45 with a pearl handle. I remember it was Mr. Anscott's pride and joy. He also took two or three other guns and a shotgun, but I don't know what kind they were. All I know they were all very expensive weapons.

"The Colt alone is worth several thousand dollars if it's in good condition," Brighton said.

"Mr. Anscott had only real expensive guns and kept them cleaned and oiled regularly."

After a time I saw his bag was pretty full," Lilly went on. "Then, finally, he walked toward the front door and left. I ran for the phone and called 911 and you, Inspector. Then the police came and I let them in the gate.

"In all the time he was with you did he ever speak?"

"No, he didn't."

"Did he wear gloves?"

"Yes."

"Do you have any idea how he got into the house?" Latimer asked.

"I've no idea, but he didn't break a door or anything. He must've had a key."

"Do you keep a key anywhere outside in case you lock yourself out, Lilly?"

"Oh my goodness, right under the big green plant in front. I put it there after I knew I'd be alone here. After all, what would I do if I locked myself out? Richard had taken it away after the murder, because he said it was not safe."

"But you put it back after they left for the beach?"

194

"Yes, I did." She started crying again.

"Officer Keller, check it out."

"No key, Sir," he reported when he returned.

"Now we know how he got in the house, don't we?"

"We're going to leave now, Lilly. Do you need anyone to stay with you?"

"I've called my sister and her husband. They should be here any minute, Sir. I'm not staying here by myself until Miss Cassie comes home."

It was five o'clock by the time Latimer got back home. He was bone tired and debated whether to go to sleep or type up the report. His body won out and he fell into bed after setting the alarm for eight o'clock. Unfortunately, he slept right through and didn't wake up until ten in the morning when the phone rang.

It was Glenda. She had called the office and Brighton filled her in on the events of last night. That's when the Sergeant told her Latimer was still home asleep since he had not shown up at the office.

"I can't believe you are still in bed at this hour, Bob."

After she told him that Brighton had told her what happened, she asked him if they should come home.

"I don't think that's necessary, Glenda. Lilly has someone staying with her and the police will place a detail in front of the gate for a few days. Cassie will still be safer down there. We will have forensics go over the house for any kind of evidence, but I'm sure it was Marten. It will take him some time to fence the items he stole and Lilly will have to go over with an officer to let us know what she thinks has been taken. We will make a list and notify the pawn shops and jewelry stores to be on the lookout for Cassie's jewelry. She'll have to get with the police to tell them what was taken in more detail."

He yawned. "I better get going or they will arrest me for loitering in bed. I will talk to you later, sweetheart. Take care, I love you."

He still felt like a truck had run over him when he walked into the office. Maybe he was getting old when one interrupted night's sleep did him in like this. He frowned at Brighton's big smile, sipped his coffee with a vengeance and walked to the Chief's office to give his report.

The Chief was in a real snit. He had never gotten over that news report which suggested his department was incompetent. Now the break-in at the Anscott Estate was like pouring salt into the wounds of his bruised ego. This could possibly be a career changer. He would love to tell Latimer to retire because he couldn't handle things any more, but he didn't have any idea how to solve this mess either. He had made his share of mistakes and was not going to announce this latest happening to the press. Let them find out for themselves. In spite of his bad mood he didn't take it out on Latimer when he walked in.

"We are still treading water and getting in deeper, Chief," Latimer said as he sat down with a heavy sigh. He actually felt sorrier for the Chief than himself. After all, he was the one who had to face the brass every day, trying to explain why they weren't getting anywhere. The worst that could happen to him was early retirement. He doubted anyone would be so ruthless as to cut his pension for being short eight months. Maybe desk duty, but he could handle that. He was stunned to realize he was considering that possibility.

Chapter 28

The Lake Worth Crime Unit got the call two days earlier about the mangled body washed up on the shore. The retired couple taking their morning walk on the beach had phoned it in. The poor woman had to be hospitalized after seeing the terrible sight.

At first it was treated as a clear case of shark attack until the coroner pronounced it murder. A bullet was lodged in the heart. There were no extremities left for fingerprint ID and the facial features were unrecognizable, partly due to the length of time the body had been in the water. The many sea creatures had done the rest along the way. It was presumed by the coroner the body had been dumped into the ocean between one and three months ago. It could have drifted for a long time in the strong current of the Gulfstream, which flows along the Florida coastline to the north. All this was more or less conjecture at this point until more tests were run on the victim's body.

With no missing persons report in the Palm Beach County vicinity or the rest of the way down to the Fort Lauderdale and Miami area, the case was put on the back burner.

Cassie and Glenda were walking on the beach in front of the condo in spite of the heat. They waded through the shallow waters lapping at the sand to cool off. It was a glorious day. The clear blue sky was reflected in the calm ocean waters. The gentle waves produced delicate white ripples before they reached the beach and disappeared into the sand as if by magic. It had the consistency of powder when dry and was soothing between their toes when wet. It was the stuff the Chamber of Commerce promised in their brochures and tourists the world over dreamed about.

Glenda collected some unusual looking shells. She could never resist and had several fancy glass containers filled with them back in her apartment in Glenridge. The problems in Glenridge seemed unreal to them and of no importance amidst this wonderful scenery.

"You don't think we need to go home, do you Glenda?" Cassie asked while sipping her bottle of water.

"Bob didn't think it was necessary. He still thinks you are much safer down here and away from the Estate. As you can see, he was right. Can you imagine what Marten might have done if he had found you there? If you ask me, he seems deranged," she added.

"I just think he is desperate, Glenda. With no money, no family and no future except prison, I can't blame him. This kind of life must be so strange and frightening for him. It would be for me. I grew up the same way he did, in a wonderful family and no worries about money. I can't imagine what I would do if I was in his place."

"It looks like you feel sorry for him, Cassie," Glenda said, careful not to upset her.

"I do in a way, but not enough to not want him to get caught. Just when I start feeling for him I remember what he has done to my parents and I get angry all over again. Besides, we can't stay here forever. There are so many things you and I have to do at the company with all the changes that have occurred. I really think working every day would keep my mind off of all this mess with Marten and my emotional state."

Her cell phone rang.

"Richard, what's up?"

The butler sounded worried.

"The manager of the Yacht Club called and wanted to know if we are going to tie up the boat for long term or leave it the way it is. He was concerned about hurricanes at this time of year, Miss Cassie. It will need to be moored securely and closed up properly if no one is going to use it."

"Didn't Marten take care of that before he left?"

"Apparently not. Should I tell the man to see to it, Miss Cassie?"

"Go ahead, ask him to add this service to the regular monthly docking fee and send it to Mr. Rathbone. Make sure he gives the boat a good overall cleaning as well."

They walked for a little while longer and then turned around toward the condo.

"I don't think anyone will use the boat for a long time. Maybe it's time to sell it," Cassie said.

"Isn't it part of the executive package at the company?" Glenda asked. "Some of those guys would not appreciate if it was no longer available to them and their families when they spend time at the condo."

"You see, there are so many things I'm not aware of. I really thought it was just for our family."

You are a poor little rich girl in some ways, Glenda thought.

They had arrived at the condo and both were ready for a nice swim in the pool before they started their work for the day.

Latimer and Brighton returned to the Estate after lunch to go over the inside of the house and the yard in great detail. Maybe there was something Marten had left behind they could use. Latimer had also requested an increase in the number of patrol cars and some plain clothes officers in the lower district to look out for Marten in case he was trying to fence his stolen items. They were instructed to pay particular attention to a man with a hoody, beard and sun glasses. In this part of town many small business establishments served as fronts for questionable purposes like drugs or fencing stolen items.

Lilly had calmed down and Latimer took the chance to ask her a few more questions about the details of the break-in. Her sister and her husband had moved in and were sitting in the kitchen munching on cookies when Latimer and Brighton arrived. They seemed to be totally blown away, according to Brighton's words, with the mansion's interior and didn't mind staying there at all. Both were a little older than Lilly. Ken, the young man, was waiting to start a new job in two weeks and Rachel, Lilly's sister, was pregnant and didn't work. It meant they could stay for as long as necessary to keep Lilly company.

They gained nothing further from Lilly. Latimer thought the whole thing was an exercise in futility as they checked every room of the house. After all, if they found any bodily specimens, like hair or any other DNA, it would only prove Marten Anscott had been there. The man had lived here for years, for heaven's sake. Latimer knew he was fishing again, which he had done a lot lately without going to Florida.

They had checked the garages as well. They found only Mr. Anscott's BMW, a blue Honda Civic belonging to Cassie, and Mrs. Anscott's Buick. Marten's red Lexus was not there. Latimer was certain he would be trying to sell it if he could risk it. With the police looking for it in every corner of the State, he doubted even Marten Anscott would take that chance.

When they got back to the office there was a message from Mark Lenhart. When Latimer called him back, he wanted to know if the investigation was at a stage where the home, office and any other properties of the Patrick Anscott family was still considered a crime scene. Apparently he had not heard about the break-in. Latimer informed him that only the Estate was still of interest to the police at the moment and then filled him in about the situation from last night. He was surprised he had not heard the news from Cassie or Glenda and seemed a little miffed about that. Latimer pretended not to notice. No need to get involved in the power struggle between Cassie and the acting CEO of Anscott Laboratories. He had enough troubles of his own to worry about.

Later on that afternoon Cassie received a call from Henry Richter, the manager of the Yacht club of West Palm Beach.
"Miss Anscott, I'm sorry to bother you, but I would really appreciate it if you could come down to the harbor to take a look at the yacht."
"Is there something wrong with it, Henry?" She was not in the mood to drive all the way down there in this heat.
"It's pretty important, Ma'am. I'll be waiting for you if you don't mind." He hung up before she could say any more.
It didn't look like he was taking no for an answer.
"Glenda, we have to go to the Club. Don't ask me why, but Henry sounds pretty insistent."

It took half an hour through traffic to get there. They parked pretty close to where the vessel was anchored, but even the short walk caused them both to be drenched in perspiration. Henry stood waiting for them.
"What is so important that you dragged us out here in this heat, Henry?" She sounded annoyed.
"Thanks for coming, Miss Anscott." He turned to Glenda and tipped his worn out gray cap. He was a handsome man in his forties, with a deep tan and showing off a beautiful set of white teeth. His brown hair was bleached blond from the sun. He fit right in among the many vessels rolling gently in the harbor.
"Please, follow me." He waved them on and boarded "The Tranquility".
Glenda and Cassie carefully stepped on the deck of the vessel, holding on to the railing with one hand and allowing Henry to pull them with the other.
"What on earth is going on, Henry?" Glenda sounded impatient.
He led them to the other side of the deck and pointed to a red stain at the side of the railing. Something had dripped down into the wooden crack. It was not large, but big enough to be more than from a small cut or nose bleed. The stain was faint because it had been exposed to the weather, but till clearly visible.

"That is blood Miss Cassie, and I'm afraid it's human blood if I'm not mistaken. The only way to find out is to call the police and have it tested." He looked at Cassie with concern. "I just wanted you to ok this before I call. Not that we can ignore this, but I feel better if I have your approval first. The Club has strict rules about this kind of thing and will insist on police involvement to avoid lawsuits, as you can imagine."

"Henry, of course you should call the police. I cannot for the life of me imagine who's blood that could possibly be. The yacht hasn't been used since Marten went fishing about four weeks ago. He never said anything about having an accident or anyone getting hurt at that time." She turned to Henry. "Could someone have come and used it without you knowing it?"

"These boats are checked pretty regularly. Detailed logs are kept when they come and go. It takes identification for anyone to come on Club property. Especially take one of the vessels without us knowing about it. I assure you that this boat has not been moved since your brother has been here. I will check the logs to be certain of the date and let you know."

"That won't be necessary, Henry. I was here at that time with my mother and Marten. He left three days earlier than Mom and I. Nobody has thought about the yacht since we left with all that's has been going on."

"My condolences, Ma'am, everyone has heard what happened, of course." Henry was clearly uncomfortable.

"Is there any chance my brother has been here since then?" Cassie asked him.

"No Ma'am, I would know even if he didn't take the boat out. When we heard what happened, we have kept a close eye on it because we figured he might have come down here to get away." Henry looked down at his sandals in embarrassment and mumbled, "I'm so sorry about all this, Miss Cassie."

"It's ok, Henry. My whole life is a mess and now this. We better call the police and get it over with. I will give them permission to do with "The Tranquility" whatever they need to do to get to the bottom of this.

"I will get right on it. Do you want to wait in the club house and get out of this heat? The dining room isn't open yet, but the small snack room has drinks and some other stuff to eat if you want."

They didn't have to wait too long until a police car entered the parking area. The two officers were greeted by Henry. He brought them into the snack room and introduced Cassie and Glenda to them.

"I'm Officer Mendoza and this is my partner Officer Carter. We understand there is a suspicious blood stain on the deck of your boat, Miss Anscott?"

Before she could answer, he looked at her with sudden recognition and said, "Are you related to Marten Anscott, Ma'am?"

"He's my brother."

"Please accept our deepest condolences, Miss Anscott."

"Thank you, officers, let's get on with it and go look at the yacht." She felt angry and embarrassed and had spoken in a sharp tone.

"Officers, I was Mr. Anscott's personal assistant and a friend of the family. This has been very hard on Miss Anscott as you can imagine and she means no disrespect. We are fully prepared to allow the police to enter the vessel and do whatever is necessary to find the source of that blood stain." Glenda used her most professional manner to put the two men at ease.

Within the hour a van with a team of forensics technicians pulled up at the dock. There was no need for Cassie and Glenda to stay and they drove back to the condo. Glenda called Latimer on his cell phone and told him what happened.

"I wonder what that could be all about. I can't imagine it having anything to do with the case, but you never know. How is Cassie handling this?"

"She is tense again as you can imagine. Here I had her to where we could relax and freely talk about things and now this. There seems to be no end to that poor girl's problems. I told the police to inform you if they have any surprising results with the blood DNA. They weren't quite sure if it was too degraded to test it."

"It's amazing what they can do these days," Latimer said. He was happy to hear her voice. "I miss you. When are you coming home?"

"After what happened at the Estate I don't think we'll be coming home any time soon. Mark Lenhart called Cassie today and the two of them had quite a heated conversation over why he was not informed about the break-in." She sighed. "I'm afraid those two are not exactly getting along these days."

"It's good to pick your fights and this one doesn't seem worth the trouble, Glenda. Maybe you can remind Cassie the man is in charge of her father's company and has a right to know about something important like that." Latimer was ready to change the conversation to more personal things when his office phone rang.

"I got to go, sweetheart. I will call you tonight and we'll talk."

Later on in the afternoon Latimer decided to call Sgt. Peters at the West Palm Beach Crime Unit.

"This is Latimer from Glenridge, Sgt. Peters. I just heard about some incident on the Anscott's yacht. Do you have anything on that? I just want to make sure it has nothing to do with my case up here."

"Inspector, I just heard. They found some suspicious blood stains on the Anscott's yacht. Forensics is on it. As you know it takes some days before they can come up with DNA. We will definitely compare it with Marten Anscott's profile. Everybody is excited about this. After all, it is a famous case and we would only be too delighted to be able to help solve it."

He sounds excited. I wish I was, Latimer thought. "At this point I would be delighted if you guys can come up with something. We need a break here. It has been a difficult case and it's not over yet. I would appreciate it, Sergeant, if you could give me a head's up the minute you have the DNA results."

"Will do, Inspector."

Latimer had no idea what he hoped to find, but it seemed like another day to go fishing.

Reports came in from the plain clothes guys and car patrol in the lower district, but with no results. They had stopped two or three men with a hoody but had to let them go because they didn't even come close to fitting Anscott's profile. In the process they arrested two drug dealers, five prostitutes and one old woman who stole some apples from a small fruit stand. Not exactly what Latimer had hoped for.

At the end of the day he decided to get take-out before he went home. Brown had invited him for dinner, but he declined because the man just wanted to gloat. He was disgusted enough and didn't need any help to feel worse. Then he remembered he was going to talk with Glenda later in the evening. As always, it cheered him up.

Cassie had a melt-down that evening. It started after dinner when they were sitting in their favorite spot in front of the big window.

"Have you ever noticed wherever I turn there is blood?" she said into the silence. "Even down here, they find it on the yacht. I can't get away from it. My whole family is gone, my brother a murderer and a pool of blood on the boat. Everybody knows. Did you catch how the police officer looked at me when he heard my name? Then he was embarrassed and didn't know what to say. I was mortified." She began to cry. "I'm supposed to build a life after all this? Who would ever want to marry me except for my money? Oh yeah, there is the money, lots of it. Who cares? I would rather have my parents back than own the company."

There was a sudden anger in her voice. "Right, I own the company. Mark Lenhart tells me what to do every minute of the day. My own father didn't do that. Who does the man think he is? I don't owe him any explanation about what goes on with my life. It's none of his business if somebody comes into my house and steals me blind." She was sobbing now.

Glenda got up and sat next to her on the sofa.

"It's ok, baby, just let it all out. This is a good thing. I know you are angry and you have a right to be. You have literally gone through hell and back during the last four weeks and now this. The thing with the boat was simply too much." She took Cassie in her arms and held her like a child. "You have been so brave all this time. It's alright to let go. I'm right here with you and I won't let you go. Besides, there is Richard and Emily and they love you like I do. We are all here for you and you are not alone." She held her until the crying stopped.

Cassie sat up and looked at her with such profound sadness, Glenda was ready to cry herself. She realized the girl was only twenty-six years old and in no way prepared to deal with such momentous tragedy. She felt helpless and the only thing she could think to do was hold her and let her know she would be there for her.

Suddenly Cassie started shaking and gasping for breath and her face turned a deathly white. She fell back against the sofa cushion and made terrible rasping sounds as if she could not breathe. Glenda jumped up and ran for the telephone and dialed 911 and then screamed for Richard and Emily to come. Together they tried to talk to her and get her to calm down, but Cassie could not stop hyperventilating.

During the twenty minutes it took for the ambulance to get there, they thought for sure Cassie was going to die of a heart attack, a stroke or hypertension. The three could not do anything but watch as the young woman struggled to breathe.

Glenda followed the ambulance to Mercy General Hospital, but not before she took Cassie's purse with her. Richard and Emily insisted to go with her since there was only one car at the condo. No one said anything on the way, but Glenda could hear Emily crying and praying alternately. Richard sat in the front with a stony face the whole way. Glenda had seen his hands shaking as he handed her the keys.

They arrived shortly after the ambulance and rushed into the Emergency room only to be told to wait until they were called. When Glenda told the secretary she had the insurance card and driver license of the patient, she was soon called to fill out the paper work.

It was an hour before a nurse came out and told them they could go in and see Cassie, two people at a time. Glenda and Emily got up and followed her through a double door into a room with lots of cubicles surrounded by a curtain. Cassie still looked pale and had an IV in her arm. A tiny smile crossed her face when she saw them.

"My wee lassie, what are ye doin'?" Emily fell back into her Scottish brogue as she took Cassie's hand and held it with both hands. "Ye gave us such a scare, child."

"I'll be fine, Emily," Cassie whispered. "The doctor said I had a panic attack.

"You gave us all one, too," Glenda said with a slight smile.

At that point the doctor walked up to the bed.

"Is this your family?"

"Yes," Cassie said, "they are my family."

"She had a panic attack combined with a hypertensive reaction and trouble breathing. We have given her something to calm her down and she should be fine. We will keep her until morning for observation. I will prescribe some medication to keep her calm and another medication if she feels another attack coming on." He turned to Cassie. "I don't know what's causing this, but I strongly suggest bed rest and avoid what is upsetting you."

"I will try, Doctor," Cassie said in a small voice.

Glenda followed the doctor out.

"Sir, may I speak to you a moment?"

"Of course, Ma'am, what can I do for you?"

"You may not realize this, but that is Cassie Anscott, the daughter of the murdered CEO of Anscott Laboratories. Also, her mother died of a massive stroke three weeks ago and her brother is wanted for a double murder. You can see that removing the stress factor is not really an option."

"Oh, good grief, I had no idea." He paused for a moment. "Since I presume money is not an option with Miss Anscott, she should be admitted into a special clinic right here in West Palm Beach. If you want I can make the arrangements for her to be transported there in the morning."

"I will speak with Cassie and let you know what she thinks about that."

"Are you related to her?"

"No, I was Mr. Anscott's personal assistant and have taken on a role of surrogate of sorts since all this tragedy has happened.

"I will be right over there at that desk, let me know as soon as you have talked to Miss Anscott."

"Are you saying they want to put me in a nut house?" She looked like she was going to cry.

"Lassie, ye have to listen to what Miss Glenda says. They will take good care of ye in that place for a few days and talk things over so ye can get yer mind straight with all the stuff ye had to go through. We will be waiting fer ye till ye come home." She leaned over and kissed Cassie on the cheek. "We love ye. If I don't let Richard come in to see ye, he will be fightin' mad with me." With that she left for the waiting room.

Richard walked in with his usual dignity.

"I'm glad you are feeling better, Miss Cassie. I want you to know you gave us quite a scare." He stood and looked at her with such love in his eyes that Cassie took his hand and held it.

"Thank you, Richard. Just knowing you all are here with me makes me feel better. The doctor is sending me to a clinic in the morning. I don't know for how long, but I'm sure I will be better real soon. It's all right with me if you and Emily want to go back to Glenridge. Glenda can stay here. When I get out we'll fly home. What do you think? I'm concerned about Lilly at the house by herself."

"I think that sounds like a splendid idea if you are ready to return to the Estate, Miss Cassie. You know things are not settled yet." He tried hard not to mention Marten. If I might suggest that you think this over when you have had a day at the clinic and feel better. I will certainly do what you think is best."

"Ok, I'm pretty tired all of sudden. I think the doctor has given me something to sleep."

It was midnight by the time they returned to the condo and too late for Glenda to call Bob. She would do it first thing in the morning.

The next morning a van from Lakeview Clinic came to pick Cassie up. Glenda had come to the hospital early to help her check out and follow the van to the clinic. She had researched the facility on line and found it to be reputable. She even called Cassie's family physician and asked him to look into it further today.

The person in charge of admissions, a Mrs. Pendergast, welcomed them at the door and showed them to Cassie's room. She assured Cassie that Lakeview Clinic was a first class facility reserved for the upscale clientele and known for its privacy and comfort.

The room certainly looked accordingly luxurious and quite large. Actually, it was a suite with a living room and a bedroom with adjoining bath. A large window looked out over a small lake surrounded by immaculate landscaping, hence the name. Glenda was impressed and wondered vaguely what all this might cost.

A young, friendly woman knocked on the door after Cassie had settled in. She introduced herself as Lisa Gonzales and came to help with the paperwork and insurance forms. It took quite a long time. Around ten Dr. Melando, a good looking, tall, dark haired woman walked in with a big smile.

"I will be your physician for the first few days until we see if you need a specialist later on." She looked at Glenda. "Miss Anscott, it is our policy to discourage visitors during your two weeks stay here. It helps you concentrate on your treatment and avoid pressures of home that might have contributed to your stress."

"Are you saying you want me to stay here for two weeks with no contact with the outside world? It sounds like prison to me." Cassie tried not to get upset, thinking of Marten.

"We have years of experience with our treatment methods and it will surprise you how fast the time will pass with all that we have planned for your recovery."

"It looks like you are going home with Richard and Emily," Cassie said after the doctor had left. "Why don't you call Mark and tell him to send the plane this afternoon?"

Glenda reached Mark Lenhart at the first ring and relayed Cassie's request. She also filled him in on the situation.

"It looks like our girl will be well taken care of, Glenda. About the plane, I'm afraid that will not be possible. It has already been scheduled for something else. Maybe you and the others can get a commercial flight today or tomorrow. I'm looking forward to seeing you in the office again."

Cassie took Glenda's phone and dialed, her mouth held in a thin line, trying to control her anger.

"Mark, this is Cassie. You have no right to tell me when I can and cannot have the company jet. Maybe you have forgotten that there is a slight difference between a CEO of a company and the owner. Do I have to ask my lawyer to tell you what that difference is? I'm tired of you treating me like a silly young girl." Her voice was calm in spite of her anger. "I've been through unbelievable tragedy in the last month and I'm no longer that girl, but a woman who has lost her entire family. All I have left now is living up to the responsibility of preserving my father's legacy. I will not ever ask your permission to use the jet or anything else I deem necessary for my personal use. When I get home the two of us will have a long discussion about what your role and mine is at Anscott Laboratories. Remember one thing, my name is Anscott, yours is not. Do I make myself clear?"

"Yes, Cassie, you do." His voice was tightly controlled. "I will see to it the plane will be at the airport at two this afternoon."

"Make sure you have it ready when I'm done here as well. I will have Glenda come and pick me up in two weeks."

"Consider it done."

Before he could say any more, Cassie hung up.

"Glenda, I will be a different person when I get out of here. I feel I have changed from that young girl to a grown woman. Maybe I was a little harsh with Mark."

"Cassie, I have no doubt you can do it. Just relax now and let them help you do that while you are here. I expect to see a smile on your face and a new sense of resolve to continue on when I come back for you."

Mark Lenhart slammed the receiver down hard and sat in stunned silence. His dream of running the company had come true in a most sudden and unexpected way. He had worked hard to earn the title of Senior VP and now CEO of Anscott Laboratories. There was no way he was going to let a young girl take it away from him until he was ready to turn it over maybe in a few years from now.

His face was a mask of anger. There is no way he would go back to answering to someone else for the decisions he made, especially not some up start like Cassie. She needed him, his expertise and guidance. He loved the power of running the company. He had earned it and would not give it up for anybody.

He would find a way to deal with Cassie like he always had with her father. As with Patrick, she would never know he was in charge. His way was to work quietly in the shadows till the proper time. Like a wise man once said, "Never let a crisis go to waste".

Chapter 29

It was five days before Latimer heard from Sgt. Peters about the DNA results from the yacht.

"The blood is without a doubt from Marten Henry Anscott, Inspector."

"That is a surprise. I know it's his boat, but no one mentioned he got hurt while he was there four weeks ago. If he did, why would he hide it?"

"On our end that clears it up, Sir. I hope you find this guy." Sgt. Peters sounded disappointed.

Latimer was confused. According to forensics, the stain, most of it only visible under special lighting, indicated a pretty large amount of blood had been there. Certainly more than a nose bleed or a scrape or cut from fishing. Once again, nothing made sense in this blasted case and he had no choice but to file away the results as just another dead end.

He was happy Glenda was back and he had invited her to a fancy restaurant on her return. They had gone out several times since and each time it was better than the last. He had no doubt he was in love with her, but wasn't sure if she felt the same way. There was still a certain reserve when he wanted to get close. He would just have to be patient.

Two weeks later, the jet picked up Cassie with Glenda on board just as she had requested. It was a joyful reunion and Anscott Estate looked good when Cassie walked in the door greeted by both Richard and Emily. She looked rested and the strained look on her face was gone.

"Welcome home, Miss Cassie," Richard said with his usual formality.

"It is so good to have ye back, Lassie," Emily cried and hugged and drew her to her ample chest. "I have fixed every dish you like and more."

Cassie walked through the door and stood in the foyer, looking around as if she had never seen it before. "It's good to be home. It's different without Mom and Dad, but it is my home."

Glenda stood with Richard and Emily watching her. There was something different about Cassie, something tougher and much older than when she had left three weeks ago. Glenda could sense a resolve to cope and survive in spite of what happened. She just hoped Cassie would not become hard and unyielding in order to survive.

"I will be back to work tomorrow, Glenda. Please inform Mark I want to see him in my office first thing in the morning."

Let the show begin, Glenda thought. *Anscott Laboratories has a new leader.*

Glenda arrived in the office early the next morning. She wanted to be there before Cassie came in and made sure her office was in perfect order. Mark Lenhart had not made any comment when she informed him to meet with Cassie in her office. She could not tell by his manner if he was upset they would meet in her office and not his.

He walked in at precisely the set time and sat down with a stony expression. He was told Cassie hadn't arrived yet. It was fifteen minutes later by the time Cassie walked in with a cheerful "Good morning".

"Would you like some coffee, Mark? I sure would. Glenda, please ask Doris to get us some?"

She's in charge, Glenda thought with a smile.

"Cassie, it is good to see you so well. We were all worried about you when we found out you had to stay in a clinic for treatment." He had gotten up and air kissed her on the cheek. "It is wonderful to have you back."

"Thank you, Mark. I'm doing well and ready for work. It's the best medicine for what I've been through. Have a seat Mark. Let's talk frankly about our situation."

"What situation would that be, Cassie?" He tried to sound casual, but there was tension hidden underneath.

She looked at him with a smile that never reached her eyes and took the coffee from Doris. As soon as the secretary had left the room, Cassie said in a calm voice, "Mark, I have had two weeks to examine myself, my situation and my life with the help of several professional counselors. I must say, at first I thought it was a waste of time, but now I realize it was necessary." She leaned back in her large leather chair. It still smelled of her father and that seemed to give her confidence. "I've been through a trauma few people have to face in their life and it devastated me as you can imagine. Life can be cruel and I found out the hard way. It is not what life does to us, but what we do with it and in spite of it. I have every intention of carrying on in my father's tradition to run this company. I will be the fourth Anscott to do so and I intend to do it to the best of my ability." She leaned forward and looked at him. "You can be at my side by teaching me all you know or you can oppose me at every corner. The choice is yours. I'm the owner of this company and you and the Board will treat me as such. You see, I don't have to prove that point to anyone, it is a fact." Her eyes had a steely look in them Mark Lenhart had never seen. "I would like nothing better than to keep you where you are Mark, because you are good at what you do. But, I will not hesitate to replace you when the time comes if you fight me every step of the way."

She got up from her seat, walked around the desk and held out her hand. "So what do you say, Mark? Are we going to run this company together, you as my mentor and I as the owner who needs you?"

Mark Lenhart was stunned. Almost in a daze he took her hand. There was a reluctant admiration in his eyes as he smiled at her.

"I know we can do this together, Cassie, you and I. You are made of tougher stuff than most of us, a true Anscott indeed. Your father and mother would be proud."

He knew he had lost the battle he came to fight before it ever started.

Glenda was surprised to see Cassie and Mark Lenhart coming out of the office smiling. She wondered what happened but was happy things turned out well. A struggle among the management team at this point could prove very damaging for the company. She had the feeling Cassie Anscott would surprise her in more ways than one in time to come.

"Glenda, I would love to have dinner with you and Inspector Latimer this evening at The Wishing Well. Can you make reservations for us, please?"

"This is a nice surprise, Cassie," Latimer said as he pulled out chairs for Cassie and Glenda. I have not seen you in a long time. You look well." He stood and looked at her intently. "There is something different about you, you look more assured and grown up, if you will allow an old man to talk like that to you."

She smiled at him and almost looked like the old Cassie.

"I'm glad you and Glenda could make it to join me for dinner. It's not all for fun, I'm sorry to say. I have a lot of questions to ask about

Marten and where the case stands. As you can imagine, the situation is extremely difficult regarding his legal rights as heir and part owner of the company. My lawyers tell me until he has been convicted he is still entitled to the shares. So you can understand why I would like to know more than what the papers are saying.

Latimer cringed. There was so little to tell.

"Before I tell you what is going on, let me ask you if Marten was hurt when he was on the boat before he left West Palm Beach?"

"No way, Mom and I would have known about it because he wore mostly shorts and t-shirts when he was with us. You can't hide a large wound like that, even if you wanted to."

"You said he left three days early without saying goodbye. Could it have been to cover up an injury?" Latimer asked.

"Now there is a thought. Wouldn't' he have needed a doctor to take care of a large wound like you say it must have been?" Cassie asked. "How do we know he didn't go to a doctor? No one would have to know."

"Can you give me his doctor's name and we will contact his office. They probably won't tell us anything because of privacy laws," Latimer said.

"I know our doctor as a family friend. He would tell me if Marten had been there. I will call him tomorrow and let you know." Cassie studied the menu with great interest. "I think I deserve a big steak tonight." She looked up at Glenda and Latimer. "Please feel free to order anything you like. This is a celebration of my return to the land of the living." She waved to the waiter to order a bottle of very expensive wine.

"Glenda, because you have been such a wonderful friend and confidante to me during this traumatic time, I want to take time to say thanks in the only way I can. I hereby give you a large raise in pay and a new title. From today on, you will be known as the personal assistant to Cassie Anscott. I know you did a wonderful job for my father and I know you will do equally well for me." She raised her glass to Glenda with a big smile. "Here is to us, Glenda." Then she turned to Latimer with a knowing look. "I had to do this right away before someone else snatches her up."

He smiled at her with a twinkle in his eyes.

"Don't think I haven't tried. She is a hard woman to snatch."

Cassie laughed and then looked at Latimer more serious.

"We need to get back to the subject of Marten. What else is there to tell me, Inspector?"

"I think it's time you called me Bob. All my friends do." Then he told her all he had up to now.

Chapter 30

The next morning Latimer had a message to call a Capt. Roger Holloway. He was with the forensic lab of the Lake Worth Police Department. Ginny had taken the call just before she left yesterday at closing time. Latimer did not recall anyone by that name. He was not familiar with Florida and had to look up the location of Lake Worth. It turned out Lake Worth was about sixty miles north of West Palm Beach on the coast.

He dialed the number and reached Holloway on the third ring.

"Inspector Latimer, it is good of you to call me back. I believe I have some information that will be of great interest to you."

"Captain Holloway, I can't imagine what the great city of Lake Worth might have that would interest me unless you want to invite me to retire there." He laughed. "I'm looking for a place in about eight months."

"While I'm all in favor of you picking our fair city to spend your golden years and your enormous pension Inspector, that's not what I'm calling about." He chuckled and cleared his throat. "Two weeks ago a mutilated body washed up on our shores. Because it was so degraded from the salt water and animal attacks, there was no way to get fingerprints or facial identification marks. We had to do a DNA profile. You know how long that takes and given the fact there were no reports of missing persons up and down the coast, there was no rush. Our lab has just now gotten the results." He paused for effect. "Are you ready for this? The victim, according to our DNA data base, is Marten Henry Anscott from Glenridge. I believe you are looking for him?"

Latimer took in a sharp breath and just stared at the phone in silence.

"Are you there, Inspector?"

"I'm sorry, but you must be mistaken. Anscott is still in Glenridge. More than that, he has not been down your way for the last six weeks. We have phone calls, a break-in and him trying to get money from his sister just in the last three weeks up here. How long has your body been in the water, Captain?"

"According to the coroner's report, he was killed with a shot to the heart and then thrown into the water about six weeks to two months ago. Given the current of the Gulfstream, the body was carried north for quite some distance. The coroner also found rope marks on the body as if he was tied to something heavy to keep it from surfacing. I will fax you the report as soon as you give the word."

"There can be no doubt about the DNA results?" Latimer was trying to conceal his doubt and confusion and not insult the man.

"None, our lab is certain. As a matter of fact, it is a hundred percent match."

"I'm totally speechless, Captain. This throws our entire case into the crapper. According to what you are telling me, the man we've been chasing is not Marten Anscott, but someone we have no idea who he is." Latimer felt a weakness in his stomach and it made him almost sick. "Then who the heck is the guy we've been chasing up here?" He was almost shouting.

"I'm sorry I can't help you with that, Inspector. If you need to get in touch with the coroner, his number is in the report. Maybe he can help you clear up some of this better than I can. I'm only the messenger."

"Thank you for calling Captain, I will be anxious to see that report." Latimer sat and stared as if in a stupor. "Who the heck is the guy we've been chasing up here?" he said again in a loud voice to himself.

"What are you talking about, Sir?" It was Brighton.

Latimer couldn't say anything, but sat there staring at the desk and then at Brighton and then back at the desk.

"Get me a cup of coffee, Kid, NOW!"

Brighton jumped up and ran to the lounge. He wondered what had the boss in such a mood. He was hoping he hadn't done anything wrong.

Latimer's mind was reeling. His entire case was destroyed. He had literally pursued a dead man for four weeks. The department would be the laughing stock statewide and that was just the beginning. The big question remained, who murdered Patrick Anscott and Camilla Preston?

Brighton came back with the coffee. Latimer looked at him with a look of such anger and confusion Brighton didn't dare say a word.

"Marten Anscott's body was found in Lake Worth, Florida. He's not the killer, because he has been dead for the last six weeks," Latimer said in a monotone voice.

"What? You are kidding, right?"

"No, Kid, I'm not. Our case is blown and we will be the laughing stock in the precinct. We've been chasing a dead man while the real killer is walking around in front of our noses. At least now we know why we couldn't catch him. We've been looking for the wrong man." Latimer seemed to shrink into his chair and his face looked tired and worn. "I'm done, Kid, finished, ready to play bingo in Florida with the seniors."

After a long moment of stunned silence, Brighton asked,

"Then who is the Marten Anscott who lived at the Estate? We saw him and talked to him and so did his family. They would have known it wasn't him."

Latimer looked at Brighton for what seemed a long time. Slowly, he raised his head and his face lit up.

"Of course, it has to be!" He was shouting and slapped his forehead. I've got it. It finally all makes sense, Brighton."

"It does, Sir?" Brighton stared at Latimer, totally clueless what he was talking about.

"Get me the report of the interview with Clara Caskel, Kid."

In his mind the case fell together like putting the last piece into a puzzle. He waited for the report and when Brighton brought it, he skimmed to the part where she told about the birth of the baby. Clara said Lora screamed over the phone that Camilla sold her baby and then someone took the phone away from her before she could go on. What Clara didn't get to hear was, Lora had not just had one baby, but two.

"Lora Weston had twins, Kid. Camilla sold one of them to the Anscotts and raised the other one after she killed Lora. Remember at the apartment, the neighbor told us she had a son living with her and his name was Paul Weston? But we know better, according to the coroner Camilla couldn't have children, and she didn't. Paul Weston is her nephew, because he is Lora's baby and Marten Anscott's twin brother." Slowly the full ramifications of these facts were beginning to form in Latimer's mind as he continued reading the report.

He was interrupted by Ginny.

"Sir, some paperwork was just faxed to us from the Lake Worth coroner's office." Ginny walked in with several sheets of paper and put them on Latimer's desk.

"Here is the proof, Kid, the autopsy report of Marten Henry Anscott's body," Latimer said as he picked it up and studied it for a long time.

"Brighton, call the Chief and tell him I have to talk to him right now."

When Latimer arrived at the Chief's office he found him in a foul mood. Rumor had it, he would be called on to report to the Chief Superintendent about the case and explain why there had been no arrest in all this time.

"Latimer, I don't need any more excuses from you why you haven't come up with a way to find this perp in spite of all our efforts."

Latimer ignored the remark.

"I do have some news Chief you might want to hear." He handed the autopsy report to him. "This is a report that shows Marten Anscott washed up on the beach in Lake Worth, Florida and has been dead for at least six weeks, Sir."

The Chief stared at him in disbelief.

"Tell me you are kidding, right, Latimer? I'm not in the mood."

"It's true, Sir. If you will allow me, I will explain the situation." It took Latimer quite a while to remind Chief Carson of the facts of the case. When he was done he leaned back and sighed deeply. "This has been the most twisted case I've ever had and it's not over yet. I think I've unraveled most of the facts. All that is left is to find and arrest Paul Weston." He suddenly remembered something. "Good heavens, it means Cassie's brother Marten is innocent and I better get over there to tell her he's also dead."

When he got back to his office he called Glenda's office, but was told neither she nor Cassie would be available until tomorrow morning. He dialed the Estate and got Richard on the phone.

"The ladies are out shopping Sir, and will be back for dinner. You may want to reach Miss Glenda on her cell phone."

Latimer told Glenda he needed to come by this evening and talk to both of them. He didn't want to talk while they were in the store. When Glenda told Cassie, she invited him to come and join them for dinner at seven. He accepted.

He sat in his office and read the entire interview with Clara Caskel, Lora Weston's sister. Her account of what happened nearly thirty years ago cleared up a lot of the questions in his mind. Now that he understood all the facts, he wanted to be sure he could explain everything to Cassie.

It was shortly before seven when he arrived at the Estate. He was glad to see Richard at the door with his usual formal greeting.

"The ladies are in the small library, Inspector. I will take you to them."

"Richard, I wonder if you and Emily could join us after dinner to hear what I have to say. I will clear it with Cassie."

"Very well, Sir."

"Bob, how good to see you," Glenda said. "I have spent my entire pay raise today and I couldn't be happier," she told him after he kissed her lightly on the cheek.

"Bob, I'm so glad you can join us. Do you have any news about Marten or the case?" Cassie asked as she greeted him with a hug. "Come, sit down and have a glass of sherry with us."

He appreciated the drink. It had been a long, difficult day and he was not looking forward to telling Cassie her brother was dead.

"Maybe we should wait until after dinner before I tell you my news. It has been a long day and I need a moment to enjoy being in the presence of two lovely ladies." He hoped he wasn't putting it on too thick.

After the delicious meal they went back into the small library. Richard had brought some snacks and a bottle of wine. He acted a little nervous because he was not used to sitting with the family. Emily walked in, unsure of why she or Richard were invited to this meeting.

"I can't imagine what it is we are supposed to hear tonight, Inspector," she said, looking to Cassie as to where to sit.

"Take your seats everyone," Cassie said, pointing to the big, comfortable leather chairs around the coffee table. "You and Richard as well, Emily." She turned to Latimer. "How long are you going to make us wait, Bob?" She smiled. "We're all ears."

Latimer cleared his throat and took a sip of wine.

"This is quite a story I have to tell. I think I'll start from the beginning." He settled in his chair and looked at Cassie." Do you remember they found a blood stain on your yacht? We concluded it was Marten's and couldn't figure out how it got there?" He hesitated for a second before he went on, trying to figure out how best to continue. "This morning I talked to Captain Holloway from the Lake Worth coroner's office down in Florida. Two weeks ago a body washed up on their beach and it took all this time to do a DNA profile." He looked at Cassie again. "Cassie, it was Marten's. I'm sorry to tell you your brother is dead."

She looked at him without seeming to comprehend what he had just told her.

"The coroner has determined he was killed with one shot in the heart and his body was thrown into the ocean at least six weeks ago." He went on. "Cassie, your brother has been dead for six weeks. He did not murder your father. Marten is innocent."

There was complete silence for what seemed a long time.

"That can't be, Bob," Glenda finally said. "He was here, we all talked to him. He was at the funeral and Cassie talked to him on the phone about the money."

Cassie just stared at Latimer, unable to speak. She took a sip of wine and a piece of chocolate from a small silver plate as if in slow motion.

"Marten is innocent," she finally said. "I have my brother back." She looked at Latimer and smiled in a sad sort of way. "He did not murder Dad and I can still love him." She started to cry.

They sat and watched her in stunned silence until Latimer expressed his condolences.

"It's strange. I would rather have him dead and innocent than alive and a double murderer. Is that terrible of me to say?" She looked at no one in particular.

"Cassie, we understand how you feel. Now you can properly grieve over him like you did with your parents. It will take a while, but in time you will have closure," Glenda said as she took Cassie's hand and held on to it.

No one spoke for a long time.

Finally Glenda said into the silence, "Bob, can you explain all this to us?"

"I can and I will if you'll bear with me. It started twenty-eight years ago when Lora Weston had twin boys. Her sister, Camilla, was part of a baby smuggling ring. She took one of the babies and sold it to a rich family, your family, Cassie. The other would have been sold as well, but I think the police got too close to uncovering the ring before she had a chance to sell the second boy. To conceal her past criminal activity and about her participation in the ring, she murdered her sister, Lora. She threw her into the river here in Glenridge for the police to find. Since they didn't know she was a twin, they thought it was Camilla and so stopped looking for her. Since there was the second baby, she had no choice but to raise the boy herself. She called him Paul. She had taken on her sister's identity and called herself Lora Weston."

Everyone sat spellbound as he went on.

"Marten grew up a fine young man in your family, Cassie, while Paul was raised by this horrible woman in the lower district of Glenridge. He must have found out from Camilla that his twin brother was living with a rich family. Camilla had probably told him he wasn't good enough. Paul Weston was not really a bad person for most of his life because he does not have a record. Something happened to him and he came up with this plan to take Marten's place in your family, Cassie. It must have taken him a long time to figure out the details and study Marten's habits and movements, probably months if not years.

The first part of the plan was to kill Marten while he was fishing on the yacht. No one would ever look for him if he threw him into the ocean and return as Marten Anscott. To the world and your family no one would miss Marten. Remember, Marten, or Paul now, did not even say goodbye and returned three days earlier than you and your mom. Richard and Emily, you recall how differently he acted, how mad he got over little things? In many ways he did a pretty good job of deceiving all of you when he entered this house and took his brother's place. Because of the murder of Patrick, everyone credited the fact he acted different, to the grief over his father."

"Why did he kill my father?" Cassie asked.

"Camilla Preston, who told your parents she was Lora Weston, Marten's birth mother, came to see your father the Friday before the murder. According to your lawyer, your father had paid her off many times over the years. Except this time, he must have told her he wasn't going to give in to her blackmail any longer. Instead, he decided to tell Marten and you about the adoption. When Camilla told Paul what Patrick had said, he could not let that happen, because it would ruin his plan to take over as Marten. That's why he killed your father the following Sunday night. Paul, after finding out Camilla had gone to see your father, realized she would probably blackmail him when Paul had control of the Anscott money. It was then he decided to kill her as well. He must have hated her for keeping him and giving Marten to a rich family. Her murder was probably committed out of hatred and revenge as well as to protect his life as Marten Anscott, the rich heir to a large fortune. Killing your father served two purposes. One, he wouldn't expose his plan and the other, Paul would be able to do as he pleased as the main heir of the company. Your mother's death was an added bonus, because now he only had you to deal with, Cassie. Since he was the oldest, he figured you were no threat to him. I'm sure if you ever crossed him, he could very well have planned to kill you as well. With you gone, there would be no one left to stand in his way." Latimer took a sip of wine before he went on.

"When the police started to suspect Paul, he knew his plan had failed. That is when he tried to get enough money out of the bank to start over somewhere else. He didn't count on the bank notifying Mr. Rathbone and have all his accounts frozen. He had no knowledge how the financial system worked. All he knew, Marten had a large trust fund and he was the owner of it. It was more money than he could ever have imagined given his poor background.

"He sounds like a twisted person and nothing like his brother Marten," Glenda said.

"The saints preserve us, Miss Cassie. We have our darling Marten back in our hearts." It was Emily. "He was the finest young man that ever lived and we will miss him terribly. I just wish your mother could have found out he was innocent." She wiped her eyes with a tissue.

"That is why Mr. Anscott looked so surprised when we found him." Richard said. "He couldn't understand why Marten would shoot at him." He tried very hard to keep his composure. "It's a sad tale all around, Miss Cassie." He stood up and looked at her with deep emotions showing on his face. "We are all so sorry this happened and if there is anything Emily and I can do to make things easier for you, please let us know."

"Thank you. I don't know what I would do without you." Cassie walked over and hugged both of them. "I will be fine. All I can think of is my brother Marten is still my wonderful brother and I will always love him."

It was as if a dam had broken and everyone was talking at once. Glenda hugged Cassie without saying anything. She couldn't find the words for this unusual situation. On the one hand, Marten was dead. On the other, everyone was glad he was not alive and a triple murderer.

Richard and Emily stood a little to the side, talking to each other. They should really go back to the kitchen and see if more refreshments should be served. Cassie walked over to them and asked Richard to get two more glasses. They would have a toast.

When Richard returned, Cassie stood up and began to speak.

"This is a sad time. My brother is dead. I loved him so much. He was a wonderful man and we were very close. I remember him protecting me from bullies in first grade." She smiled. "I was his little sister and he took care of me. All we can do now is remember him in our hearts. I know he is with God, because he had a deep faith. He got that from Dad, I think. My father was such a good example to both of us and so was Mom." She wiped her eyes. "All three of them are in heaven and looking out for me. I will make it and I will do them proud. The only thing I'm sorry about is the terrible feelings I had when I thought he was bad. I should have loved him anyway and forgiven him instead of hating him for what I thought he did. I simply should have continued to believe he was a good man and couldn't have possibly done those awful things. Maybe I will get another chance and prove myself and learn to love my friends and those who love me the way I should have loved Marten."

She looked around at everyone. And all of you are my friends. I want to be a better person and I know you will all help me to do that. She lifted her glass.

"To my father, my mother and Marten." They all raised their glasses to her. "And to our friendship." She turned to Richard and Emily. "That goes for you two as well. I think I would also like for you to stand in for my family. From now on, please call me Cassie and understand that the three of us will be a family at Anscott Estate." She walked over to them and drew them in to the circle around the coffee table. "Let's toast each other and seal the deal." She smiled when Richard's face turned red and his hands trembled slightly. Emily began to cry and her little rotund body shook with emotion.

"I don't know what to say, Mi.., Cassie. There ain't words for it. You are the dearest child to do us such an honor. Isn't that right, Richard?" She turned to her husband, but Richard just stood, erect and proper as always.

"It is one thing to say you love somebody, it is another to put it into action." Cassie was still talking to the couple. "I will see to it that the two of you are given enough money to be totally independent. I will use Marten's trust fund to do it since it is now mine. In other words, you won't have to work anymore if you don't wish to. I want you to stay with me because you feel you have a place here as my family."

The couple stood speechless while everyone else broke out in cheers.

Emily was crying while Richard smiled at Cassie with a look of deep affection.

Latimer looked at Glenda.

"I think it's time for me to go. I'm sorry to be the bearer of such a terrible tale, but at least we now know to look for Paul Weston and not Marten Anscott." He turned to Cassie, "I'm happy, Cassie, that your family name will be restored and so will Marten's reputation. I will see to that as soon as I get to the office in the morning."

He looked at Glenda. "We need to talk sweetheart, how about dinner tomorrow?"

"That sounds good, Bob. I'll call you at the office."

She walked him to his car.

"This is the most incredible story I've ever heard. You're going to be quite busy tomorrow setting the record straight about Marten."

"I will, but you and I need to talk about us. When I heard what Cassie did for Richard and Emily, I thought about us. Life is too short to waste it. Why are we living alone when we can be happy together?"

"What are you saying, Bob?" She sounded reserved.

"Let's talk about it at dinner tomorrow." He took her in his arms and kissed her. She held back a little, wondering what exactly he was talking about.

Chapter 31

The man had been sitting in the waiting room of the free clinic for two hours. He was getting restless. He wanted to get up and leave or yell at the receptionist. He had a terrible headache and he was dizzy. All he was here for was his medicine.

"Paul Weston, come with me please." The nurse stood and waited for him to follow. "How are you, Paul? It's been a long time since we've seen you. Are you ok?" She was just making conversation. She knew him. He was close to going over the edge judging from his demeanor. "Step on the scale for me." He was shaking visibly. "Sit down right here and let me take your blood pressure. You should not have waited so long between visits." She smiled at him. You've grown a beard. I wouldn't have recognized you if I hadn't seen your name on the chart.

"I feel bad. My head hurts and I need medicine." His voice was flat.

"The doctor will be just a minute."

He sat in the small room. He felt claustrophobic and wished she hadn't closed the door. It made him angry. She should know better.

The young doctor walked in and gave him a big smile. He was familiar with this patient.

"Hello Paul, I can see you are not feeling well. I would like to check you into the hospital. They will take good care of you and help you get rid of the headaches."

"I'm not going to the hospital. They will stick needles in me and do things like open up my head." He was getting extremely agitated. "All I want is my medicine and I'll be fine, doctor."

"I'm afraid I can't give it to you this time unless you let me check you in, Paul. You have a brain tumor and it is growing and making you feel bad. You will die if you don't let me help you." The young doctor sounded concerned.

Paul looked at the physician with pleading eyes and then took his arm and held it. "All I want is my medicine." He was close to tears now. "Why won't you give it to me?" There was a sudden hint of menace in his voice.

The doctor stood very still.

"Ok, Paul, I will write you a prescription, but you must let go of my arm. It's the last time. If you come back, we will not see you unless you agree to go to the hospital, do you understand?"

"I will, just write it just one more time." He was trembling.

"The doctor sat down and took out a prescription pad and started writing. He knew how dangerous this patient could become if provoked and he was afraid.

"Here it is, Paul. Don't wait too long to fill it or you will become very sick." The doctor opened the door and let Paul walk out without stopping him. He was bound by patient confidentiality and could not force this man to check into a hospital. At the same time, he knew Paul Weston was a ticking time bomb.

Paul went to his tiny apartment after filling the prescription. He took two pills, closed the blinds of the bedroom, covered his eyes with a towel and waited for the headache to go away. He was still shaking and felt nauseated. He had not eaten since yesterday, but he wasn't hungry. He was afraid to go to sleep because of the nightmares. They wouldn't stop haunting him. He couldn't tell anymore what was real and what was not. Maybe the medicine would help. It had in the past. The moment he closed his eyes he would see Marten's face on the yacht as he walked toward him laughing. Then all he could see was blood everywhere. It was like shooting himself, because Marten's face was exactly like his own.

He fell into a semi dream-like state. He had failed. Camilla said he was a nobody. He was still a nobody. Every time she got mad at him when he was a boy she would tell him he was second best. He never knew why until many years later. One night, when she was drunk, she told him about his twin brother, Marten Anscott. That same night she even bragged about killing his mother and throwing her in the river. She didn't remember any of it the next morning, but he did. It was then he devised the plan to become Marten. It would be his turn to be rich and live in a mansion. It was justice.

It hadn't worked. He was still a nobody. Now Cassie had all the money and he had nothing. She could have shared it with him. Instead, she had lied and called the police. She was his sister and still she wouldn't share with him. He was second best to her, just like with Camilla. He could change that if he wanted to. She would be sorry, just like Camilla had been in the end. He would tell Cassie who he really was before he….

He was falling asleep. The medicine was working. He knew it would.

Chapter 32

This time Latimer was in charge of the press conference. The Chief had insisted. The media was there in full force. The Governor had made sure of it after being informed of the details. He was determined to clear the name of his greatest financial supporter, Patrick Anscott. He personally called Cassie to let her know he never had any doubt Marten was innocent. She had just smiled and graciously accepted his assurances. Politicians are so predictable, although she was sure many of her business associates will probably do the same after the press conference. She did not blame them and wished she had believed in Marten instead of hating him when she thought he was guilty.

The national media had picked up the story. Latimer felt nervous. Not just because of the cameras, but there was still the matter of answering why the murderer had not been caught. He would have to come up with an explanation, while truthful, did not damage the reputation of the department. *I'm going to sound just like the Chief,* he thought.

The crowd of reporters was instantly silent when he stepped up to the microphone and introduced himself and Brighton. The Sergeant stood next to him with an expression of utter terror. He had never been good in front of a crowd and this was definitely the mother of all crowds in his opinion.

"There has been an astonishing new development in the case of the murder of Patrick Marten Anscott and Camilla Preston," he said. "The Glenridge Major Crime Unit has been tireless in its effort to uncover the facts and apprehend the perpetrator of these two brutal crimes. I want to report to you that another murder has been uncovered which was committed by the same person. It is my sad duty to tell you that Marten Henry Anscott's body was found washed up on the beach of Lake Worth, Florida. According to the coroner's findings he was killed with a single gunshot in the heart seven weeks ago."

After a stunned silence, a surprised murmur arose from the crowd. Latimer waved for silence.

"Please let me explain. Because of these developments we can tell you unequivocally that Marten Henry Anscott is innocent of all charges and was the first victim in this string of murders. In a surprising twist and due to the diligence of the Major Crime Unit, we have uncovered that a man named Paul Weston has committed these terrible acts. You will be surprised to know that Paul Weston is the twin brother of Marten Anscott."

The reporters rose up in an electrified uproar and shouted questions all at once. Latimer simply stood there for a moment and then waved them into silence.

"If you will give me a chance I will explain everything to you."

When he was finished with his story he spent thirty minutes answering questions. One reporter from one of the larger networks asked what he was doing to apprehend the new suspect.

"I'm glad you brought that up. Paul Weston looks identical to Marten Anscott. However, we believe he has grown a full beard and is therefore not easily identified. I have asked Sgt. Brighton here to disseminate a computer composite of the man and what he would look like with a beard. The Glenridge Major Crime Unit would appreciate if you would show this computer generated image in your reports. I'm sure with your help we will have no trouble finding the suspect. The one hundred thousand dollar reward money is still in force.

The sensational story went out nationwide and was the topic of endless conversations, opinions and discussions on the blogosphere, twitter and all the other ways of modern communication.

The Chief was elated. His department had come out smelling like a rose.

"Good job, Latimer. Now all we have to do is find this guy."

"There is that," Latimer said with a little smile.

Brighton was still in a daze when he got back to the office.

"We're famous, Sir. I can't believe it." His smile was bright enough to light up the room. "Do you think people will recognize us in the street?"

"I hope not, Kid. Besides, this kind of fame is here today and gone tomorrow. Don't let it go to your head. We still have a killer to find."

"So, where do we go from here, Sir?"

It was Brighton's favorite question and as usual, he didn't have an answer.

"I think you need to help out with the hotline, Kid. This time it will be even worse with calls coming in from all over the US."

Brighton groaned. "Not again."

"That's what fame will do for you."

Latimer leaned back in his chair with a cup of coffee in hand. There was nothing he could do but wait. Surely someone in the lower district remembered Paul Weston now with the beard and his real name. The reward money should be a real boost to jog people's memory.

The phone rang. It was Glenda.

"Are you still talking to us mere mortals, Inspector? That was a fabulous press conference. You handled it like you do this for a living." She sounded exuberant.

"Ah, it was nothing." He chuckled. "If you had any idea how scared Brighton and I were, you would be amazed."

"I am amazed. You came across like a real pro. I think we should celebrate tonight with dinner, what do you think?"

"That sounds great. I will pick you up at seven at your place."

The doorman greeted him with a smile of recognition.

"Mrs. Hinsley wants you to go up to her place, Inspector Latimer."

"Thank you."

Latimer was surprised. He thought they were going out to dinner.

"Come in, my hero," she said. "Your dinner is ready. I have slaved over it all day. I don't get to cook for a famous celebrity every day."

He grinned at her with a touch of embarrassment.

"Ah, it was nothing," he added with a mock gesture of modesty. "It's all in a day's work."

Her cooking was wonderful as usual. *I could get used to this*, he thought as he pushed the plate away. "This was great, Glenda, thank you."

"Let's go in the living room, shall we? I will pour us a glass of wine and you tell me all about the press conference. I like to hear the details behind the scenes, an insider's view you might say.

"There isn't much more to say than what you saw on TV. Let's hope we find Paul Weston or all this euphoria is out the window." He motioned for her to sit with him on the couch. "I would much rather talk about us."

She looked at him with a touch of apprehension, but remained silent.

"We've been going out for quite some time now and I have enjoyed our being together each time." He cleared his throat in the way he did when he didn't know quite how to put into words what he wanted to say. "I've been through a tough time with this case and every night when I come home to my empty apartment I wish you were there."

Glenda sat up and looked at him with a frown on her face.

"Bob, I told you, I will never live with anyone or spend the night without marriage." She withdrew from him and moved to the end of the couch. "I thought I made that very clear." Her tone was almost business like.

"I remember. I have never asked for anything inappropriate, have I? And I won't now." His hand went into his pants pocket and came out with a small jewelry case. Very carefully he took out a diamond ring and held it up to her. "Glenda, would you do me the honor of becoming my wife? I love you more than I could ever put into words. At my age, I don't have years to waste and let happiness slip away from my fingers. I would love to get old with you, sweetheart." His smile was that of a man deeply in love.

Glenda looked at him and fumbled with her glass. Then, slowly, a smile appeared on her face and she put the glass on the coffee table.

"Robert Latimer, I would be honored to become your wife."

In spite of hoping she would say just that, he was stunned and couldn't move.

"Well, are you going to kiss me or just sit there?" She was laughing at him and moved close to him.

He took her face in both hands and gently, ever so gently, kissed her.

"I do love you, Glenda."

"I love you, too, Bob."

They sat and held on to each other without saying a word for a long time.

"When will you marry me, sweetheart?" Latimer asked.

"How about when the case is solved and we both have more time to enjoy our new life together?" Glenda snuggled up closer. "I'm looking forward to spending my life with you, Bob. I have been quite lonely for a long time and never thought I would find someone."

"Are you going to make me wait that long? What if the case never gets solved?" He was teasing.

"Then you better get it done pronto, Inspector." She smiled up at him and they kissed.

All the way home in the car Latimer whistled a happy little tune.

The next morning it was a mad house at the precinct. The phones had been ringing all night and still hadn't let up. Tips of sightings came from all over the US instead of just the State. This time Latimer didn't let it get to him. Instead, he called Cassie on her cell phone.

"You were wonderful, Bob. Thank you for clearing Marten's name. Our phones at home and the office have not stopped ringing. Poor Glenda is overwhelmed I'm sure." She sounded excited. "I have no doubt with all this publicity we will find Paul Weston soon, don't you think?"

"All we can do is hope, Cassie. I will continue to do my best."

"I know you will, Bob. By the way, can you tell me if I can get my brother's body transported up here? We need to have a funeral service for him."

"Cassie, I spoke to the coroner down there. He thought it would be better to have the body cremated, for obvious reasons. The choice is yours. The ashes could be picked up by your company jet and then you can plan a memorial service." He was careful to pick the right words so he wouldn't have to go into details of the terrible state of Marten's remains.

"You know, that sounds good. He can still be buried next to Mom and Dad, can't he? Somebody here will see to the arrangements if you will make sure the coroner is ready to release the body."

"They are done with the autopsy, Cassie. There is no reason why he can't be turned over to the proper place for cremation."

"Thanks Bob. By the way, Glenda told me the good news about you two. Congratulations, I'm so happy for you both." She paused for a moment. "Bob, I have not said anything to Glenda, but would you like to have the wedding here at the Estate? It would be my wedding gift to you both."

"That sounds great to me, Cassie, but I'm going to be a married man soon and now I answer to a higher authority. You better ask Glenda about this." He chuckled.

"I can see you have been trained well in these matters," she said, laughing.

Chapter 33

The funeral turned out to be a highly publicized, huge event. The major networks and the local media were there to report in detail as each invited guest entered the church. Once again, every politician, business leader and community personality had come and each of them were discussed at great length. Police protection made sure Cassie and her family had unhindered access to the church. A murmur went through the congregation as they entered the sanctuary. Cassie looked composed at the arm of a relative.

This time Latimer sat right behind the immediate family next to Glenda and Mark Lenhart and his wife. It had taken a number of days to put this all together and he hadn't seen much of Glenda since the proposal.

Once again, he was invited to attend the select group of invited guests for a gathering at the Estate after the service. This time it was as a guest and not as a member of the police. The Chief was not invited and grumbled something about some people in the lower ranks having certain privileges for obvious reasons. Latimer pretended he didn't hear. He smiled on the way out, making sure the Chief didn't see it.

In spite of the intense publicity, Paul Weston was still missing. A knot formed in Latimer's stomach every time he thought about that. What if they couldn't find him? He tried to put it out of his mind for today at least. There was time enough to worry about it tomorrow.

The gate at the Estate was open and after showing his ID he was waved through by security personnel. He was one of the first to arrive since he left immediately after the service ended through a side door so he wouldn't have to talk to the many reporters. He was sure they wanted to know if he had made an arrest yet.

The front door at the Estate was wide open and he slowly wandered into the drawing room. This place had become familiar to him in the last few months. He saw Richard and Emily directing the extra hired help to get things ready for the soon to be arriving crowd of important people. Lilly waved to him as he passed by the open door. She didn't have time to stop and talk to him.

"Can I get you something, Sir?" It was Richard. "You may also go into the dining area. The food is ready and the bartender will be glad to fix you a drink."

"I'm fine, Richard. Don't worry, I will help myself. You are too busy to worry about me," Latimer said, walking towards the dining room. He asked the young man behind the bar for a glass of white wine and looked around while he waited. This house had seen a lot of sadness in the last three months. Hopefully this was the end of it and the next occasion would be his wedding.

The first guests were arriving. Cassie and the family walked in shortly thereafter and the room slowly filled with a crowd strangely familiar from the last two funerals. He could tell for many it was awkward to be back again so soon for the same sad reason and the atmosphere was subdued. Most people spoke in hushed tones as they waited to offer their condolences to Cassie. Latimer thought she carried herself extremely well. She actually tried to make people feel comfortable as she shook their hand with a warm smile. *What an amazing young woman,* Latimer thought as he watched her.

Suddenly Latimer heard a commotion coming from the front door. A woman's screams stopped the conversation in the room instantly. Everyone looked startled and stood still in their place. Latimer felt for his gun and took it out of his holster. He held it behind his back where no one could see it.

And then he saw him. A man was holding a woman in front of him standing in the door of the drawing room. She was whimpering. It had to be Paul Weston, but he couldn't be sure. The brown beard hid most of his face. His curly hair looked disheveled. His shirt was crumpled and hung half out of his tattered jeans. His brown eyes had a wild look about them that left no doubt he would use the gun he held in his shaky hand.

Latimer moved to hide behind a heavy-set man, his gun held in both hands. If he could stay out of sight of the man, he could try to take him down when and if it became necessary.

"I want to talk to Cassie." It was Paul Weston. The voice was unmistakable.

"I'm here, Paul." Cassie stepped forward and looked him straight in the eyes. Her voice was shaking. "Why don't you let these people go and we will talk."

"You have taken everything from me, Cassie. I'm your brother and you lied to me by going to the police. All I wanted was some money to go away, but you wouldn't give it to me. You want all the money for yourself." He was trembling now, but held on to the woman in front of him. "I didn't mean to hurt anybody, but I had no choice. Marten was my brother and he was always first and I was second best. I thought if I killed him and took his place I could be first." He was almost crying now. "Don't you see, Cassie, I could have been your brother if you had let me. But you think I'm only second best just like Camilla did."

"You are my brother, Paul, because Marten was." Cassie's voice was stronger now. "I will help you if you put the gun down and let Mrs. Polk go."

"You lie just like you lied before, I know it." He waved the gun at Cassie. "I don't want your money now. I just want you dead like your father and mother and Marten are dead. Then I'm the only one left and I will not be second best anymore." He pushed the woman further into the room toward Cassie.

Cassie moved backward and away from him.

"Don't you dare move or I'll shoot you and everybody in this room. That will show them I'm somebody. It's justice, don't you see?" His face contorted and he put his hand to his head. "I have a terrible headache."

When the woman started to move away from him he grabbed her again and said in a monotone voice, "You move lady and I'll kill you." She whimpered and stood perfectly still.

Cassie took a step toward him.

"Marten, you know I love you," she said in a soft voice, pretending he was her brother. "You are my brother and the two of us are the only ones left. You can come back and live with me again, just like in the old days." She held out her hand. "I know you didn't do all those things, it was just your headaches giving you nightmares. We will have Dr. Cameron take a look at you and give you some medicine and you will be fine." She smiled at him and stepped closer.

"I don't believe you. Don't you see I have to kill you to have the things I never had? I wanted to be like Marten. He had everything and I had nothing all my life." His body was shaking again. "You stay right where you are." He shook his gun at her when she moved closer.

"Paul, I know you don't feel well. I forgive you for what you've done. I truly believe you couldn't help it. I see that now. Because you are Marten's brother, you will be my brother as well and I'll take care of you. I will share with you all that I have. Together we can make it."

Latimer stepped out from behind the heavy-set man until he had a clear shot at Weston. At the same moment Weston moved so that Mrs. Polk was in the line of fire. He had no choice but to inch out further. If Weston turned around he would see him. Some people watched what he was doing and he shook his head at them not to look in his direction.

"Cassie, I don't feel good. The medicine isn't working very well anymore." Paul looked at her with pleading eyes. "I'll never be anybody, will I, Sis?" He let go of the woman and raised his gun toward Cassie. "There is no other way."

"Hold it, Police. Move that gun one more inch and I will shoot."

Paul turned around and aimed his weapon at Latimer.

The noise of the shot was overpowering. Paul Weston fell to the floor instantly. Latimer ran to him and took the gun out of his lifeless hand.

He looked at Cassie, ignoring the screams of the crowd in the room. She was safe.

She ran up to Latimer and threw her arms around him and started sobbing uncontrollably.

"I would have taken care of him. I would have. He was Marten's brother and he was sick."

She let go of Latimer and knelt by the body. "You are somebody to me, Paul," she said in a whisper. "I do forgive you. I know God will, too."

The room had quieted down. Everyone's eyes were riveted on Cassie. Some women cried. The men stood in stony silence.

After what seemed a long time, Richard walked in and in his calm, professional way asked the crowd to follow him out of the room. Latimer took Cassie's arm and helped her up.

"Let's allow the police to do what they need to do, honey," he said in a gentle voice. "He is at peace now."

She looked up at him and took his hand in hers.

"I know."

They were sitting in the morning room, Cassie, Glenda, Richard, Emily and Latimer. Everybody else had left, including the coroner and the forensics team.

"You are probably the pluckiest woman I've ever met, Cassie," Latimer said, sipping on a cup of coffee.

"It's really over, isn't it?" she said with a deep sigh. "I don't think I've ever been so scared in all my life." Cassie sat in her mother's chair with a cup of coffee in her hand. "There are no words that come to mind to thank you, Bob. I will forever be in your debt."

"It was in the line of duty and anyone at the precinct would have done the same thing if they had been here." He sounded definite.

"Thank you for saving my life, Bob. I don't care, it was truly a heroic deed. You saved this damsel in distress." She looked at him with a warm smile.

"I believe when the coroner's report comes in they will find he had a mental illness of some kind. With his headaches, it was probably a brain tumor," Latimer said.

"I would have taken care of him," she said. "I really would have and maybe they could have operated on him." Everyone sat in thoughtful silence.

"You are a forgiving person, Cassie." It was Glenda. "Not many people would feel that way after what he has done."

"I wanted to make up for failing with Marten and I believe God gave me that chance with Paul." She smiled at the group. "It's amazing, but I feel at peace in spite of it all." She looked at them all and smiled.

"It also means that when an appropriate time has passed and all this is put out of our minds, I promise we will have the grandest wedding in this house the city of Glenridge has ever seen." She looked at Richard and Emily. "Isn't that right?"

"It is, Cassie." It was the first time the butler had called her by her first name.

Several days later Latimer received the coroner's report. He was not surprised to find out Paul Weston would have died within the next six months because of a large brain tumor. He must have suffered from delusions, fits of anger and violent headaches for quite a while, because of the area it was located in.

Latimer called Cassie right away and she started to cry.

"That means he wasn't responsible for what he did, doesn't it?"

"Yes, it does. You were right. The coroner says he must have suffered terrible bouts of depression over quite some time before all this happened."

"I feel so sorry for him. Thank goodness I did not act hateful toward him at the end." Cassie sounded relieved.

"I think you acted quite admirable, all things considered, Cassie. I don't know if I could have done the same in your situation," Latimer said.

"Don't you see, I got another chance to make up for the way I acted with Marten. I still feel guilty about the way I felt when I thought he was guilty. It looks like we are going to have another funeral. I hope people will come to honor Paul Weston the same way they did the rest of my family, because I will." She suddenly sounded strong and at peace with herself.

It was on a clear, beautiful day in January, three months before his retirement, Latimer and Glenda were married. As promised, it was a grand wedding. To Latimer, the best part was when they boarded the company jet and were whisked away to a certain posh condo in West Palm Beach.

The End

I hope you have enjoyed reading my book as much as I have loved writing it. It has been my goal to entertain my readers with a great plot told without the usual offensive language, excessive violence or sexually permissive setting so prevalent today.

The story about Robert Latimer, now a private eye with his own detective agency, will continue with the next book called "HIS PERFECT TARGET". He is referred by Cassie to solve the murder of her friend's father, Peter Bellami, the owner and CEO of a large trucking firm in Glenridge. All the major characters are still there to participate in this twisted, stunning plot with a surprising outcome. The book will come out in October of 2014.

In the third book of the trilogy, called "HIS PERFECT LEGACY", a wealthy investor dies and leaves a Will in which he accuses one of his five children of murdering him. Once again, the main characters are still part of the story. The book will come out in time for Christmas.

If you would take the time to go on Amazon.com and write a review I would so appreciate it. Your comments make the difference between success and failure for any author.

I have also written a WWII historical novel about the experiences of my mother as she flees from the East to escape the

Russian front right into the carpet bombing of the Allies during the last six months of the war in Nazi Germany. "**When the East Wind Blows**" has a 4.5 star rating and is available for Kindle.

To buy it in paperback please go to my website: **www.BarbaraHMartin.com**, where you can see other books I have written or engage me as a speaker for your organization, conference or club. I have been a professional speaker for over twenty years and have traveled widely with my books.

www.ingramcontent.com/pod-product-compliance
Lightning Source LLC
Chambersburg PA
CBHW071451040426
42444CB00008B/1290